The Book of
Okehampton

HERITAGE OF A TOWN

Roy and Ursula Radford

HALSGROVE

First published in Great Britain in 2002

British Library Cataloguing-in-Publication Data
A CIP record for this title is available from the British Library

ISBN 1 84114 1550

HALSGROVE

Halsgrove House
Lower Moor Way
Tiverton, Devon EX16 6SS
Tel: 01884 243242
Fax: 01884 243325
email: sales@halsgrove.com
website: http://www.halsgrove.com

Frontispiece photograph: *Okehampton and Torrington Fire Brigades attended the fire at Heanton Satchville,
the home of Lord Clinton Huish, on December 19th 1932.*

Printed and bound in Great Britain by Bookcraft Ltd, Midsomer Norton

CONTENTS

Acknowledgements

Researching the heritage of Okehampton has already brought us three times more information than is printed here so, while we're only just opening the door to a fascinating past, we are very grateful for the help received from so many people and organisations including:

Mr Ian Bailey; Mr and Mrs Ray Balkwill; Mr and Mrs Fred Barlow BEM; Mr Colin Beer; Dr Tom Bell; Mr and Mrs M. Brint; Mr Norman Butlin; Brigit Barrett; Mr Ted Cann; Mrs Margaret Case; Lt/Col (Rtd) A. Clark – Commander Okehampton Firing Ranges; Ted and Rosemary Coombes; Mr and Mrs W. Cornish; Mr and Mrs Jeffe Cunliffe; Mr Ian Donovan; Mr A. Ewens; Mrs Lilian Finch; Revd P. Fitzpatrick; Mr B. Hain – Australia; Mr Paul Hambling; Mr P. Hammond; Mr and Mrs F. Harper; Mr John Hawking; Mr and Mrs R. Hayes; Mrs C. Heard; Ron and Gloria Hooper; Jane Hopper; Benita King; Revd M. Koppell; Mrs Iris Lee; Mr R. Letchford; Cllr Gill Lower; Mr and Mrs P. Luckett – Berlin; Mr and Mrs D. Luxton; Cllr Christine Marsh – Town Mayor; Mrs Christine McPhee; Mrs W. Mitchell; Mr G. Payne; Mr Brian Pinney MBE; Mr and Mrs Roger Partridge; Mr and Mrs W. Passmore; Miss Joan Pauley; Mrs K.M. Pavely; Mr J. Pope; Mr and Mrs P. Powell; Col (Rtd) McA Pyman – Cmdt Okehampton Camp; Mr N. Reader; Mr and Mrs B. Rendle; Mrs J. Richards; Mr Jim Sampson; Mr G.R. Scantlebury MBE; Dr Jean Shields; Mr Ian Snell; Mr and Mrs David Terry; Mr R. Thomas; Mr and Mrs C. Trigger; Cllr Perry Vallance; Mr David Vick; Mr David Voaden; Mrs Voaden (senr); Mr Brian Weaver; Mrs M. Webber – Curator Okehampton Museum; Mr Peter Woodgate; Mrs R. Young; Cinnabar Photography – Okehampton; Dartmoor National Park Authority – Dr. N. Atkinson, and members of staff; Devon County Libraries – West Country Studies; Devon Records Office; The Devonshire Association; Carmel Harnett – Dublin University; Joanna Finegan – National Library, Dublin; The Royal Dublin Society; Exeter Diocesan Stewardship Office; Editors Steve Hall – *Exeter Express and Echo*, Barrie Williams – *Western Morning News* and Colin Slade – *Okehampton Times*; The Maryland Historical Society, USA – War Record Division.

With special thanks to Okehampton Librarian Susie Hewitt and members of staff; Town Clerk, Mr J. Winchester, and staff members Hilary Bacon, Rosemarie Richards and Graham Smith for putting up with us rummaging through the records and to Mr Jack Hellier, town reporter for half a century, for reading our manuscript. It has been a privilege to work with so many supportive people in beginning to show that Okehampton has never been just another country town but has held an important role in history.

Roy and Ursula Radford
September 2002

Meldon Valley, before the dam, and wistfully remembered by many.

1

The Early Years

The heritage of Okehampton shared by its people today has origins that take us back far beyond the bounds of written history. History nowadays seems to be served to pupils in small doses. 'We're doing the Romans this term,' we hear children say, and a few weeks later they are asking us about the Victorians, not only because they seem to believe we lived in those times but because that is the subject of the new term's 'project'. They are then quite likely to move swiftly on to their next topic, perhaps the Elizabethans, and the one after that which is just as likely to be about the Normans.

That rich highway of history which was unrolled with vivid explanation by enthusiastic history teachers a generation or so ago, to disciplined listeners, established a road that connected prehistoric times with the present day. Unconnected, unrelated projects fail to achieve the all-important connection of past with present but serve admirably those that would divorce us from our past. It is not, therefore, surprising that quiet, unassuming Okehampton, set sleepily beside Dartmoor, and close enough to remaining wild regions of Exmoor and Bodmin Moor, appears to many to be just another town in the countryside that must have been of no significance to anyone, other than tax- and toll-collectors, as the tide of history flowed elsewhere.

None of this, of course, is true. Okehampton's importance, we will suggest, has been recognised since the earliest of wanderers came this way, and whose prehistoric traces can still be found so close to the present town. Its values, other than as a provider of funds for kings or earls, have been recognised by many down through the centuries – until, that is, the town has come to be seen by some to be critically, if not terminally, bypassed since the age of the railway, motorway and air transport. But such views are misplaced. The very reason that Okehampton was established and thrived in the first place could again provide it with yet another important role to play in the region – given clear vision and political will.

For the moment though we will turn our attention away from the present to see where Okehampton has been placed on that highway of history. Three or four thousand years ago people of the Bronze Age were settling on Dartmoor and on the hills around where Okehampton now stands. Stand within the remains of Okehampton's castle and look towards the rising ground of the moor and you will be looking at the area known to and used by our ancient predecessors. Their burial places can still be found and where stone was readily available it was simply piled up to create a cairn. The people that built cairns lived nearby; early farmers who settled here to grow their annual crops and benefit from a little hunting.

A cairn eight metres in diameter (Scheduled Monument 28749) can be found on the heathland above Moor Brook by the military ranges and another lies on the neck of land towards East Hill, but they can also be found in groups; prehistoric cemeteries. For example, on the southern slope of the West Okement River valley, near the A30 trunk road, there is a group of more than 25 cairns and nearby there is the evidence of local agriculture with a 36-foot-diameter stone hut circle and the visible remains of at least five fields. But beware; anyone looking for

'Oakhampton' taken from a drawing dated 1666.

some of these sites must bear in mind the proximity of the Army firing ranges and establish whether or not they are in use at the time.

The fields clearly indicate that the Bronze-Age settlers had developed farming techniques which provided them with annual corn crops and cereals for themselves and their animals. Their moorland homes, the round huts, would have had a post in the centre or a ring of posts to support a conical roof of wood or thatch of ferns with space to let the smoke out from the hearth below. The hut was not just a circle of stones but a circle that overlapped itself to make an entrance passage to provide added protection against the weather. Animal skins, stretched on a wooden frame, would have made a cover, or door, at the entrance.

During the later Bronze Age the people were producing gold ornaments, axes and scythes, weapons such as socketed spearheads for hunting and fighting and rapiers – all of which kept their smiths very busy. Ladies were not overlooked and their desire for pins, elaborate neck rings and arm rings among many other things was being satisfied by the village bronzesmiths.

An outstanding Okehampton tapestry created by the Okehampton Quilters as a millennium project; it can now be seen, in glorious colour, in the Charter Hall.

An artist's impression of Okehampton Castle published by R. Jennings and W. Chaplin of 62 Cheapside in 1830.

Main: *Elmead Farm, 1939.*
Below left: *At work, and perhaps a little play, at Webber Hill Farm in the 1920s.*
Below right: *It is 1935 and young John Hawking is unsure about riding with his grandfather William Hawking at Elmead Farm.*

Bronze requires tin, which is a comparatively rare metal, and while the moorland region had a share the greater quantities were to be found further down the peninsula. From around 750BC the local farmers would have been participating in a bronze-working boom, when market demands across the country enabled smiths to expand production and introduce new designs for swords and tools, which included a socketed axe to replace the palstave.

Society had changed. These were not ignorant people but ones skilled in farming, metalwork and many of the crafts that survive today. Farmers were extending the cultivation of land as far as they could and with the high moorland's bad weather stimulating the development of peat and eroding areas of arable and grazing land it seems highly likely that their attention turned to the land in the valley where the farmers of the Okehampton hamlets still survive.

The increased production of spears provides the first indication that people were feeling unsafe and that the arrival of the next incomers to the area was imminent. Virtually relegated to the 'myths and legends' story-telling time in schools are the Celts and their Druids, the priesthood and religious leaders who, as a sect within the tribes, are still commonly remembered as being responsible for the sacrifice of children to satisfy some pagan god. The trouble with the Celts was that they did not leave a written record of their times for historians to sift through later. The original priesthood of Druids therefore left no connections extending down through the centuries to the 'new Druids' of today. In the absence of recorded Celtic history, today's Druids have more recently invented a colourful costumed way of life that inspires interests in music, art and the preservation of language that might otherwise be lost – and a jolly good job they make of it.

What the Celts brought with them was a wider knowledge of metals and civilising arts connected with that knowledge; they came with bronze vessels elaborately decorated with geometric patterns, armed with bronze weapons, and the swiftly developing knowledge of the manufacture and use of iron. They also brought beliefs in many 'gods' and nothing was more sacred to them than the mistletoe, especially if it grew on an oak which they sought for their sacred groves. Rivers and wells were sacred power sources for these incomers to their new lands.

Okehampton as Trading Centre

This photograph of Fore Street, c.1888, provides a reminder of the benefits of reasonable roads and street cleaning.

The ebb and flow of Okehampton's prosperity during the spring depended for centuries on its March fair that added to the hustle and bustle of market day.

Okehampton as Trading Centre

Trade has always been vital to Okehampton. This picture, dated 1899, is believed to be of the men who built and developed the Victorian Arcade, connecting Fore Street to St James' Street, which remains a popular shopping centre within the town.

Fore Street to the west in the late 1880s with its unmade roads. In c.1906 David Stanbury, a farmer, walked down Rosemary Row (to the right) in the darkness of night and evidently walked into the river. His body was found near Knowle Bridge. The inquest jury called the Town Council's attention to the dangerous state of Rosemary Row, the lack of lighting, and the unfenced river.

First came the Alpine people called Goidels, or Gaels, who gave their name to Gaul, who spread rapidly over the whole of our island and through the South West and Wales into Ireland. Then came the Brythons, of whom Pytheas wrote in 325BC. A Greek mathematician and explorer, he sailed around a Britain that he then called the Bretannic Isles, into the waters of the Severn Sea and around our south-west peninsula, referring to it in his writings as 'Belerion'. Only later did Ptolemy use this name for Land's End. While the Greeks were capable of navigating the globe as far as Norway, the Brythons were still only ushering the Iron Age into our county. They also followed the old tracks and highways across the region as they opened up commerce with the people of the Mediterranean. The language they brought with them would eventually oust the Gaelic tongue. The last Celts to reach Britain were the Belgæ, who had become dominant in the South of England by the time the Romans arrived.

Of these three waves of Celts, according to Sir John Rhys, the lingering old language of Devon and Cornwall provides a clear indication that the Dumnonii tribe that held this land descended from those early Alpine incomers, the Gauls. Their Dumnonian peninsula encompassed Cornwall, Devon and stretched back into parts of Somerset and Wiltshire. It was they who also left behind them the origins of names for rivers and places; the Exe and Axe, Dunster and Dawlish are just a few to bear names with a Gaelic origin.

But what did the little valley where the twin Okements now join offer these incomers? Trees, water, high ground for security, fertile lands, access to the western regions in an area already established by the folk who lived on the hill – these were just a few of the local benefits.

With the coming of the Gauls a civilisation began in which villages were to become clusters of round huts surrounded by a stockade or earth ramparts. Thatch-covered huts were partly sunk in the ground and there could be 80 or 90 huts protected by the outer walls. A 'village' of 350–450 souls would not have been unusual and these 'villages' would have been linked with each other and with the hill-forts by a system of high roads or trackways. Who can tell what the streets of Okehampton hide beneath them?

These were a people who were capable of smelting lead ore for spindle whorls, working in tin and using bronze for personal ornaments. They smelted iron to make edged tools such as axes, saws and bill-hooks – much like those in use today. They made daggers, swords and spears, but they could also spin and weave and use looms to make textile fabrics.

These ancestors of ours were capable of bringing down a duck in flight using a sling-and-clay shot but their main food was lamb or mutton, horse flesh, pork and goat and, later, beef. Outside of the walls protecting their villages they were cultivating wheat and barley which they could grind in rotary and saddle-stone mills. They were cultivating peas and beans and they collected wild fruits, such as blackberries and sloes.

These people had small oxen and horses which were used unshod to draw carts and sledges on the tracks and highways; there is mention of sledges in Devon still being used in the late-nineteenth century. As early traders they already had a form of currency, coins made of tin, and bars of iron of varying size. The tribes living up and down the Dumnonian peninsula were more than capable of dealing with other tribes throughout the Bretannic Isles or with those on the continent from Amorica across the channel to the Mediterranean.

The steady expansion of Rome's empire brought Roman traders to these shores long before its invading armies. Those seeking tin or lead trod well-travelled inland tracks up the backbone of the peninsula that soldiers would follow in the other direction a century or more later. They encountered a people that were using light chariots drawn by horses whose domination of these areas, we will suggest, was vitally important in establishing and developing a village settlement that in time would become Okehampton.

It appears to be 'known' in the district, and vaguely understood by many visitors from overseas, that Drewsteignton, 'the Druids town on the Teign', was an important area for Druids in the district. There is nary a mention of Okehampton but, despite this, we stand by our convictions that with the Bronze-Age settlements already well established the incoming Druids of the Gauls would certainly have found the converging east and west rivers in their valley of too great a value to their naturalistic beliefs to be ignored. The trackways already in use down the spine of the peninsula were an added bonus.

Like all things, however, the time of the Celts we are told came to end when they were chased out of the country, with the Druids massacred at Anglesey; although a few must have hidden in Cornwall if the county is to prove its independence and continuity as a Celtic kingdom. It is not so long ago that historians and other academics were telling us often enough to make it believable that the Romans never reached that Celtic kingdom. The Roman invasion, they confidently professed, ended at Exeter and a line stretching roughly from Exeter to Gloucester (Isca Dumnoniorum to Glevum) was marked as being virtually the outer western edge of the Roman Empire. The Romans had reached Exeter before AD48, and were working the lead mines in the Mendips a year later. The Second Augustan Legion was garrisoned at Exeter, under its legate Vespasian, a soldier destined to become the Emperor of Rome who would see the destruction of Jerusalem and the building of the Colosseum. We now understand that his legion's task, assisted by auxiliaries, was to annex the domain of the Dumnonii, which included the tin deposits that would have been a great attraction. Since that domain stretched down the south-west peninsula to the end of the land, it is not surprising that the history of the Romans in the South West continues to be revised. There can be little doubt that the future Emperor was well acquainted with the lie of the land that provided him with access to the far South West. Where Okehampton now stands, the future Emperor once walked; or more probably rode.

The Second Legion based at Exeter was below its full strength, so it seems; Vespasian could hardly have considered that he would have much trouble in keeping secure the lands of the Dumnonii. The invading Romans built a chain of forts soon after AD55 which of necessity must have been linked by roads, pre-existing or newly laid. A small fort at Wiveliscombe held a garrison at the time and there is evidence of a camp near Tiverton, indicating a route down the Exe Valley.

The North Tawton area provided at least a temporary camp, or depot, where interest continues in a fort, since excavations in the area have produced first-century Roman pottery. The fort at Knowle confirms the route of the Romans as they pressed westwards into the area where they would have crossed the Okement or, taking the strategic benefits of the land between the East and West Okements, crossed them above their merging.

Overseeing such a position, and the countryside around it, the small site found near Okehampton's church then becomes a very useful signalling station. The Romans marching across Sourton Down would have been following an already well-established route westwards, passing fortlets on the way, towards Nanstallon, on the Camel, where a sizeable fort was built, capable of containing and sustaining 500 infantrymen and cavalrymen.

The Roman occupation of the region undoubtedly saw them passing to and fro through the area. The observation point near the church, another possibly at Sourton and the occupied fort at Knowle indicate that the area was important to the legion's access to the South West. From the high ground of the tors and hills, all routes could be observed and warning given of any danger to those warriors using the route to the west.

Where soldiers make camp, there have always been those nearby, ready and prepared to provide for their needs and replenish their depleted stores. The 'annexed' village of the Celts on the hillside and valley below is not difficult to visualise as a source of supplies. In helping Rome, its occupants, willingly or otherwise, would have been assisting the permanent foundation of a future town.

On October 6th 1897 a man named Mr R. Furze was working in Okehampton Park, above the railway station, and close by the old Roman road when he found a hoard of Roman coins under a rock. He took his treasure to Dr Young in Okehampton who,

excited by the find, contacted the Dartmoor Exploration Committee which arranged for further inspection of the area of the find by a deputation. Six days later the investigators met Dr Young and Mr Furze at the site and the latter showed them where he had found the coins, under a rock on the side of the hill. Mr Furze had originally found about 160 coins and another 40 or more were discovered by the investigators. Many of the coins were broken or corroded but about a third of those discovered were later identified with a Roman ruler and then dated.

Speculation down the years has variously suggested that the coins had belonged to a beggar sitting beside the road and begging from soldiers; or that a soldier hid them before setting off to settle some dispute somewhere down the Dumnonian peninsula and either never returned or, on doing so, failed to find 'his' granite bank among many rocks of a likeness on the hillside; another suggestion is that the coins were loot, hidden after a robbery, ill-gotten gains for which the criminal failed to return. The soldier theory appeals to us, but it may just be because of a tale told in the area of a Roman soldier walking the hillside, 'seen' by many people at different times who all mention that he appears to be looking for something.

After financial arrangements were made with Mr Furze and agreement reached with Mrs Trevor Roper and Mrs Lees, owners of the manor at the time who kept some coins, the remainder were presented to Plymouth's Municipal Museum. The coins, examined by experts of the British Museum, were associated with the period AD320–30.

The Roman occupation ended in 410, to all intents and purposes, with the withdrawal of its legions after Alaric, King of the Goths, sacked Rome. With their departure the land lapsed into an era generally regarded as the Dark Ages, during which time the raiding parties from Ireland continued.

The first waves of the Angle, Saxon and Jute invasions were imminent. During those Dark Ages, over 600 tortuous and trying years, hitherto unconsidered events were to take place that enabled those who populated this area by the rock-mocking waters of merging rivers to turn a settlement into a town.

By the time of the Norman Conquest, and with William confirmed as Conqueror and eager to learn what taxes could be wrung from his newly-acquired land or, rather, from its people, 'Ochementone' was well established. William's inspectors came upon a borough possessing a castle and a market, 31 villeins and land for 30 ploughs (which would have been around 2,000 acres), with burgesses to run its civic affairs. All of this was confirmed when William sent out his recorders to add information on this area to what was to become the Domesday Book. The question which this raises – why had our small, mid-west-Devon area been important enough to have grown to prominence before those turbulent times? – we will address elsewhere.

Above: *West End, with the Okehampton Bank between the Tavistock road on the left and Rosemary Row on the right leading down to the river's ford.*

Right: *Pigs, anciently used as free-roaming daytime street-cleaning scavengers, were secured here at night. Note also the historic sign of three balls of business that continues.*

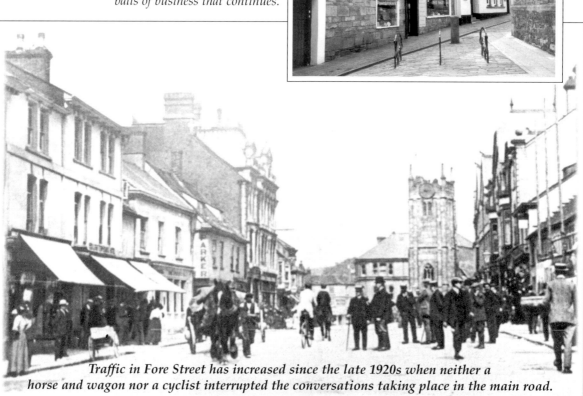

Traffic in Fore Street has increased since the late 1920s when neither a horse and wagon nor a cyclist interrupted the conversations taking place in the main road.

2

1066 & All... or Some of What it Led To

By the time of the Domesday survey the borough of Ockmenton, the town on the Ock, with its four burgesses and market, owed fealty to a noble adventurer who had become the Sheriff of Devon named Baldwyn De Brionys (aka De Molis or De Sap depending on which records are used). Baldwyn was the second son of Count Gilbert Crispin who in turn was directly related, albeit apparently on the wrong side of the blankets, to Richard, Duke of Normandy.

Baldwyn's pedigree, blessed by carnal pleasures of the past, brought him close to the invader, William the Conqueror, himself the bastard son of Robert I, Duke of Normandy, from an illicit relationship with Herleve (or Arlette), a tanner's daughter from the town of Falaise.

In 1068, less than two years after the Battle of Hastings, William was obviously sufficiently satisfied with his warrior-relative from Brionne to place him in command of the fortress he was building at Exeter and, in making him Sheriff within a further year or so, gave him control of a wide area.

It is thought that William was not only responsible for initiating the building of Exeter's Rougemont fortress but also instigated the building of Okehampton's castle on the site of Saxon fortifications as his campaigns took him further westwards. The near-20-year period from invasion to the Domesday survey of land is unlikely to have been sufficient to convert Okehampton from a settlement into an established town, which indicates that Okehampton had found a role in the area that it had filled long before the Conquest.

William, in recognising both that earlier role and the strategic positioning of the town, emphasised its importance by providing it with a castle. By 1086 Baldwyn had made the castle one of his regional administrative centres, since by then he possessed almost 200 rural manors in the region and property in Barnstaple as well as in Exeter. Evidence of the town's importance to the incoming Normans lies in its very inclusion in their Domesday survey, despite it being a lesser town than nearby Lydford, and others.

As he received lands, so Baldwyn bestowed lands on others. To his steward, Rainer, went the manor of Kigbeare, while Chichacott was bestowed upon Roger de Molis, a Norman whose family came from Meules, an area owned by Baldwyn. To the beaten Britons, the castle that emerged at Baldwyn's bidding dominated not only the road and rivers but became a despised symbol of the Norman domination over them as a barbaric aristocracy swallowed up their lands.

Baldwyn, who divided his time between his fortress and castle did not enjoy his position and privileges for long after the Domesday survey was completed; he died c.1090, outliving the Conqueror who had given him power by three years.

Baldwyn had three sons who succeeded him. William and Robert had interests elsewhere that ensured they had little time for their father's prized possession, Okehampton. Robert spent much of his time dealing with the family's affairs in Normandy, while William, more like his warrior father, embarked on the conquest of South Wales. It was left to the third son, Richard Fitz Baldwyn, to find time for nurturing the borough, a task he readily undertook.

Another continuing tradition – beating the bounds in August 2000.

13

Okehampton, as a borough, was an area already made subject to a court of its own, within which tenants, in lieu of providing services to the lord of the manor, could purchase acre plots, and landowners could buy or sell their property at will. In Okehampton, free tenure had taken the place of villeinage tenure – a situation achieved through either a grant made by a king or baron with the royal consent, relinquishing to the borough part of the jurisdiction which he was entitled to wield.

At Brightley, north of Okehampton, there is a barn now converted to use as offices for a business that contains all that remains of a chapel built by Richard when he founded a religious house for a Cistercian order in 1133. On May 3rd 1136, a superior (also named Richard) and 12 monks arrived from Waverley Abbey to build a new monastery on the site. The death of their founder on June 25th 1137 and the demise of their first prior so unsettled the monks that they lost the will to develop the site and decided to abandon it.

Adelice, Richard Fitz Baldwyn's sister and successor, provided them with another site at Ford in 1141 on which they established Ford Abbey. Mention of appointments to what appears to be have been known as the Perpetual Chantry of the Chapel of St Mary, Brightleigh, can be found in the Bishops' Registers and it appears that at times the chapel was probably served by the incumbent of Sampford Courtenay.

Brightley Priory & Mill

Andy Ewen, with more Priory stone found on his property.

Left: *This window is the last sizeable item remaining from the twelfth-century Brightley Priory and it is now in the building that houses the offices of the Okehampton Glass Company Ltd.*

Below: *A cottage in the old Brightley Priory ground has probably been built and rebuilt many times with stone from the Priory. This one was renovated in 1895 by men from Exeter and practically rebuilt again by it is present owner a few years ago, using the original stone.*

Brightley Mill in the early 1900s with, it is thought, Joshua Watts and his family.

Above: *Bees have been kept for centuries. In 1971 Okehampton apiarists formed a group that became the Okehampton branch of the Devon Bee Keepers Association. They took on Holsworthy branch in a quiz night.* Left to right, back row: *George Tonkin, Jim Sampson, George Gennes (questionmaster), Percy Haymor, Will Dunning;* seated (Holsworthy): *Tom Shaxson, Roger Lancaster, Bill Paddison, Gordon Bates.*

Inset: *Mr Dudley Luxton with a flailing stone. Probably more than 500 years old, it was once regularly used to remove ears of corn but leave the sheaf intact for use in thatching.*

George and Winnie Hawking preparing to mow hay, 1937.

These were disturbing and perilous times and events that divided the country could hardly have passed unnoticed in West Devon. Since the death of the Conqueror the country had suffered rule by William Rufus who had immediately set out to extract more taxes from the barons, who had in turn extracted more taxes from their people. The 'accidental' loss of an arrow that killed the king during a hunt also let loose Henry (I), who had been present, to take the throne and commandeer the country's treasures and royal insignia.

He toured the country, as Saxon kings had done earlier, collecting taxes and dues, dispensing brutal justice and producing a large number of illegitimate

children. As his heir he nominated his daughter Matilda, forcing his barons to swear that they would accept her as Queen when the time came.

Okehampton, its owners and its people and those living off the land around it could not have avoided the continual demands for taxes, nor the political manoeuvrings of the times; but worse was to come. At Henry's death in 1135 the barons reneged on their promises and Stephen, the son of Count Stephen of Blois and Adela, daughter of William the Conqueror, seized the throne with the support of his brother Henry of Blois, Bishop of Winchester, and a majority of the nobility. Within four years the nation was in a state of anarchy. Matilda, coming to claim her throne, supported by her illegitimate half-brother, Robert of Gloucester, set herself up in London, earned immediate unpopularity because of her arrogance and was driven out of the city while the barons used the civil war to settle old scores.

Matilda soon gained control of most of the West, and the local people were faced with providing for a new army that took men, young and old, away from their toil on the land to battles across the country. A now almost forgotten anarchic civil war engulfed the country, accompanied by the barbaric settling of private feuds across the South West. The farms on the prized estates around Okehampton, the small holdings and peasant plots, like others across the land, were pillaged for supplies of food for warring parties and their horses; everything was taken without mercy being shown to skin-and-bone adults or starving children.

In the mid-twelfth century the townsfolk of Okehampton had a foretaste of the type of war that would erupt again a little over 200 years later (in the Peasants Revolt) and, as their descendants would also do, they took commercial advantage of each side in the bloody conflict. Okehampton's castle alone among many avoided attack, whilst from Bampton and Barnstaple in the north, to Plympton in the south, blood-soaked battles took their toll; for 13 years the common people suffered terribly. Historian Professor Christopher Brooke aptly summed up Stephen: 'his real weakness as king was that he could neither control his friends nor subdue his enemies.' Peace, of a kind, returned to these lands in 1153 when Stephen acknowledged Matilda's son, who became his successor a year later as Henry II and restored order.

It was Henry's marriage to Eleanor of Acquitaine that was to take Okehampton a step forward in terms of its relative importance in the South West. With the prosperous provinces of south-west France under English control there were political and economic benefits soon to be gained for the region with the development of Fowey and Exeter as ports.

Adelice (Adeliza) who had received the barony of Okehampton and the wealth it provided when her brother Richard died, did not survive the civil war conflict; she died in 1142. For over 30 years the family fortunes continued to be handed on by other heiresses, the husband of one of whom, also conceived on the wrong side of the blankets, was a bastard son of the first King Henry.

It was during this period that the French connection with the South West stimulated the growth of Fowey, with wine being imported and cloth being exported. Okehampton was strategically established at the hub of the most successful ports – Exeter, Plymouth, Fowey and Dartmouth. Poor though the locality was, it provided the basis of an enormous industry and for Okehampton passing trade of any kind provided opportunities for financial benefits to be gained that would not have been ignored.

Some 31 years after the death of Adelice Okehampton came into the hands of a rather determined lady, Hawisia (or Hawvis) de Aincourt, who married into the Courtenay family; not just once, but twice, at least. Whatever the reason – love, a lusting for wealth and power, or political manoeuvring – Hawisia's marriages ensured that the Courtenays took a tight hold of Okehampton. In 1173 she married Reginald Courtenay who had arrived in England in the service of Queen Eleanor of Acquitaine some 20 years previously. To their marriage Hawisia brought the castle, estates and lands that would keep the Courtenays associated with Okehampton with little interruption for over 350 years. For his part Reginald only held Sutton, in Berkshire, granted to him by Henry II, prompted perhaps by Eleanor.

In 1178 Pope Alexander III, who canonised Thomas à Becket, granted the right to have a free chapel to Reginald de Courtenay who enjoyed the benefit until he died on September 27th 1194, to be buried on the north side of the presbytery of Ford Abbey. Some time soon after Reginald's death Hawisia married another Reginald, who may also have been named William. Upon his marriage to Hawisia, Reginald the Younger, or William, De Courtenay paid on succession 50ℓ and 5 palfreys for possession of the Honour of Okehampton.

More confusing than the names of the men Hawisia married is the mysterious question of whether or not her marriages ceased with the second Reginald. Hawisia is said to have died on July 15th 1209, and was buried at Ford Abbey on the south side of the presbytery, according to the monk of Ford. Such records seem quite acceptable, particularly in view of the fact that Reginald, husband number one, was buried on the north side of the presbytery of Ford Abbey. Other records, however, indicate that Hawisia, accounted to the Exchequer in 1210, was considered to have been a marriageable widow in 1217, and was later said to have died on July 31st 1219. Whatever the truth, she was a remarkable lady, living in an adventurous age at a time when legend was created.

In 1189 that hero of medieval legend, Richard I, whose military exploits earned him the sobriquet Lionheart, had come to the throne. A year later he was setting out on his third Crusade, funded by his new source of revenue, his subjects in England. The romanticised stories of the Crusades omit the fact that it took men and money to launch them. Richard I ransacked England's wealth throughout his reign, despite spending less than a year in the country himself during his time on the throne. Ever more exorbitant taxes were demanded of the barons and landowners, and in Okehampton as a developing town and in the flourishing countryside around it those tax demands fell heavily on the people, not excluding the poorest among them. Such taxes, however, did not go directly to Richard since he assigned the royal revenues of Devon, together with those of Cornwall, Somerset, Dorset, Derby and Nottingham, to his brother John; who, also holding the Honour of Gloucester, later relied upon his power base and supporters in the South West.

Reginald de Courtenay died in 1190 and was succeeded by his son, Robert, who married Maria (Mary), daughter of William, son of Baldwyn de Redvers, Earl of Devon and founder of Cowick Priory. Facing danger both from France and from his brother John, c.1193–94, King Richard ordered the renovation of his royal and baronial castles, which increased work opportunities for carpenters, masons and other skilled craftsmen in and around Okehampton; who could then afford to pay their taxes of course, until they were increased again.

Robert de Courtenay was Sheriff of Devonshire in 1215 and 1217 but one of his claims to local folklore fame is that in c.1221 he paid King Henry III five marks and a palfrey to gain the right to hold a fair yearly in his manor of Okehampton, on the vigil day of St Thomas the Apostle; which some say appears to be the origin of what is called Okehampton's 'great market' held on the Saturday before Christmas. Whatever the truth is about the horse trading, Okehampton gained a borough charter granted to the burgesses of the town by Robert de Courtenay which is not dated, but which was probably written in or soon after the year 1219. In that document Robert de Courtenay's words indicate the growing importance of the town, addressing 'all Christian people' to know that the deed was 'confirmed, with the assent and consent of Mary my wife and of my heirs, to my Burgesses of my free Borough of Okehampton' that they should continue to enjoy all rights and privileges and possession of their 'tenements and free customs' that had been theirs since the time of Richard, the son of Baldwyn. There were 'fees' for such privileges of course, to be paid yearly:

... for every burgage to me and to my heirs, by the hands of my Provost (Portreeve) of the Borough, at the festival of St Michael 12d. for all services and demands,

Above: *Inside Town Mill, c.1975. Okehampton's mill was mentioned in the Domesday survey and it continued to serve the town for almost another 900 years.*

Right: *The old Town Mill, during its latter days. It was sold in 1978 and has since been converted to provide comfortable homes.*

pertaining to me and to my heirs and to them and to their heirs...

But by such financial arrangement they were to be secure in their 'holding':

... by right of inheritance freely, quietly, peaceably and honourably for evermore in wood and in plain, in ways and paths, in marshes and in common pastures, in waters and in mills, and in all places where Robert, and his heirs may reasonably warrant.

The burgesses of the 'free Borough' were also granted to annually 'of their own council, elect and depose a Provost and a Cryer (an assistant official); the Provost shall be quit of his rent, the Cryer of sixpence.' Anyone wishing to settle in the town paid 4d. to the borough and to the lord in order to be admitted to the 'freedom'. Thus, in addition to provost and cryer there was one or more 'local government officer', an early borough treasurer and financial member of staff, receiving and accounting for incoming funds and fines, serving the burgesses, villeins, serfs and vassals.

Anyone in the borough deserving punishment by the lord could escape it on payment of 12d., unless they were an habitual offender, whereupon they were to face the judgement of the burgesses and the lord's steward, according to the seriousness of the crime.

Burgesses, or their children, wishing to marry or be given in marriage were given permission to do so, 'quietly, and wherever they will'. Furthermore, every burgess was to be entitled to keep a sow and four little pigs 'quit of pannage in my wood of Okehampton'.

The charter excluded those from outside the borough trading within it, with tolls imposed if they were found trading illegally, and it made the provost (portreeve) responsible for collecting tolls, from which he received '12d. from the toll and the quittance of his rent for this service'. The commission the provost, or portreeve, was to earn was from tolls levied: for a horse 1d.; for an ox $^1/_2$ d.; for five sheep 1d.; for five pigs 1d. For corn and grain their was no charge. Anyone evading paying the toll was subject to further tolls: for a farthing toll 5s.; for a halfpenny 10s.; and for a penny 20s. Stiff penalties indeed.

A burgess could sell his burgage to whomsoever he wished, except to religious houses, and could depart without challenge on giving: to the lord 12d.; to the provost 4d.; and to the borough 4d. But, if a burgess died, his widow and heirs could 'quietly receive his tenements'.

For the charter and its benefits the burgesses gave Robert ten marks as consideration and in order that it remained fixed and firm for ever, he sealed and confirmed it in the presence of witnesses including, among others:

Main: *Jeweller and clockmaker Mr Drew in the mid 1870s standing before his shop attached to St James' Church.*
He emigrated to Brisbane, Australia, in time for that city's worst floods on record.
Inset: *Brisbane, 1893. Mr Drew's shop was on the right.*

Lord Reginald de Courtenay, William de Nymet, (Sheriff of Devon), Robert the Bastard, William de Albamara, Baldwin de Belstone, Elia Coffin, Ralph Fitz Ralph, Roger de Mules, William de Ley, Augero de Wile, and Geoffrey de la Hag.

Two decades or so later, in 1240, the chapel in the castle was appropriated, with the Parish Church, to Cowick Priory, Exeter, under an agreement stipulating that Mass would be said daily in the chapel, either by the priory's vicar or the chaplain of the then lord.

Robert died two years later and was succeeded by John Courtenay, who died in 1274 leaving Okehampton to his son and heir, Hugh Courtenay (1). Hugh managed to quarrel with the monks of Ford Abbey in 1288, and in an act of revenge impounded their cattle and drove them on to the moor on his Okehampton estate. He died three or four years later leaving his estates and fortune to his 16-year-old son Hugh (2). Since Hugh (2) would not come of age for another five years the estates returned to the hands of Edward I, whose purchase of other lands was to deny young Hugh (2) his inheritance.

Isabella de Fortibus, sister of the last Earl of the Redvers family, died in 1293, and previous marriages, having connected the Redvers with the Courtenays, now brought the former's estates and their Devon castle of Plympton to the Courtenays. Edward I, however, had purchased the Redvers' estates in Hampshire and the Isle of Wight just before Isabella's death and, with Hugh (2) his ward, he allowed the earldom of Devon to lapse. The Courtenays' lands were his.

Hugh (2) was knighted by the Prince of Wales (later Edward II) in 1306, quarrelled with the people of Exeter over rights of the River Exe, seemingly did little for Okehampton and did not regain his inheritance until it was restored to him by Edward III in February 1335. Hugh (2) died on December 23rd 1340. As 'Sir Hugh' de Courtenay he lived long enough to see an important population movement and Okehampton's countryside become ever more attractive to those who sought to obtain burgage settlements from the lord or who saw their future in trade. Larger towns like Plymouth drew such enterprising people from the other end of the peninsula; smaller ones, like Okehampton, from closer to home. W.G. Hoskins (*Devon*) provides a plausible reason for the migration by those who were probably 'sons of the numerous peasant-freeholders in the backwoods who were free to leave the ancestral farm,' continuing: 'Only the eldest son could succeed to small peasant property: it was too small to divide up: and the other sons and daughters had to fend for themselves.' He also notes that the tax rolls of 1332 confirm this migration.

As the colonisation began these enthusiastic people started to open the moorland for new farms, and to conquer and clear the forest ways as they reached new sources of timber. Others opened up shops and added to market stalls for the sale of produce, while the more industrially minded established mills and forges to grind flour and provide tools for the new farmers.

Okehampton, and the entire country, was embarking on a roller-coaster of a ride that was to take it to heights of wealth creation and to depths of despair that are almost beyond our imagination today.

Sir Hugh de Courtenay also lived long enough to see Edward III, by claiming the French throne, begin a war in 1337 that would last 100 years. Men and ships were going to be required, not forgetting money, and Okehampton and the estates were capable of providing all of these. Timber was needed for more ships as Edward's navy, including mariners from Devon, began winning impressive victories, starting at Sluys in 1340. The human losses of war were not contained in battles but losses in commerce and industry fell upon the county and Okehampton paid its due. Trade between England and France virtually ended, Devon's ports felt the loss as much as the centres of commerce and industry and the county began to sink into a century of decline and decay. Few places felt this worse than market towns like Okehampton and Crediton, while nearby Tavistock, and others with their tin trade, suffered least of all.

Like his predecessors Edward looked to his barons and nobles to find the funds necessary to continue the intermittent fighting. But it was not war with France that was to have the only impact on Okehampton. Originating in China, a far more deadly enemy came knocking at the door. It was bubonic plague that would decimate England and demoralise society. By 1349 between a third and one half of the population of Okehampton, as with the rest of England, had succumbed to a dreadful death. Wave after wave of the plague swept across the country taking high-born and peasant alike; and the plague took three forms. The country people of Okehampton and their rural kin around them were suddenly confronted by an horrific illness that their potions and remedies could not combat. The swelling of glands in the groin, armpit or neck was followed by blood vessels beneath the skin breaking, causing bright spots and rashes and agonising pain that was unremitting, day and night; the victim usu-

ally died within a week. Wailing children could only look on as their mothers or fathers, or both, succumbed to the silent killer that stalked the country. Weary mothers could do nothing for their young, farmland and plots of ground remained untended, trees unfelled, and the strongest of men fell before the onslaught. When the miller died, the mill ceased to operate, when the blacksmith died his forge fire was extinguished too. When supplies could not be found, shopkeepers remained with their share of misery behind closed doors.

The wounds of war or infections caught at home was all, and often more, that most could cope with. But many faced the second type of plague in their homes, a violent fever. Continually coughing up blood, few were released from their suffering in less than three days; and during those agonising hours they spread the disease with every cough that convulsed their weakening bodies.

Those that fell to the third variant of the disease were, perhaps, the fortunate ones. It is difficult for us today to imagine an Okehampton, flea-ridden, lacking anything that we could remotely consider as sanitation, when we cannot even really understand, closer to our own times, the Dickensian squalor described by a man who bore witness to hard times. Nothing can have been so hard as that plague-ridden period endured by our ancestors on whose flesh the human flea fed, and in so feeding infected the bloodstream and brought death within hours.

Even for those that survived the 1348–49 epidemic, the 'normal' death rate was high. They entered the second half of the fourteenth century aware of that, fearing the return of the plague and facing drastic changes in the countryside; with a population that was probably halved.

On the brighter side there was more land available for cottagers and smallholders that had survived and yet more could acquire their first piece of land; all as beneficiaries of the dead. If more than 200 souls survived the onset of the plague there could only have been a few more. What they needed though was more time for themselves and less devoted to the lord of the manor. The reduction in population also brought increased wages, lower rents, and the barons turning to Parliament to try to freeze prices as well as wages and seek a means to keep labourers under control. A ploughman earning 2s.(10p) before the plague of 1348–49 was earning nearer to 8s. (40p) in 1350, and more than 10s. (50p) a year later. The Statute of Labour enacted by Parliament in 1351 was, *inter alia*, intended to stop labourers, bond or free, from breaking their contracts or changing residence.

Villeins had been able to commute their work services by the payment of rent since the twelfth century, and for a further century there had been plenty of men to do the baron's bidding, but now there was a manpower shortage. The 1351 Statute

Dartmoor Stonemasons

Below left: *It is no longer in church but this is a font nevertheless and a tribute to the ancient skills of the Dartmoor stonemason.*

Below right: *The skill of an unknown Dartmoor stonemason ensured that the circular sharpening stone sank into the matching granite groove.*

Above: *This circular granite trough was made by a craftsman from one piece of granite and could be several centuries old.*

was perhaps, in modern parlance, a knee-jerk reaction designed to reverse the effects on wages of that shortage. Employers were to return to the level of wages that applied before the period of the Black Death and all men not landowners were compelled to take work at those rates. Wages fell, and discontent rose. The worker that once had 10s. (50p) in his purse for his week's pay, now did the same work for just over half that amount.

The Statute was unpopular with landowners who still found labour in short supply, it contributed to the Peasants' Revolt and can be considered to have failed because labourers could not be contained. The partial recovery of Okehampton swiftly faded as more and more Okehamptonian villeins increased their landholdings in an effort to escape serfdom, provide food for their families and extra for the wider community. Their time could not be divided – many of those allowed to either pay rent or provide labour chose the former. Then came the poll tax. It was the first time that every person in Okehampton over the age of 16 was subject to a graduated direct tax that moved part of the tax burden off the shoulders of the lord of the manor, the rich and the property owners, on to the poor. Those that recall the more recent attempts to introduce such a tax on individuals, and the riots that ensued, will know that the events of the late-fourteenth century were far more bloodthirsty.

Across the land there was revolution. Manor houses were attacked and records of dues owed by villeins to lords were burnt. A rebel army rose up in the east, led by Wat Tyler, and Canterbury fell, among others. On Blackheath, the 'mad priest' John Ball

preached that nothing would go right for England until there was 'neither vassal nor lord'. In London, the headquarters of the legal profession in the Temple was burnt down, as was the home of John of Gaunt, Duke of Lancaster. The Archbishop of Canterbury was beheaded; he was, after all, also the Lord Chancellor. The Lord Treasurer lost his head too.

Many historians point to the East and the revolt in Essex, Kent and Anglia, but the tax that induced the uprisings was universal. So, would not the unfair imposition have been felt as heavily in the South West as elsewhere? Suffice to add here that the South West was not some backwater that events passed by.

For the moment, however, the appearance of John of Gaunt must take us forward, to consider another chapter of bloody history that the people of Okehampton would help pay for through taxes or bastard feudalism. From 1337 until 1445, the so-called Hundred Years War had engaged three generations of Okehampton volunteers or pressed men into war at sea and battles in France, between long periods of truce or fretful peace. The need for men, money and arms varied at times but any or all needed to be available whenever required; and with minimum delay. From the countryside and town the equivalent of 'standing armies' were created from indentured retainers; armies which were available for service not only to their lords but also to the king. Corruption and coercion were prominent in the maintenance of such paid and often uniformed military forces as, two years after the long war ended, Okehampton families, with others the length and breadth of the land, faced civil war; with each side adding a rose, of red or white, to their uniform.

3

Hamlets & Manors Maketh Okehampton

Some claim that had there not been an 'Okehampton' there would never have been any 'hamlets', but this flies in the face of all evidence pointing to the fact that it was the land in this area that first attracted our ancestors in prehistoric times. Our iron-using, bronze-bearing ancestors found the land and what it contained of value and in settling here they placed their mark on the ground that still yields up a reason for some to remain here, though not as many now as in some years past.

The fertile land provided the first farmers with all that was needed to totally sustain their community, a value that was only diminished in very recent years. As centuries passed by it was in the areas we regard as 'the hamlets' (within which even Okehampton Castle falls) that the matters of importance to Okehampton and its development took place. It was an area sufficiently well established by the time of the Conquest for the invaders to record in their survey, in addition to the entries regarding Ochementon (Okehampton), the details of two other manors, Cacheberga (Kigbere) and Cicecota (Chichacott).

Later records, the Testa de Nevil of 1241, provide us with information on yet more manors – Crofte, Maddeford, Alfardesdune, Meledune, La Hoke and Stackelegh. Each of these relates to areas of productive land that could, through its residents, produce wealth for the owner and a meagre living for his tenants. Each of the manors provided Okehampton with the support it needed and while we would prefer to explore all manors to reveal the foundations of the inheritance that is Okehampton's today, space in a small volume restricts us to explore but a few, and, even then, only briefly in passing.

In 1086 Baldwyn's manor of Cacheberga, previously owned by an Anglo-Saxon called Sawin,

Mr 'Bert Luxton (left), and Mr Charlie Sprague were keen followers of tradition, especially beating the bounds.

was held by Baldwyn's servant, Raner, whose holding was described in Domesday as follows:

... in demesne, 1 ferding and 1 plough, and the villeins have 3 ferdings and 3 ploughs. There Raner had 6 villeins, 5 bordars, 1 serf, 5 beasts, 30 sheep, 3 swine, 2 acres of woodland, 12 acres of meadow and 20 acres of pasture. Worth 30s. (£1.50) a year.

Then, 80 years later, the manor formed part of four fees held by Roger de Langford of Robert Fitz Regis of the Honour of Okehampton. The Langford connection with the manor was to last, with some interruption, for nearly 300 years. In 1303 Roger de Langeford is recorded as holding what appears to be two tenements, Cakebere and Cadekebere, of Hugh de Courtenay, together with Crofte for half of a knight's fee. After Roger died in c.1310, on June 8th that year, King Edward II instructed Walter de Gloucester, escheator, not to meddle further with the hamlet of Cadekebere, Devon, which was taken into the King's hands by reason of the death of Roger de Langeford, as it appeared by Inquisition he did not hold any lands in chief of the King, except certain tenements in Chale and Newenham on the Isle of Wight, as of the castle of Caresbrook by the service of half part of a knight's fee.

Six years later, Cadekebere is mentioned in tax records together with Brixton, Inwardlegh, Gorhywys and Ayshbury, for all of which Adam de Brodenimet was answerable. The Langford connection reappears in 1343 when John de Langeford was the holder of Cadekebeare, of Hugh de Courtenay, on February 16th; although his holding seems to have been short-lived since it is Thomas de Langeford, on September 21st that year, who granted to Simon de Asshe and Walter de Yldishe, clerk, his manors of Langeford and Cachebere.

Farming Around the Parish

Mr Woods and others take a harvest break in the field, 1931.

Top left: *Haymaking, c.1938, at Elmead Farm with Gale and Emily Hawking on the cart, George and Winnie Hawking with Gale senr, and John and Roy.*

Above: *During the winter of 1937 the children had not been so keen to help Winnie and George at Elmead Farm.*

Right: *Mr and Mrs Horn at Webber Hill Farm in the 1920s.*

The rabbit catch from the corn crop at Glendon Farm in the 1940s.

Above: *Mr and Mrs Hawking were at Chichacott Farm by 1953.*

Clapps Mill. The mill area from above West Bridge to Somerfield supermarket included a warren of small cottages, condemned by MOH Dr J. Allen Price in June 1936, and subject of a clearance order in 1937.

Held for half a fee, Cadekebere and Crofton, of the Honour of Ockampton, were in the hands Thomas de Langafford in 1346. In 1348 the Black Death arrived in Dorset, carried by terrified men who fled from France to escape it, but instead brought the pestilence with them. With devastating speed it swept through Devon, spread by fleas carried by rats. The local population suffered severely. It was an unnamed number of heirs of a 'William Langford' that held half a fee in Cakebury and Crofton in 1428, which 'old Thomas' Langford had at one time held, but none of them apparently held a complete quarter part.

By this time the Langfords were losing their grip on the manor and the names Devyok, Deviock or Devick, relating to a family from St Germans in Cornwall, begin to appear in the borough records and Kigbere became theirs. We cross paths with Edmund Devyok in 1475 and John Devyok, armiger, in October 1481. The following month, on November 10th, John Asshe and Margaret his wife granted their land in Kympleigh to John Devyok, Johanna his wife and Edmond their son. In c.1499–1500, Edmond Devyok is again mentioned, as a feoffee. Kigbere left the hands of the Devyock family c.1520 when it passed, by way of marriage, to the Cary family when Jane, the daughter and heir of Edmund Deviok of Okehampton, was wed to John Cary.

John Cary was the eldest son of Robert and Jane Cary of Cockington and grandson of Sir William Cary who was slain on the Bloody Meadow during the Battle of Tewkesbury on May 4th 1471. John Cary

of Okehampton, esquire, and Robert his son and heir apparent, are recorded as conveying the manor of 'North Lew' to Thomas Cary of Cockington in November 1544. Thereafter appears in the records what may well be a series of incidents that occur to one person, a Henry Cary. In 1586 he is mentioned as a trustee under the will of Richard Brock, the man who gave almshouses to the town.

By this time, having prospered during Mary's brief reign and the first three decades of the Elizabethan era, the town boasted grist-mills, fulling-mills and tanneries. Boot making was a major trade and looms were exploited to the full to produce a popular white woollen cloth for the Exeter market and for overseas. Okehampton's own market flourished and had become famous for its cheese, though farmers had problems then that might still be recognised. It was at that time recorded that 'the oats which they sow be all spoiled oats and the drink they do make thereof spoiled drink,' simply because 'all the year throughout commonly it raineth or is foul weather.'

On June 20th 1589 one Henry Cary was appointed a feoffee of the borough property; and just before 1600 Henry Cary of Kigbere, who had married Willmott, daughter of Edmund Cann, a 'burgess of Oketon', moved off to Launceston. In 1609 Lancelott Cary of Cadicabere, gent., gave by will 'three score pounds to put out apprentices and for relief of the poore upon good securitie and to continue for ever.' Ten pounds of this sum were to be employed for the inhabitants of Kigbere. This generosity did nothing to offset the town portreeve who, with others, was not happy with Henry Cary who had earlier departed for Launceston, and in 1610 a bill in Chancery was brought by the portreeve, John Rattenbury, and the late portreeve, William Calmady, and others against Henry, and other feoffees, for refusing to make a new feoffment as was required. Further, the said Henry, it was claimed:

... had dwelled for 13 years or thereabouts in the Burrough of Launceston, by reason whereof he ought not to hold the premises any longer; but was to graunt same over, as aforesaid, or to be excluded from medling therein.

They obviously wanted Henry out.

Chichacott or Chissacott Manor

In 1086 Baldwyn held a manor called Cicecota, which Brismar the Saxon had previously held:

... and it paid geld for ½ virgate. This 3 ploughs can till. Now Roger holds it of Baldwyn. There Roger has 1 plough in demesne, and the villeins till with 2 oxen. There Roger has 4 villeins, 1 bordar, 1 serf, 13 beasts, 3 swine, 32 sheep, 30 acres of wood [land], 3 acres of meadow, and 3 acres of pasture. Worth 15s a year, and was worth the same when Baldwyn received it.

Besides Cicecota, Brismar the Saxon had held many other manors before the Conquest, of which 17 were subsequently given to Baldwyn, who actually held 186 Devonshire manors and from those one 'Roger', or Roger de Molis, held nine: Chichacott, Lew Trenchard, Waddlescot in Lew Trenchard, Exbourne, Highampton, Lashbrook, Mules in Bradford Dabernon, George Teign in Ashton, Pennycot in Shobrook and Smallicombe in Northleigh. In 1166, in the Honour of Okehampton, Johel de Molis held lands for four fees, of Robert Fitz Regis. The lands were not specified, but may well have been those in the possession of Roger de Molis in 1086 and inherited by John de Molis in 1241, by which time fees held by the Honour of Okehampton included:

Lashbrook, Bradford	)	
Dornaford, Sampford Courtenay	)	
Exbourne	) John de Molis	2½
Highampton	)	

Historian Dr Edward Young believed that Chichacott must in some way represent Dornaford (Higher and Lower Dornaford Farms in Sampford Courtenay) since Dornaford is not found in Domesday, unless it formed part of the manor of Sanfort, identified as Sampford Courtenay parish, and held by Baldwyn himself; Sanfort was valued at 12ℓ as compared with Okehampton, only 10ℓ. He considered it likely that Roger de Molis made his home at Chichacott, as one of the chief vassals of his countryman Baldwyn de Sap, de Molis, de Execestre (to give him his full titles). By doing so Roger was within reach of the castle and he farmed as his holding the lands of Dornaford; the two tenements forming one manor.

Okehampton certainly had a school and a teacher by the time that Peter and Susannah Ebbsworthy were making an agreement in 1611 with Giles Iglett, concerning the manor of Chichacott and other lands in Okehampton. John Alford, Susannah's father, came from Okehampton and a later reference, in 1632, also mentions his name when his elder daughter Ursula, her husband John Calmady and their son and heir John, conveyed a moiety of the manor of Chissacott to the Revd John Hussey, the vicar of Okehampton.

Turn the clock on 28 years and it is Simon Hussey, the son of the Revd Thomas Hussey, who is then recorded as conveying to his brother, Thomas, lands in the manor of Chichacott. Thomas and Edith Hussey produced a son named Henry, described in 1678 as a yeoman, and it was in that year that the family conveyed to John Northmore of Okehampton and Thomas Yendall the moiety of the manor of Chichacott, and also conveyed a moiety of Chichacott to Benjamin Gayer; but as far as Mr Gayer was concerned the Husseys excluded a tenement called Easter Place and Broadmeet Meadow from their conveyance.

Benjamin Gayer, burgess and Mayor of Okehampton, lived in a house near St James' Chapel, and, according to legend, was a sinful man since, after he died at Kigbere, he was condemned for his evil ways to labour forever at Cranmere Pool, or, if

Left: The Mayor, Cllr Christine Marsh, attended by the Town Clerk, Mr Winchester, preceded by mace-bearers, prepares to lead to the procession to the Civic Service, June 13th 1999.

Below: Civic Sunday, 1999, and the Okehampton Excelsior Silver Band prepares for the procession to All Saints Church.

not forever, at least until he emptied the pool with a sieve. Over the centuries the 'pool' has dried out many times, which permits some to say that he perhaps succeeded, while others claim that the 'pool' has always retained some water, so Mr Benjamin Gayer continues his penance. In a time when witchcraft trials were far from unknown there is much to consider about suggestions made that Mr Gayer and his family had been associated with passing sentence on so-called witches, such as those tried in the 1650s that we mention elsewhere. A 'curse' upon Gayer then, or his family, would easily be carried down the years in a tale that contrasts with the little-known tablet from his time that is in the vestry of the Parish Church and which testifies to Gayer's good name.

The name of Thomas Hiern, surgeon and four-times Mayor of Okehampton, can be associated with Chichacott in 1727, but also for some years prior to that, because on May 15th he died and left a moiety of Chichacott to his son Thomas.

In 1801 Thomas B. Luxmoore sold Mary Hiern one moiety of Chissacott and it is her will of 1818 in which the descent of Chissacott manor is recorded.

Bowerland

Mention of the farmland between the Holsworthy and Plymouth roads is found in reference to the receipt of scutage, at half a fee, in 1284, when Richard de Heuuishe held Borlond in the manor of Okehampton. In 1291 la Bourlonde was held by Ernina de Hywisshe for half a fee. Silvester Danvers, the son of Thomas and Margaret Danvers of Dauncy, Wiltshire, sold Leonard Yeo his share in the manors of Northe Hewysche, Stofford (Stowford) and Bowrlonde in Okampton, on April 29th 1548, including the power to nominate clergy to three churches, for £85.13s.4d.

On May 18th 1578 Edward Barkeley of Wotton-under-Edge, Gloucester, and his wife Elizabeth sold their portion of Huysshe (N. Huish), Stowford and 'one mancion house or farme' called Bowerland to George Yeo of Fyshlieghe, for £51.12s.6d.

Robert Tayllor, the tenant of 'Bowerlande', was among those witnessing the conveyance, and paying one penny as a portion of the attorney's fee. George Yeo was seemingly gathering in fragmented parts of the earlier Bowerland estate because on September 16th, for £61, he purchased the shares of the estate, described in each case as 'one part in fifteen and one-third of a fifteenth', held by Thomas Throkmurton of Tortwoorthe, Gloucester. On the same day Henry Poole of Saperton, Gloucester, sold one-third of a fifteenth of the estate to him for £12. The following year, 1579, George Yeo continued his shopping spree on March 8th, by purchasing for £40 the share in the estate held by Hugh Jones of Dancye, co. Wilcester. That George Yeo may not have been acting on his own behalf begins to be revealed on February 10th

1580 when Thomas Bodenham from Herefordshire sold Leonard Yeo of Totton his share (one part in fifteen) of the estate for £70. Less than a year later, on January 10th 1581, George Yeo conveyed his holdings in the estate to Leonard Yeo, his father, and kept things further in the family by having Robert Yeo acting as attorney – who took payment of 1d. from the tenants.

The estate that had been put together by the purchasing spree was fully revealed in October 1586 after Leonard Yeo had died. His holdings amounted to nine parts of a messuage, 160 acres of land, 30 acres of meadow, 200 acres of pasture and 200 acres of gorse and heath called Bowerland divided into 15 parts – all this held of the heirs of the late Earl of Devon as of his Honour of Okehampton by fealty. Value 24s.

In the marriage settlement ten years later of Leonard Yeo (2), Bowerland is described as being in the tenure of Robert Taylor but records of 15 November 1596 show that George Yeo had gained most of his father's estate. George and his wife Elizabeth, living at Hatherley, are by this time recorded as having been worth nine parts of the manor and advowson of Stowford and of 20 messuages, 2 dove-cots, 20 gardens, 20 apple-orchards, 600 acres of land, 80 acres of meadow, 60 acres of pasture and 600 acres of gorse and heath, divided into 15 parts, in Stowford, Bowerland and Okehampton.

George and Elizabeth appear not to have been blessed with children and, when George died around March 15th 1607, his heir, John Trelawny, was a minor. The estate returned to the King, until John came of age, and was in the care of the Reynald Mohun, Nicholas Halls, knight, John Courtenay and Hannibal Vivian as of the Honour of Okehampton. Leonard Yeo (2), may have been in ill health by November 1621 because on November 28th he appointed trustees to care for his lands which amounted to nine parts, of 15, of a messuage, 100 acres of land, 5 acres of meadow, and 300 acres of gorse and heath in Bowerland and Okehampton, described as his right and inheritance. Leonard (2) may also have had a son later in life as an action taken by a further Leonard (3) against one John Pawlyn, on January 27th 1663, seems to suggest. The action, regarding a fine levied on Pawlyn at Easter 1659, and presumably unpaid, also records that 5 parts of a messuage, a garden, 100 acres of land, 4 acres of meadow, 20 acres of pasture, 200 acres of furze and heath, and 100 acres of moor divided into 15 parts in Bowerland, was deemed to be to the sole use of George Yeo.

Do we see in all of this two lines of one family, or succeeding generations preferring the names Leonard and George for their offspring? By October 10th 1682 Leonard and Joane Yeo of Huish, and their son George, gentleman, appointed trustees to 14 of 15 parts of their estate of Bowerland, among other lands held by the family.

Halstock Manor

While being the site of early Anglo-Saxon settlements, but not being mentioned until after the Domesday Book, the Dartmoor area of Halstock is shown to have once belonged to Cowick Priory and was probably a foundation gift made by William Fitz Baldwyn in c.1090. In 1295 John Bere de Holdstocke was the provost of Okehampton. With the destruction of Cowick Priory by fire in 1445, its possessions were seized by the Crown, and Henry VI handed them over to his new foundation at Eton in 1451. Edward IV, however, removed the land and rights from Eton 13 years later and gave Halstock to Tavistock Abbey. In February 1482, Roger Bowden, the son of John Bowden of Halstock, received from the Abbot of Tavystoke, by the hand of Ralph Pouvoen, his overseer, a tenement for which he paid 40s. John, the abbot at the time, died ten years later and it was the abbot Richard (Banham) of Tavistock who, on December 30th 1495, approved land to be received by William Fursse, Alicia his wife and their son John on payment of 20s.

Henry Dynham, monk and abbot's overseer, dealt with the transaction and similarly acted on behalf of the abbot on February 16th 1496 when John Caddyng, Matilda his wife and their son received a tenure which Agnes Boughdon actually held, but which would be theirs after her death, for the term of their lives, for 26s.8d. to be paid at each Michaelmas.

Such reversions of tenement were a popular means of pre-arranging for continued income from land and its tenure. As lord of the manor of Halstoke, John (Perynne), the abbot of Tavystoke in 1524, approved a reversion of a tenement between father and son, whereby John Whyte (junr) would eventually receive the tenement held by his father, John Whyte (senr), for which arrangement the former paid the abbot 66s.8d.

On September 10th 1543 Richard Andrewes, of Hayles, Gloucestershire, and Nicholas Temple, holders of messuages and lands in Halstok, obtained a licence of alienation, for 6s.8d., permitting them to transfer their holdings to Leonard Yeo, gentleman. Wasting little time, the transaction was concluded on payment of £20 on October 20th when the men sold, 'to Leonard Yowe, gentleman, Halstocke; held for $^1/_{20}$ fee and the annual rent 2s.1$^1/_2$d.'

So significant was the sale that the appointed attorneys, John Yowe, gentleman, and William Lovey, yeoman, had it witnessed by seven local worthies: John Alworde; Wylliam Hopar of Ockehampton, the elder; John Caner, the elder, of Hatherley; John Bowdon; John Cadynge; John Whyte; and Walter Horrell, of Halstock.

In 1550 Leonard Yeo of Hatherlegh, gent., let to John Fursse of Ockenton 'the Chapell grond' in the manor of Halstocke, for 99 years, paying 4s.8d. yearly, 'with suyte at my court att Halstocke and discharge of venwell rent.' A modest income perhaps but lump sums were not unknown, as shown in 1552 when Jone, wife of John Caddyng and Edmonde his son, paid Leonard Yeo £13.6s.8d. for the reversion of a tenement in Halstock, for 99 years at 2s.8$^1/_2$d. yearly.

Brother and sister, Wyllyam and Maude Bowden, obtained for 20 marks from Leonard Yeo, on February 28th 1560, the reversion of a tenement in Halstock, which John Whyte was holding until his decease. The tenement was theirs and their heirs' for 99 years at 2s.4d. annually.

Two years later it was Leonard Yooe of Tottnes who was gaining even more from the letting of messauges in Holstocke, as on June 6th when, for £15, he let to John, son of Walter and Mawte Horwyll, their messuage in Holstocke for 99 years at 3s.2d. yearly. Discharge of 'venwell' rent and best beast as 'heryott' were undertaken.

For the better part of two decades, at least, Leonarde Yeo continued to be associated with the transactions dealing with messauges of Holstocke, during which time 'local' family names appear here as they do also in other manors. Thomas Weeke and Alice his wife secured their future in 1569 with land at 4s.1$^1/_2$d. yearly, but 'only for pasture and not to tyllage without lycence.' John Cadinge's son William, having paid £20 in 1574, awaited the death of John Bowscott (or his early retirement) so that he could then take over. Later, Edward Baggetor would await William's departure from the same land.

Ladies too took up land leases from Leonarde Yeo, one being Kateryne Weke, wife of Thomas who was after the messuage held by 'Thomas and John his son', and paid £20 to secure it for 99 years, with an agreed 4s.1d. annual rent. Reason suggests that Kateryne was at least the second wife of Thomas who had a son by a previous marriage. The landholder could have been her father-in-law, but that is less likely. The done deal was witnessed by three people; Richard Latchebroke, Richard Rowke and William Caddeng. There were other Caddinges about at the time with an interest in Holstocke, or lack of it in Edmunde Caddinge's case. He surrendered to Leonarde Yeo his claim in 'messuages' in Halstock which John Caddinge his father held and had this withdrawal witnessed by no less than four: Richard Northleighe; John Furse, of Crediton; John Seywarde; and Nicholas Truyt.

At the same time, though, James Caddinge and William Caddinge his brother had Leonarde Yeo grant to them the 'ferme letten' messuages in Halstock, lately held by John Bouscott, for 99 years, at 3s. annual rent. The following was recorded: 'Heriott and suit at Courte of Halstocke. Tenants to discharge venvill rent but to receive howse boote.' This agreement was witnessed by Nicholas Potte and Wylliam Cloke.

Three years later, on August 21st 1580, William Caddinge surrendered his share in the presence of

Pascall Brook and William Clooke. Edmund Caddinge's disinterest in his father's holdings in Halstoke (look back a little way) may be explained by a record of an agreement made in August 1578 when William Caddinge and Marye his wife, for £20, leased the 'moytie or halfindele of messuages' in Halstock in the tenure of Johan Caddinge, widower, and Edmund Caddinge. Edmund obviously had enough on his hands. Leonarde Yeo was still dealing with leases in 1585 but his residence by then was in Exeter so, unless we have two, Leonarde appears to have moved from Tottnes (sic). It may have been a move prompted by ill heath since this Leonarde had only a year left to live. It was on July 15th 1585 that he agreed, for £10, to lease Edwarde Baggtor of Okehampton, husbondman, and Johane his wife, certain messuages in Halstock for 99 years, to commence after the death or surrender of John Guscote. The agreement called for payment of 3s. yearly, suit at the 'Courts of Halstocke,' and best beast as heriot, or 33s.4d.

In October of the same year Leonarde Yeo of Exeter, and George Yeo his son and heir of Hatherley, leased to John Horwyll of Hollestocke, Alyce his wife, and William son of Matthew Rattenberye, deceased, 'messuages late in the tenure of William Bowedon, deceased, and which Hughe Hytchue then held.' The agreement was for 99 years at 2s.4d. yearly and was witnessed by William Bennett alias Clook and Richard Call.

Leonarde Yeo, gent., of Exeter died on May 30th 1586. An enquiry held at Exeter Castle in October, before the escheator, Hugh Sayer, confirmed that Leonarde Yeo had held, with other estates, 6 messuages, 100 acres of land, 40 acres of meadow, 100 acres of pasture, 30 acres of wood, and 20 acres of gorse and heath in Hulstocke which was held of the Queen in chief for the service of one-twentieth part of a knight's fee and the rent of 2s.$1\frac{1}{2}$d. George Yeo, gent., aged 50 years and more, was his son and heir, who surrendered a schedule of his possessions on November 3rd 1586, including the above valued at 21s.

Eleven months later, a licence under the great seal of Queen Elizabeth confirmed that George Yeo and his wife Elizabeth now had, among other possessions, the manor of Halstock. This was to be theirs for little more than ten years. In ill health by 1605, George leased to Nicholas Yeo, his fourth son, 'Chapell landes in the manor of Halstocke' for 90 years, on the death or surrender of Leonard Cottell the holder at the time, paying '4s.8d. yearly and suit at the Courts of Halstocke. Venwell rents to be discharged, the best beast or 30s. as heriot.' By paying 6s.8d. Nicholas could terminate the lease.

On March 15th 1607 George Yeo died, leaving his estate to his son Leonard who, 18 months later, leased to Thomasyn, wife of William Yolland of Belstone, those messuages in the manor of Holstock late in the tenure of William 'Caddyn', deceased, for 99 years,

on the lives of Richard Yolland, Elynor Yolland and Elizabeth Yolland their children. They were to pay £60.8s.0d. yearly rent. The agreement excluded 'one house latelie fallen downe at the North end of the barne.'

Halstock was financially beneficial to Leonard who agreed in 1612, for £56.8s.0d. yearly, to lease to Erkinwalde Arscotte of Okehampton, husbondman, and Wilmote his wife, the messuages, etc., in Halstock 'late in the tenure of Walter Arnolle, by right of Johanna his wife, deceased.'

Halstock also provided security for an £80 annuity in April 1621 in the marriage agreement between George Yeo, gent., heir of Leonard Yeo of Hewish, esq., and Elizabeth Bassett, one of the daughters of Sir Robert Bassett of Heanton Punchardon.

The following month a licence from the Court of Alienation under the great seal of James I to Leonard Yeo, esq., diverted the manor of Halstock and 5 messuages, 5 gardens, 30 acres of land, 10 acres of meadow, 30 acres of pasture, 20 acres of wood, 100 acres of gorse and heath and common of pasture for all beasts in Halstock, Dartemoore and Okehampton, as well as other estates, to the use of George Yeo. Halstock subsequently passed to Lord Courtenay, who sold it to Mr Charles Luxmoore.

Maddaford Manor

According to the records of 1086, Maddeford was part of Kigbere in 1086, held of Baldwyn by Raner, his steward, but how it came to be so named is unclear. In 1241 it was held for a quarter fee by the heir of Peter de Syrefuntayne, of John de Curtenay, lord of Okemeton. In 1295 Philip Byestecombe granted to William the son of John de Maddeford and to Ennotia his wife, daughter of Philip Byestecombe, freedom of common through his land of Blakedon for all animals; except when corn was growing. A generation later, in 1336, William's sons, John and Robert de Madefford, retained a family hold on the manor, still for half a fee of the Honour of Ockampton but, somewhere within the next 60 years or so, the family connection was broken and the manor changed hands.

On June 29th 1390 it was Robert Donsta and Cristina his wife who were able to grant to Robert Tayllour of Okehampton and Lawrence Kyng 'all lands, tenements, rents and services in Maddeford, in the tithing of Cadekebeare.' The agreement was witnessed by Robert Cotelegh, then the portreeve of Okehampton, Roger att Pytt, then 'Bailiff of the Borough of Okehampton', and others.

In the same year the lands, etc., at Maddeford, were confirmed as: 4 messuages, 3 tenements, 20 acres of corn land, 27 acres of meadow, 6 acres of wood, and common pasturage on Blakedon. When the Tayllour-Kyng partnership ended, with the death of the former, Laurence Kyng, on June 8th 1421,

Maddaford and the common right passed to his son John Kyng of Okehampton in a deed witnessed by Okehampton's portreeve and others and an Inquisition was held on July 1st at the Hundred Court of Blaketoryton before William Blench, seneschal.

Versions of many local family names can be found among those of the jury which consisted of Walter Madeford, John Fordeman, John Rithdon, Thomas Knapman, Nicholas Davy, Thomas Wodelond, John Biset, Thomas Hayside, Richard Underhill, Richard Poleworthy, Richard Taillor and Robert Viell. The jurymen said on oath that Laurence Kyng acquired the lands, etc., from Robert Donsta and Cristina his wife, by deed dated in 1390, and that John Kyng his son was the rightful heir.

Only two years later, on September 30th 1423, an indentured deed testified that John Jamme, John Berne, John More and John Pynta leased to Edward Maddeford all the messuages, lands, tenements, etc., in Maddaford, with pasturage in the wood, for 38 years. The rent was 30s. and 3s. to be paid to the lord of the manor; at his death the best beast as heriot.

Edward was responsible for maintaining a cattle enclosure and a barn and keeping in repair all closes and ditches. He was to have reasonable 'house-bote' and 'hay-bote' from the wood by consent of the keeper of the store of St James' Chapel, Okehampton.

Following names down through the centuries can either confirm or confuse the present-day local family's connection with the past. John Rithdon served on a jury in 1390 and almost a century later, in 1486, a Richard Rysedon is one among a group described as enfeoffed when dealing with a lease to Walter Wonecote and Edith his wife of all messuages, etc., in Maddaford, for the term of their lives at a rent of 16s. and the best beast as heriot on the death of Walter. Did the Rithdons become Rysedons and then the Risdons of today? Some, following their family tree, believe so. The names Wolcote, Furse and Estebroke all appear at this time and have been brought to our attention by other family-tree followers.

John Hodge at the Okehampton Show, c.1974. The event has served town and country for over a century.

Above: *A recently experienced whiteout on Dartmoor reminds us of conditions experienced more regularly by our ancestors.*

Left: *The old method of using a pole and ropes to take hay up for rick-making, as here at Glendon Farm, was tried and tested through centuries before mechanisation lifted the load.*

4

The Coming of Education

From 1536 parishes held the responsibility for providing children with basic reading lessons and religious instruction and generally added these duties to those already being undertaken by the vicar. By 1547 there were grammar schools in most major market towns. Laymen were also being licensed to teach boys arithmetic and writing, using, for the latter, the abecedarium, the book of latin letters. He was not a local trader, but the fact that a 'fishmonger' was granted a licence by the Archbishop of Canterbury in 1596 confirms that licensed teachers came from differing backgrounds. It was their task to teach reading, writing, and the casting of accounts. The three Rs were traditionally considered important, as things to be taught by following a given process and it was a system that was to serve the art of education well for almost four centuries.

For young children, below the age of seven, towards the end of the sixteenth century, there were the 'dame schools' in which girls were instructed in spinning, weaving perhaps and knitting, but rarely in reading or writing.

That parents with the inclination are recorded as having been able to borrow and use textbooks at home for the private instruction of their children, or servants, indicates that 'learning' was somewhat limited to those children whose parents were wealthy enough to employ help in the home. There were other teaching aids, notably the horn book, a primer shaped like a table-tennis bat with a sheet containing a 'cross' below which were the letters of the alphabet, covered by a sheet of transparent horn, fixed to the 'bat' frame. There were sometimes two sets of letters, in capitals and lower case called Christ's Cross Rows, below which was printed the Lord's Prayer and a set of numerals. For some children, this teaching aid that could be carried with them at work or to school helped them immensely but, for others, it was noted that some could not, 'tell six of their letters at twelve months' end'. Literacy and numeracy for all had yet to be achieved but the first steps on the road towards that end had clearly been well established long before the Civil War.

In 1610 a feoffment detailing the obligations of the town for the education of Okehampton's young makes mention of 'the keeping of a schoolmaster there'. For almost the next 200 years the post of schoolmaster was held by the chaplain of St James' Chapel under the jurisdiction of the Corporation, and they were to be expected to: teach scholars at the School House of the town and borough during 'the pleasure of the Mayor, Principal Burgesses and Assistants'; read Common Prayer at the chapel morning and evening; preach sermons at four Quarter Sessions every year; and instruct free of charge six or eight poor children selected by the Mayor.

In consideration of their exercising these duties to the satisfaction of the Mayor the teacher was at liberty to dwell in the school house, and was to receive £15 yearly in the form of a gift from the Mayor and burgesses in recompense for his pains. The chaplain increased his income from fees charged to others.

It was also a term of employment that the teacher/chaplains should preach a sermon once every year at the election of the Mayor, unless the Mayor chose another to perform the duty.

The original 'grammar' schools established in the Middle Ages were preparatory institutions for university or for jobs where a knowledge of Latin was essential. By 1722 the Okehampton school certainly complied and was referred to as a grammar school but the inclusion a century earlier of between six and eight poor children in the school appears to indicate a more far-sighted approach to education than simply providing tuition for the children of the wealthy minority.

A century beforehand, in 1619, the Receiver's Book includes the note: 'Paid to Mr. Peter Bolt, Minister, for reading prayers at the Chapel, and for teaching children of the town as scholars.' Such 'painful and learned schoolmasters' were expected to 'bring up the youth in the fear of God and good letters' – an expectation mentioned frequently in the schoolmasters' agreements; which sometimes appears to have been an expectation unfulfilled.

Schoolmaster Peter Bolt was not without his tribulations. In 1622 John Anstey was accused of abusing Bolt and two others, of being drunk and profaning the name of Christ; he was ordered to appear at sessions, pay five shillings to the poor and confess publicly in church. It was Bolt also who must have seen his classes decimated, empty stools where pupils once sat, as the town struggled to survive during the disaster of 1625–26 when the town, and the county as a whole, was hit by an unusually severe outbreak of plague when it was said that there were many young people among the 300 people in the parish who died. Some of those children had no doubt been receiving their education at the small school, a thatched building on the far side of the West Bridge, close to the house of the chaplain/schoolmaster, Mr Bolt.

The town had bought back the endowments of the chapel, which had been confiscated in 1549 under the Act for suppressing chantries, and these endowments were now applied by the Corporation for the maintenance of the chapel and the upkeep of the school.

Whether or not Peter Bolt survived the plague it was instead a Mr Christopher Williams who, in 1634, was charged with neglecting his teaching in t own and endeavouring to teach at Jacobstowe. Concerned about the matter, Bishop Hale wrote to the Revd John Hussey, the vicar of Okehampton:

Salute in Christ.
I hear that, which I am sorry to hear, the Liturgie of the Church is much neglected in your chapple at Okehampton, being not fully read at any time by the Curate there, and not at all by the Lecturer, and not well frequented by the people when it is imperfectly read; this thing you know to be contrary to the Laws and Canons of the Church and His Majesty's late instructions...

The Bishop made it quite clear that he would expect an explanation from the Mayor regarding this situation when he next visited the town.

The Mayor promptly sent for Mr Williams, instructing him to come to the Town Hall but the errant teacher advised the Sergeant delivering the summons to tell the Mayor that he would not do so. The Mayor despatched the Sergeant a second time with the same message, to which he added the threat that, unless Mr Williams appeared, his pay would be withheld. Deciding to face the enemy, the teacher made his way to Okehampton where he advised the Mayor that he would not stay, not even for £60 a year in salary. Attempts to negotiate a settlement of their differences failed but during them, as the records show, Mr Williams used:

... many unfitting speeches in a choleric and domineering way towards the Company present; Whereupon he had to leave at Lady-Day, unless he do crave some reasonable small time longer, and do and shall during that time behave himself in the place as becometh him.

Mr Williams had no intention of putting up with being dismissed by the Corporation in such a way, and appealed to the Bishop. The Bishop, writing to the vicar of Okehampton, on May 31st, said of the Corporation: 'If they shall take upon them to place and remove Curates, they must know I may not beare so injurious an encroachment upon Episcopal power.' The burgesses' response to this was not conciliatory. They wrote: 'that albeit the Lord Bishop hath power to replace and remove Curates, yet the Corporation hath power to withhold the pay, if they see cause.'

The Corporation must have reached some short-term agreement with Mr Williams who remained in office but, on April 30th 1635, he asked if he could stay until Midsummer Day, agreeing that he would read prayers in the chapel. This appears to have concluded Mr Williams' engagement in the education of Okehampton children as Mr Wm Newbery was engaged, on trial, to teach school until Midsummer Day. His salary for the period was £2, and it came with a promise of future employment, if he proved satisfactory, at £15 per annum, together with the school house.

Five years later Mr Newbery has obviously found employment elsewhere since the Mayor and Corporation were by this time having trouble with a teacher named Bartholomew Caunter to whom, the town records reveal, they felt impelled to write:

Mr. Caunter, you may well call to mind that yor acceptance and entrance here, though upon some recommendation and yet not without much dissention, were only upon loyal and good behaviour. And your admittance after and continuance here were and are but upon yor carefull pformance and paynfull discharge of the duty of yor place.
Some speciall notice haveinge been formerly taken of yor often absence, and, what is more, yor too much neglect of teachings and instructinge yor schollers whereby some have been compelled to place their children elsewhere.

This was an unsatisfactory situation and the Mayor and Corporation concluded their correspondence in an appropriate manner:

... wee whose names are subscribed by the will of the dead, and charged by the duty of our place in their behalf have thought fitt hereby to give you notice and advise you either speedily to reform what hath been and is amyss therein, or else that upon a quarter's warning you provide yourself of another place and wee of a more carefull and paynfull schoolmaster.
yor lovinge friends
14 ffeb 1642

It is desired and expected that you give us yor answer hereunto written under your hande.

With the country erupting into Civil War, Mr Caunter did not want to be seeking a new job at such a difficult time and, judging by his response, decided that he would be better off remaining among 'lovinge friends':

Such unhappy differences of late have fallen out amongst the states of this land that many subjects are as it were to their wit's ends, by reason of which said distractions and jealousy, many (I believe) could not follow their vocation according to their former and wonted course, and therefore whatever you or any other of my accusers have found me negligent in, or remiss of, I shall readily and willingly use the utmost of my power to reform it and remayne yor servant as long as I may
Bartholomew Caunter

The standards expected of a 'carefull and paynfull schoolmaster' by this time included being skilful in Greek or Latin, of solid religious belief, grave in behaviour and sober in conversation. The elected individual was warned that he 'should not a tippler be, nor a frequenter of ale-houses or bawdy premises' – and that he should not smoke.

During the republican period and military dictatorship, the dismissal of a teacher could be achieved in the event of him being found guilty, among other things, of adultery, fornication, perjury, drunkenness, playing cards or dice, fighting or using irreverent or blasphemous language. Encouraging or practising the traditional 'holiday' festivities or wakes was sufficient to earn dismissal, especially if they were associated with Morris dancing, stage plays, May Day or moon festivals, excluding Easter but including Whitsun with its ale festivities.

Apparently Mr Caunter's ploy pacified his 'friends', for a while at least, but in 1645 Richard Mervyn, the vicar of Okehampton, or one in his place, appears to have taken over the duties of educating Okehampton's young ones. Those pupils were still experiencing the draughts and icy blasts that so easily penetrated windows filled only with wooden shutters. Glass windows, when they came, regularly added a new cost to education, the expense of replacement. After some heavy expenditure caused by wayward pupils in 1652, Mr Thomas Fynner, who was by then the teacher, was advised, after a window was broken, that he was to have:

... the school house repaired, with the glass in the school, and if it shall be broken afterwards the schoolmaster is to amend it at his own cost. And to take order that the scholars behave themselves civilly and orderly in coming and going to and from the school, and at the church and chapel.

The chaplain may well have reconsidered his position as chaplain/teacher since his salary was reduced to £10.

On October 29th 1670, Mr John Randall was forced out of his school, not because he would not read prayers but, perhaps, because the children's had been answered:

There happened a fire in the school house chimney which occasioned the burning down of the school, that is all the thatch to a very small matter, but most of the timber was preserved; it fell out on a Saturday in the afternoon.

Whatever the children's wishes, their school was rebuilt and improved the following year: 'This Spring the School was new built with a chamber over it, and new heated, which was before a thatched school without a chamber over it.'

On May 13th 1672, the children did at least have a day off school to enjoy one of the traditions still maintained:

This day Mr. Mayor, with many of the inhabitants of the town, together with Mr. Hussey (Vicar) and Mr. Randall (Schoolmaster) and divers both young and old viewed the bounds of Dartmoor common belonging to this parish.

The prosperity of their parish, if not all of its people, had grown over the years, despite the Civil War, a fact demonstrated by the growth of the Vicarage at this time. In 1602 Mr Hussey's predecessor had enjoyed 'only' ten rooms, with a kitchen, 'pastry' and dairy. There were also a malt-house and a brew-house because the vicar brewed his own beer, and some farm buildings, as the vicar farmed his own glebe of about 150 acres. By Mr Hussey's time, however, the ten rooms remained but other buildings had been added, including a cider cellar with an apple chamber over it, a shippen and a stable and an ox-house; oxen used for ploughing and heavy work continued for more than another 300 years. Soon, there would also be a walled court and several gardens, complete with summer-house. The relative affluence of some was reflected in the generous education being provided to the few.

On February 13th 1695, following a scholarship examination taken by 'Free Scholars', it ordered that:

John, the son of Thomas Bassut, be taught at the free school the English and Latin Tongue, and Roger, the son of Roger Jole, and Matthias, the son of John Spragge, and John, the son of John Palmer, and Samuel, the son of Walter Merrifield And John, the son of Henry Coram be likewise taught.

Many of these boys were later to play leading roles in the civic life of the town as either Mayor or Town Clerk.

In 1695 Richard Carter was appointed as the schoolmaster for one year, but stayed for 11 during bustling and prosperous times. The woollen trade recovered and the town obtained, at a cost, two

31

additional fairs from Charles II. Like many towns, Okehampton had been forced to surrender its old charter in 1684, but the townsfolk were pleased enough with the additional privileges the new one gave them. The population was increasing and the vicar, Mr Hussey, numbered the inhabitants in 1676 at 1,207 in the whole parish, with, to his satisfaction, only one Papist and seven Dissenters among them.

An organisation that was to influence education came into being in 1698; the Society for the Promotion of Christian Knowledge, which had as its first purpose the promotion and encouragement of the erection of 'charity schools' in all parts of England. In Okehampton, however, it was local benefactors who supported schooling, and during the term of office of schoolmaster Mr J. Amyatt (in 1713) the school received a legacy of £120 in the will of John Northmore. It was a land-based legacy that was to provide, through interest earned, for the schoolmaster of Okehampton and his successors, to teach the Latin tongue for so long as the free school should continue. William Northmore was John's executor, and during his lifetime ensured that the schoolmaster received the interest on the legacy. Later, William, his son, continued to pay the interest until about two years before he died but he had wasted his late uncle's assets and mortgaged all his lands for £20,000. Two decades or so after being given, the annual benefit from the legacy lapsed.

To become a schoolmaster required the vicar to recommend the applicant to the Bishop who then granted the licence. In 1719 John Coram was recommended as 'an object of charity and not able to get a living if my lord doth not grant him licence for keeping the English school... he is no other way able to get a farthing.' When appointing licensed teachers, the Corporation sometimes seemed to anticipate problems, as, for example, in 1722, when Timothy Edwards, the vicar of Okehampton, was appointed teacher in the town for at least the trial period of one year, the agreement being noted that:

... the said Mr. T. Edwards shall yield up the schoolhouse at the end of the said one year quietly and peaceably into the hands and possession of the said Mayor, Burgesses and Assistants or within three months the next after if the said Mr. Edwards be not chosen, and the said Mayor, Burgesses and Assistants shall require the same.

His agreement with the Corporation also set the times of chapel at 7a.m. and 5p.m. but these times may not have suited him. Mr Edwards, apparently, also did not like the school house for some reason and decided that he would teach his pupils closer to his home, the Vicarage. His decision was not favoured by his employers and a letter from the Mayor and Corporation was duly despatched to him on November 17th 1722:

We whose names are subscribed hereunder do consent and agree that the Grammar School of Okehampton shall hereafter be held and kept at the School-House within the said town and borough, being the usual accustomed place. And we whose names are hereunder written do agree that whosoever shall be chosen Schoolmaster for the said borough shall serve as Chaplain, and read Prayers in the Chapel at the usual hours as we agree, and shall have for his pains the usual salary.

This prompted a swift reply from Mr Edwards:

I have a licence from my Lord Bishop to teach school in the town and parish of Okehampton, and by virtue of that shall continue to keep it at my vicarage house.

What had really upset the Mayor and Corporation was that the vicar had installed a tenant in their school house and a writ was served upon him for repossession; his tenants were thrown out.

On June 21st 1726, Mr Edwards resigned, claiming unpaid salary for which the Mayor, Burgesses and Assistants promised that he would 'be paid the sum of £36 and £15 out of the Corporation stock and revenue and demand.' Mr Edwards emerged from all this as the first vicar to become one of the school governors.

Teacher/chaplains such as John Roberts of Northhill in Cornwall, appointed in 1726, Thomas Bate of Colebrooke, and M.J. Silke of Northlew, who was appointed in 1738, all kept on their other appointments at the same time as serving Okehampton. This situation rather riled the Bishop of the diocese, who provided the incumbent with a licence to teach.

On September 8th 1738, the Corporation despatched a letter to the 'Right Rev. Father in God, Stephen, Lord Bishop of Exon'. It contained the following:

Whereas the Mayor, Vicar, Principal Burgesses and Assistants of this town Borough and Parish in the county of Devon, within your Lordship's diocese have nominated and made choice of the Rev. M.T. Silke, Curate of North Lew in the County of Devon to teach the Grammar School within this town and borough and read prayers twice a day in the Chapel, which is now become vacant by the resignation of the Rev. T. Bate, may it please your Lordship to grant unto the said Mr Silke your licence to teach the schools and read prayers in the chapel accordingly.

John Lethbridge. Mayor.

Mr Silke also presented his Corporation contract to the Bishop, who then refused the licence on the grounds that the contract did not bear the common seal and, *inter alia*, that Mr Silke, at Northlew, was too far from Okehampton to devote time there in pursuit of teaching and/or prayer duties daily.

Okehampton's leaders, slighted by the Bishop's refusal to accept their chosen man, swiftly added the seal and information previously missing regarding Mr Silke's salary, and wrote again to the Bishop addressing his remaining objection:

... we humbly conceive in the distance of his cure which is not above five miles. However, if your Lordship think Proper to continue him in this, or appoint him a cure which is nearer, of £30 yearly, besides the school, he is, I daresay, willing to accept of either although the present cure brings him in £50 a year. If both these are denied, the youth must be of necessity debarred of their education, and the town deprived of the inestimable benefit of prayer twice a day.

All must have been resolved since it appears that Mr Silke served the town until he was replaced in 1748 by Mr J. Vickry of Belstone who remained in the position until 1767.

During this period, the vicar, John Hockin (1744–78), expressed his belief and proposed, that if a physician analysed and recommended, the local mineral springs, Okehampton might become a health resort similar to, but smaller than, Bath or Tunbridge Wells. Of much more value was his work in establishing charity schools – one for 20 boys and another for the same number of girls

However, when Mr J. Walter, of Bratton Clovelly, took over the post of schoolmaster/preacher the Corporation had amended the contract of employment in a manner that would have satisfied Mr Edwards over 40 years earlier. Mr Walter was appointed for three years, and given the option of dwelling in the school house or letting it out at rent; an option that continued thereafter.

Succeeding Corporations and Bishops appear to have harmoniously agreed for the remainder of the eighteenth century but somewhere during those years the education of the young in the town suffered radical change and in 1806, when the Revd W. Hole, of Belstone, was appointed Chaplain of St James' there was no mention of the schoolmaster's duties; and the stipend was reduced to five guineas per annum. The school had ceased to exist. A publication in 1822 includes the observation: 'There is still a school room and a school house, but the funds are wholly lost, and no master has of late been appointed.' The funds, however, had not been lost, but had been passed to the borough charities as shown in a deed of December 22nd 1821, in which the Mayor and burgesses received on trust certain charities, including one for the maintenance of a grammar school.

Still belonging to the town, but let out on life leases, were the schoolroom and school house close to the Western Bridge, and where the houses known as the Old Post Office once stood. The older of two houses that had faced obliquely the West Bridge was in all probability the schoolmaster's house. Okehampton Grammar School had continued until 1806, when charity schools were started, but during the course of the centuries many local boys benefited from their learning gained there, including one whose record, before an ill-fated fire, could be found on a mural tablet in the south aisle of the Parish Church:

To the memory of John Haynes Esq. a native of this town, born of honest and industrious parents, though of low and obscure condition; first instructed as a poor scholar, then going to London by the benevolence of Mrs. Rebecca Hussey, widow of Jeremy Hussey, once Vicar of this Parish, and a man eminent both for his piety and learning, was happily recommended to the most Rev. Archbishop Tillotson's family as Clerk to the Secretary, 1692, continuing with Archbishop Tenison 1715, who had appointed him his Registrar of the Diocese and Province of Canterbury for life. Born 1672, married Feb. 1708 and died Feb. 1st. 1719.

By a deed of 1836 a site in North Lane, later North Street, was conveyed to the vicar and churchwardens on which a school was to be built in union with the National Society. The town's National School was opened a year later, built partly by private subscription and with grants from the National Society which was also assisting to finance Church schools.

As previously mentioned, the management organisation of the school included one member of the managers of the charity school, confirming the existence of such a school until this time. Okehampton had been well endowed with charities and, by the arrangement made in 1873, three-sevenths of their income was devoted solely to education.

An infants' school was established in 1848 in Fairfield Place, North Lane and lessons were conducted in a schoolroom adjoining and belonging to the Independent Chapel, built there just over 60 years earlier.

In 1856 Joseph Sprague of West Bridge is recorded as the 'school master' in the town and Miss Elizabeth Hooper, who lived at Providence Place, as the 'school mistress'.

The Education Act of 1870 made elementary education free, universal and compulsory and a school board was formed on January 9th 1872 which then assumed responsibility for the National School and later took over the other schools, paying a rental for each establishment of £10 per annum to the Church authorities and the Independent Chapel trustees respectively. The board's chairman was James Hunt Holley Esq., and its members were Revd Charles Wm Hunt Holley, residing at Oaklands, Revd Henry Trigg (Congregational), of Ivy Cottage, and Messrs Henry Drew, a farmer living at Castle Villa, and Henry Newcombe, a farmer from Kigbeare, all of whom decided to build new schools for 200 pupils, in North Street, close to the National School.

The new schools opened in 1874, at a cost to the board of £1,500, to provide teaching, separately, to older boys and girls. The infants took over the former National School and the chapel schoolroom in Fairfield Place ceased to be used as a day school.

At this time, Miss B. Hill was the board schoolmistress at North Street but there were other schools; Miss Clara Trigg, also of Ivy Cottage, is recorded as having a 'ladies' school', presumably held at the cottage, and Miss Grashina Hudd was running a ladies' boarding-school at 32 East Street. Miss Maria Pile is mentioned in records of the time as an 'infant school-mistress' whose address was given as 'the Post Office', so she could have been providing private tutorial services for children in the town, or may otherwise have been helping Miss Hill at the new schools.

Roy Walker, John Hawking, Gordon Branch and Charlie Curtis on a nature ramble with school-friends, c.1938.

Over the following two decades the population of Okehampton rose and by 1896 the school board was forced to extend the girls' section of their school buildings. A year later the intake of infants to the former National School had grown to such an extent that the school was declared inadequate to cope with requirements. Again the board was required to provide the necessary accommodation and built a school in Exeter Road; but only for older boys. Girls of the same age groups were then moved into the boys' part

of the North Lane School which left their original schoolrooms empty and available for use by the overcrowded infants. The old National School appears to have then reverted back to the Church authorities as it became known and used as the 'church rooms'.

As the nineteenth century was about to enter its final decade a number of 'private' educational facilities were available in Okehampton. One such was provided by John William Besley, MA (London), who was principal of the 'Moorside School For Boys', another by Mrs Emma Amelia Dufty, who had established a day- and boarding-school for ladies called 'Park House School'. Both of these, according to local directories, organised 'excellent centres of education'. There are others listed, but not highlighted in editorial comment, who presumably could not afford additional advertisements. Miss Elizabeth Angel ran a day-school for girls in Kempley Road and Mrs Frank Landick another day-school for girls in West Street.

After the Education Act of 1902 all elementary schools in Okehampton were placed under the jurisdiction of the Local Education Authority as 'Council' schools. Four years later local charities which supported education were brought under a separate foundation, known as the Okehampton

Boys of Okehampton Senior School, 1923–24. Back row includes: *? Vanstone, E. Day, W. Glover, W. Pike, B. Horn, B. Cockwill, ? Pedrick, L. Mills, ? Pugsly;* middle, left to right: *T. Farley, N. Wellham, ?, W. Letchford, T. Hodge, R. Turner, R. Bolt, ? Pedrick, G. Alford, R. Lock, ? Paul, ? Piper;* front, left to right: *J. Kelly, W. Kelly, W. Dustan, G. Vanstone, G. Newcombe, R. Barkwill, ? Cox, ?, ? Farley.*

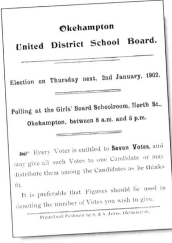

Okehampton

United District School Board.

Election on Thursday next, 2nd January, 1902.

Polling at the Girls' Board Schoolroom, North St., Okehampton, between 8 a.m. and 8 p.m.

Every Voter is entitled to **Seven Votes**, and may give all such Votes to one Candidate or may distribute them among the Candidates as he thinks fit.

It is preferable that Figures should be used in denoting the number of Votes you wish to give.

Printed and Published by S. & A. Janes, Okehampton.

United Educational Foundation. The county authorities built a higher elementary school in Mill Road in 1911 to provide 'education of an advanced elementary type'; £1,500 was granted from the charities fund towards the building, together with an annual subsidy of £100. The *Okehampton Charities Government Report* of 1913, referring to the Mill Road school, stated that, once more funds had accumulated, the school was to become a secondary school for boys and girls. That hope became a reality surprisingly quickly, with the school being reorganised as a public secondary school for boys and girls in September 1918.

The newly appointed governors suggested to the Board of Education that the school should be known as the Okehampton Grammar School, and the gap of more than a century was bridged when Okehampton Grammar School reopened its doors.

A preparatory school at Upcott was also doing good work at this time. Within less than a decade, overcrowding at North Street brought about further changes and in 1928 the girls' school joined the boys in Exeter Road, which then became the mixed senior school. Down the road in North Street the infants were now able to take over the area vacated by the girls in what many, at the time of writing, still remember with affection as either the Junior Mixed and Infants' School, or the County Primary School – depending on whether they had attended before or after the First World War.

The baby boom of post-war years increased, in time, the numbers of infants attending school. The demand for extra places for children continued through the 1950s with children having to use the Church Hall, a short distance from the school, while others had to go into different parts of the town for school purposes.

Without any space for expansion on the site, it became necessary to provide the school with three additional classrooms on the opposite bank of the East Okement river and in November 1961 the classrooms, linked to the old premises by a bridge, were opened by Mr G.U. Fulford, a member of the Devon Education Committee, who did much to bring about the extension.

A class at work in 1960.

Included here are the North Road Primary School rooms, across the water.

G.U. Fulford of Devon Education Committee at the opening of the classroom extensions.

Primary School teachers in 1975. Left to right, back row: Graham Madge,
Vic Lancaster, M. Greenslade, G. Gay, L. Knight, M. Wonnacott, S. Gow, M. Nottage;
front: *D. Gale, J. Hawking, H. Piddington, G. Lower, J. Laws (head), L. King, J. Pauley, M. Davies, L. Hosgood.*

Primary School teachers in November 1979. Left to right, back row: V. Lancaster, S. Gow,
G. Gay, L. Knight, S. Glynn (head), L. Finch, M. Wonnacott, M. Nottage, T. Gazzard;
front: *B. Dodd, H. Piddington, J. Pauley, D. Gale, G. Lower, S. Daniel, C. Cowley, J. Hawking.*

Both bridge and new classrooms were designed under the direction of the County Architect, Mr H.V. De Courcey Hague, but their very presence dashed the hopes of those who firmly believed that a new, purpose-built school was needed. The hope had been to build a new secondary modern school adjoining the then Okehampton Grammar School, but permission had not been given. Mr Fulford, in his comments, paid tribute to the teachers and the headmaster Mr G.W.R. Knapp, who was soon to leave, all of whom had worked under appalling conditions.

With prospects for a new school now being represented by less than a glimmer of hope, the primary-school staff continued to provide the best education possible in better, but not adequate, facilities as classes filled and attendance figures increased.

A little overdue, the school celebrated its centenary in July 1976 after it was found that while, according to an Okehampton historian, the school had opened in 1877, the school's original log-books referred to the new school opening in October 1874. A local newspaper reporter clarified the situation:

SIDE BY SIDE
Under the (1870) Act, a school board was set up and a new school built at the end of 1874. Both schools continued to exist side by side, with girls in one and boys in the other, until some time before 1935, when the present school became a mixed junior school and after that a mixed junior-infant school. Before additional classrooms were provided, the children continued to attend classes both in the old national schoolroom and the Congregational schoolroom. The idea eventually is to build a new primary school on the site of the old one after taking in more land but it is not expected to take shape for many years because of the cut-backs in education.
WITHIN CAPACITY
Including the nursery, the attendance figure is 413 which, with the extra classrooms, brings the numbers just within the school's capacity.

The headmaster, Mr. James Laws, does not envisage any accommodation problem at the moment. He said, "A peak was reached in 1956 with 450 children, dropping to 350 in 1961. Our numbers will fluctuate from time to time but Okehampton's population has remained more or less static since 1900. There could be a problem if Okehampton develops at the rate many people, including the Development Commission, wants it to. Pressures will then be on for a new school."

Mr Laws' comments regarding development problems were something of a prophecy. Headmaster for 22 years, Mr Laws retired to be succeeded by Mr. R.S. Glynn, from Kingston-on-Thames, who became another very popular and hard-working headmaster during almost six years in Okehampton before accepting headship of Boringdon County Primary School at Plympton.

Speaking to the *Okehampton Times* reporter he said

that he praised the efforts of parents, governors, other individuals, and many local organisations for their help: 'We could not have done anything without them behind the school. Their support has always been magnificent.'

Behind his words however lay the hopes of many that major improvements in educational premises and facilities would be provided in the not too distant future. New schools and upgraded premises were needed. Six years on and those hopes and aspirations had been dashed. A newspaper cutting from Friday 29 January 1988 reveals all:

THE OKEHAMPTON 'SAVE OUR SCHOOLS' CAMPAIGN IS GATHERING STRENGTH

Almost every shop in Okehampton itself and in the towns and villages whose youngsters go to school at the College is collecting petitions.
Newspapers and County Council officials and councillors have been flooded with indignant letters.

The campaign, launched by the governors of the College and of the Primary School, was based on a firm belief that the town and district had been given a raw deal after the building programmes for both schools were suddenly dropped from the priority lists, which they'd been on for many years, in favour of a new School building programme in Tavistock.

According to the furious Okehampton school authorities, Tavistock had not even been on the priority list and local MP, Emma Nicholson, was summoned to meet an angry deputation that included both County Councillors for the area, Mrs Mary Vick and Mr Bill Cann, the heads of the College and Primary School, Mr Phillip Herriman, and Mr Jim Wiltshire, the chairman and other members of the two sets of governors, representatives of the PTA, and the Mayor of Okehampton, Mr Jack Hughes.

The MP was left in no doubt that not only did Okehampton feel that it has been ignored but that the issue affected all the 17,000 people in the Okehampton district who resented the downgrading in County estimates of the two longstanding school building projects. After the meeting the MP told the Okehampton Times, 'I am seriously concerned about the position of Okehampton on the educational capital programme – or rather its lack of position. I have undertaken to go to County Hall to get all the papers and talk to officials, who are the ones responsible for putting up proposals for councillors to consider.'

The eventual outcome was to provide Okehampton with the schools it possesses as we write and these have grown and developed thanks to succeeding headmasters. But the warning of the mid 1970s by headmaster, Mr James Laws, that 'there could be a problem if Okehampton develops at the rate many people, including the Development Commission wants it to' has returned to haunt the town.

Red-Letter Days

Above: *The cast of* Peach Blossom, *an operetta by L. Ramsey produced in 1950. Characters include: Emperor (John Holland), Peach Blossom (Erica Barnes), Ching-Ching (Trevor Collins), Hi-Ti (James Little); Fusi-Yama (Michael Evans), courtiers (Marion Cockwill, Eileen Kelly, Rosemary Nash, Alan Gaywood, John Hanniford, Roger Slee); flowers (Ann Day, Kathleen Curtis, Jean Bevan, Trixee Spencer, June Soby, Nita Jago, June Harris, Vera Stanley); bird chorus (Barry Grant, Bobbie Green, Trevor Hutchings), chorus (P. Bray, B. Middleton, G. Bird, J. Lee, L. Vernon, B. Ware, P. Voaden, N. McKay, J. Wayborn, P. Russel, J.Westlake, D. McKenzie, M. Saunders, V. Baker). The play was produced by Miss J. Pauley, with musical instruction and accompaniment provided by Mrs V. Hayward.*

Above: *On December 17th 1959 Okehampton Primary School children had obviously learned the value and joy of taking presents to the local hospital.*

Right: *One of Okehampton College's 'big bands' that the town is proud of – here entertaining the public in Charter Hall, Christmas 2001.*

Red-Letter Days

Above: *On March 2nd 1961 a meeting took place to start fund-raising for a Youth Centre in Westcott's Yard, School Way; there are flats there now.*

Above: *February 1966 and the first parade of 2443 Squadron ATC at Upcott House School.*

Right: *Many still remember the old swimming pool in Castle Road and this photograph is said to be of the opening day, when town benefactor Mr Simmons was present.*

School Sports

Left: *Maypole dancing was taught at the primary school and was very much a part of the children's calendar in the 1950s.*

Below far left: *Sports Day invariably included the sack race and none of the participants spoken to recently can remember anyone getting seriously hurt.*

Below centre and right: *Skipping races, c.1953.*

Bottom: *Grammar School sports; Chris Tolley, senior boys champion, making his winning dive. Mr Jennison takes notes.*

5

Ochenemitona & Meldune

Ochenemitona

Baldwyn, the Sheriff, had a manor called Ochenemitona, the same manor that Osfers had held 'on the day on which King Edward was alive and dead.' At the time of Domesday it was:

> ... a manor rendering geld for 3 virgates and 1 ferding which 30 ploughs could till. Thereof Baldwyn has 3 virgates 1 ferding and 4 ploughes in demesne, and the villeins 2 virgates and 20 ploughs. There Baldwyn has 31 villeins, 11 bordars, 18 serfs, 6 swine herds, 1 rouncey, 52 beasts, 80 sheep, 1 mill which renders 6s.8d. a year, woodland 3 leagues in length by 1 in breadth, 5 acres of meadow, pasturage 1 league in length by ¹/₂ league wide, and on the land stood the castle of Ochenemitone. There Baldwyn has 4 burgesses, and a market which rendered 4s. a year.

The burgesses were all of those householders who were also residents and who, as a condition, paid 'scot' and bore 'lot', and were sworn and enrolled at the Court Leet. Among those who could not become burgesses were females, minors, men of the cloth, villains, those of infamous character, lunatics and peers.

One of the earliest differences 'twixt town and country was based on taxation; in the country the tax was levied by the Crown on individuals but towns paid a lump sum. Thus one had to be a resident of a town to qualify for the right to become a burgess. A further difference was that of the court. Originally, while 'all freemen', rich or poor landowners alike, had the right to attend the Sheriff's (County) Court and have their voice heard, it was the burgesses that generally 'selected' those going. Similarly, they chose from among themselves those to go to court to represent the borough. When the boroughs began to purchase privileges from the Crown, however, among the earliest purchases was the right of a borough to hold its own Court Leet; thereby making itself independent of the Sheriff and the County Court.

As a borough, Ochenemitona was an area set aside in a manor and made subject to its own court. Its tenants payed a fixed sum for acre plots and, as owners, bought or sold property as they wished. Villeinage tenure was replaced with free tenure and the lord of the manor placed some of the matters that he alone had previously dealt with under the jurisdiction of the burgesses. Nevertheless, Ochenemitona was much more than an Anglo-Saxon meeting-place by a muddy ford by the time that the Normans arrived, as we have already ascertained.

Baldwyn did not create Okehampton but he did develop what was already there. Pleased with what Baldwyn had achieved in Exeter, William the Conqueror started showering him with manors, Baldwyn recognised the potential of this settlement, and those around it, and worked to increase their value.

The charter granted by Robert de Courtenay, c.1219, clearly states that since the days of Baldwyn's son Richard, the burgesses had possessed their 'tenements and free customs'. Robert confirmed and added to those rights, addressing his charter 'to my Burgesses of my free Borough of Okehampton'.

Okehampton and its castle was his administrative centre attended by those who owed allegiance to the lord – those owing suit at the Court of the Honour of Okehampton (the knights), and those who leased the manors of the Honour of Okehampton (the tenants, landowners and traders). Burgesses were paying 12d. each year, at Michaelmas, for each burgage they held. For this sum their rights were established 'in woods and in uplands, in ways and in paths, in common of pastures, in waters and in mills.' They were permitted to turn a sow and four pigs out to feed in Lord Courtenay's forest.

The provost, or portreeve as he became known, previously appointed by the lord of the manor, could now be elected each year by the burgesses, as could the crier, or beadle, but the gallows (furcas) and ducking stool (tumbarel) remained under the control of the lord.

For the best part of 80 years the charter suited all parties but towards the end of the century, c.1290, there was growing friction over the burgesses' rights 'in common of pasture' in the woods and ground to the south of the castle in particular. The conflict resulted in a deed signed in the 20th year of the reign

Okehampton Castle preservation work being carried out, c.1976.

of King Edward I, on the Feast of St Thomas of Canterbury, the martyred Thomas à Becket, and in that deed 'privileges' were redefined. The portreeve and commonalty gave up their rights to 'common of pasture' in all the baron's woods and ground to the south side of the castle and in other parts of the manor. They and their heirs and assigns would be granted certain privileges by the lord of the manor which they were to receive in return for two 'tunnes' of wine given to Sir Hugh (in advance). These privileges included:

... common pasture for all animals throughout his [the lord's] whole wastes between his arable land of Byrham towards the south and the borders of Dartmoor throughout the whole year, with free and peaceable ingress and egress from the said Borough through the middle of the said South wood, by way of Rodmore unto the said Waste.

In addition, from Michaelmas until mid-March they were to have 'common of pasture for all their beasts throughout the whole demesne of the said Hugh of Okehampton.' One further privilege was granted to the burgesses. Each could have:

... a sow and four little pigs in his wood called Hokwood in the northern part of the said Borough, at the time of mastage, free from pannage, throughout the whole of the said wood.

The lord then added a clause saying that the pigs would have to go if he or his heirs needed to enclose any of the area at a later date. Hugh also undertook in writing, on his own behalf and that of his heirs, that they would:

... warrant and defend for ever the above mentioned common pasture of the lord and the pannage of pigs to the before mentioned Commonalty, their heirs and assigns, without disturbance by the said Hugh or any of his servants.

There is some confusion as to the date on which this document was signed, due to the calendar of the time, but it was either December 29th 1292 or January 1st, also 1292. What is certain, however, is that it was witnessed by: Lord Henry de Raleghe, Robert Beaupel, knights, Nicholas de la Hoke, Elya Coffin, William de Cockyscombe, Roger de Durneford, Walter atte Byare and others. The festival of St Thomas the Martyr was December 29th. Edward I came to the throne in 1272 so his 20th year is not difficult to calculate.

Clarification of the 'customs and services of customary tenants, &c.' in the Okehampton manor were much later revealed by Richard Shebbeare, in his diary. He drew information from a document in possession of a former Town Clerk, Thomas Austyn, which included these extracts:

Every tenant holding of the lord a tenement by copy for terme of life shall yield to the lord at the day of his death ffor ye same if he haud it in possession at the time of his death, his best beast;

· *If he have two or three tenements hee shall pay two or three of his best beasts, if he hold more he shall pay more, always provided he have the estate in his possession at the time of his death.*

If these tenements be graunted to three severall p'sons to hold joyntly; and, if one of them dye, he shall pay three of his beasts for heriotts. And, if the third dye, he shall pay but three of his beasts for heriotts, although he be in possession of the whole three tenements. And if any of them have no Quick Cattle, hee shall pay soe many p'cells of his best moveable goods. And, if they agree amongst themselves and make petition, that every tenant shall have but one tenement and soe shall the first dye, seized but of one tenement. This shall not defeate the lord of his heriott, for, allbeit that any of them bee seized indeed but of one tenement, yet he is seized in right from the lord of all the third part of all the three tenements.

This continues to deal in detail with tenants holding 'the moiety, third part, fowerth part or fifth part of any tenement', and onwards. It was stated that in all cases:

... if any Customary tenant, being seized of his aforesayd bargain and sell the same by way of surrender or exchange the same, he shall then yield unto the lord but sixpence for heriott.

This was a payment for moving on, rather than dying, at which time the best beast or moveable goods would be due and the lord who, much like the Inland Revenue, would take every penny he could get his hands on. Every avenue of escape for the tenant was closed, and his wife was barely treated any better; especially if she were not co-tenant with her husband:

Noe wife, after the death of her husband, shall have any widowe's estate of any lands within the mannor, either Customary or Barton, unless shee bee named in the Copye with her husband, and then shall injoy the same according to this grant.

All the tenants of manor or borough did enjoy 'commons upon the King's fforest of Dertmore for all manner of cattle', but driving them to market through the manor lands could incur a fee for every beast of $1^1/_2$d. and for every score of sheep a similar sum.

The true relevance of the burgesses in society at this time was to be demonstrated at the end of the century when burgesses Robertus Cissor and Thomas de Tanton (de Tawton) were summoned to Edward's Parliament at Lincoln; from around the kingdom, knights and others called were ordered to be there... unless they were dead, or too ill. It was Parliament, but not as we know it. It petitioned the King for redress of grievances, sanctioned legislation already initiated, and Edward collected the debts from the people which he considered due to him for carrying on the government of the country.

Some 12 years later, on October 11th 1312, John de Honiton and Henricus Welych were, according to a writ of that date, chosen and returned as burgesses for Okehampton. Another writ, dated July 26th 1314, confirms that the burgesses chosen to go to Parliament to represent the town were Henry Gloube and Richard Bourman; Okehampton's people enjoyed representation at the seat of power at last – or at least some of them did. For the majority, increasing expenditure meant increased tolls and taxes and it cost 2s.0d. (10p) per day to keep a burgess at Parliament representing the town.

Parliament's early popularity with the boroughs soon wore thin and, later, many often did not bother to send representatives; considering that costs made this a burden rather than a privilege. And besides the cost, the dangers of a journey from the South West made potential borough delegates think twice; knights of the shire, too, entertained doubts, despite the fact that they were paid 4s.0d. per day. The system became wide open to bribery and corruption by any who wanted their viewpoint represented in Parliament; how little change there has been.

Meldon

Okehampton as a borough always co-existed with the manors around it and traders in shops or markets down through the centuries have relied on their 'rural' neighbours coming into town. Each manor with which we are here concerned has its own history but while visitors enjoy the countryside, it is in just one manor that industry commands their attention.

The open wound on Dartmoor that is Meldon Quarry impacts on the memory of every traveller that passes by. While most other quarries in the area are now dormant, Meldon dominates the landscape as it continues, with a few workers, to take what lies beneath the moorland. It is also a living memorial to times when it was employing men by the hundred; and making a mint.

In 1241, Meledune was 'held by Robert de Maledune for one-sixth fee, of John de Curtenay.' Convened in Okehampton to determine local holdings in 1274, the jurymen John Fitz Decani, Richard Osmund, Michael de Porta, Martin Faber, Walter Halpeni, Walter Taylfer, Geoffrey Osmund, Richard the Hare, Geoffrey de Molend, Randolph Globbe, Richard Fitz Faber and John Pictor declared on oath that Hugh de Curtenay held 'ninety-two fees of the lord King in chief by the service of two knights for forty days.' With regard to the manor of Meledune they knew that, *inter alia*: 'Robert de Meledon holds of the lord Hugh $^1/_4$ part of a fee and for what time, and by what homage and service they know not.'

The Courtenays had considerable holdings in the county, were incredibly wealthy, but at times were prone to losing their heads when it came to taking sides in matters of war. While the fighting times in what Sir Walter Scott would later christen 'the Wars of the Roses' amounted to only a matter of weeks during more than a generation, the pitched battles at Tewkesbury, Towton and Northampton are among the highlights of history. The Courtenays were there, taking with them men from their manors, fighting for Lancaster and York, as they saw fit at the time.

The future of Meldon at least, if not the throne, was resting on the shoulders of Thomas Courtenay, 6th Earl of Devon, in mid-March 1461 as he led his men, including those raised from the manors of Okehampton, northwards to join the forces of King Henry VI. Previous victories for the Lancastrians at Wakefield and St Albans encouraged Courtenay's men to be confident of a swift return to Devon, but the long cold winter that would soon be extending into April was sapping their spirits. Yorkists from London heading north, led by the young Prince Edward, were warmed by their simmering anger at the execution of prisoners after the Battle of St Albans and heartened as their ranks were swelled by those joining them at Pontefract.

On the bitterly cold eve of Palm Sunday the two forces came face to face between the hamlet of Towton and the village of Saxton. On Towton Ridge Courtenay's men lined up beside those of the Dukes of Northumberland and Somerset, with the River Cock on their right. Along the ridge fires were lit and men huddled around them, sometimes gazing past the leaping flames towards the fires below Castle Hill Wood to the south, around which their lord's enemies huddled for warmth. The few that managed to sleep at all that night were forced awake by the winds and driven snow come dawn on a fateful March 29th.

The cold light of day brought joyful confirmation that Lancastrians outnumbered Yorkists but, as the former's archers stood to press their advantage, even the Devon men among them misjudged the wind and distance. Their arrows fell short and were used against them by the advancing Yorkists. Somerset and Northumberland urged their men forward, but Warwick's men, opposing them, stood their ground. Prince Edward's forces reeled back in Castle Wood as Northumberland pressed forward again. For two hours opposing forces fought back and forth until the outnumbered Yorkists were relieved to see the late arrival of the Duke of Norfolk's men.

Despite being without their leader, Norfolk's forces rallied the Yorkists, outflanked the Lancastrians' left wing, and forced the hard-pressed men towards the river. Men from Meldon and other Okehampton manors must have been among the many who drowned that day.

Those that lived to limp away, homewards, were soon to be overtaken by the news that, after the battle, Thomas Courtenay, 6th Earl of Devon, had been beheaded. Meldon was granted to Thomas Fulford, knight. At Westminster, on November 23rd 1464, letters patent were issued granting to Thomas Fulford and his heirs and assigns 'all messuages, lands and possessions in Widefield, Meldon, Yoldych, Folle, Okehampton, Bradford, etc.' He enjoyed his war-won gains for over 25 years, dying in February 1490:

... seised of 5 messuages, 200 acres of land, 80 acres of meadow, and 600 acres of pasture in Wydefield [Widefield], *Meldon, Folle* [Fowley] *and Yolditch* [Youlditch] *worth 40s., held of the Earl of Devon, of the Honour of Okehampton for* $^1/_{12}$ *fee.*

Almost a century later, on May 20th 1585, his descendant Thomas Fulforde, and his wife Ursula, sold Meldon and Sowerton 'with 12d. and one horse shoe naile' for high rent, total value 6ℓ 11s.8d. and the horse-shoe nail, to John Fytz of Fytzforde, Esq. Leases at that time included:

Stonewyke, held by Thomas Wonnacott, his son
    John and others;
Yollande, a tenement held by Richard and Johane
    Kennacote, and son Thomas;
Folleighe, a tenement held by James Arnell, and son
    Wylliam;

Yoldich, a tenement held by John and Margeria
    Gaskeyna and Robert their son.
Karslake, a 'capitall mansione' held by Robert and
    Elizabeth Wylliams, and William Huntte and;
Wydefeilde, a tenement held by Richard and
    Mawde Smythe and Robert their son.

One Thomas Horwell held an interest, in 1671, in two
messuages, Meldon North and South Downs, that
had of late been in the tenure of Robert Wonnacott.
Horwell's interest was dealt with legally by local
attorneys Henry Hawkings and Nicholas Prior.
Witnesses to the recorded interest were Ric.
Underdowne, Thomas Haine and James Yendall. It is
worth noting that in one transaction we find seven
surnames that appear in the local telephone books
today. Any descendants of the Bowyers, 'vellmon-
gers' of Okehampton during the latter part of the
seventeenth century, may also be interested to learn
that Richard Bowyer paid £15 in 1673 for the eighth
part of two tenements in Meldon – one called
Stondon and the other Wonnacott's. Those descendants, however, may well have the name Boyer now
because, perhaps by coincidence, a record over 40
years later links the same two tenements to people of
that name:

August 10th 1715; Indenture tripartite between (i)
Richard Boyer, the elder, of Okehampton, yeoman, and
Richard Boyer, the younger, his son and heir, of Bratton
Clovelly, weaver; (2) Francis Waldron of Okehampton,
maltster; (3) Robert Incledon and Henry Sanford of
New Inn, Middlesex, gentlemen. Incledon and Sanford
pay 10s. to the Boyers and Waldron to gain, among
other properties, the eighth part of the two tenements,
Standon and Wonnacott's.

For those with a particular interest in tracing names
through the transfer of leases and other similar agreements the records for the following century will
prove a goldmine. Aside from an unexpected John
Bowyer turning up there are rich encounters to enjoy
with well-known names linked with the manor of
Meldon: Gertrude, Duchess of Bedford; Robert, Lord
Clive; Edward, Lord Clive; John, Earl Spencer;
George John, Earl Spencer; Walter Meryfield the

Okehampton weaver; and Thomas Clack, clerk of
Moretonhampstead. Also of note is a widow lady of
Okehampton, Margaret Cudmore, who left the messuage in Meldon called Warren's tenement to her two
sisters-in-law, Amy and Martha Cudmore, on the
basis that it went to Walter Meryfield the weaver
when they died. By the time that Margaret herself
had died and her will was proved, in 1776, Amy and
Martha were dead and Walter came into his inheritance earlier than he had expected. To make the most
of his good fortune Walter got weaving and then
sold the fee simple to Clack the clerk from
Moretonhampstead for £42 and promptly gave up
weaving. Incidentally, the tenement, together with
right of Commons on North and South Downs in the
manor of Meldon, had been in the tenure of John
'Bowyer'. Was he related to the Richard Bowyer of a
century earlier we are left to wonder.

Space in this brief volume is obviously limited
and as we approach the Meldon of the nineteenth
century we are well aware that a new and more
industrial era is opening up. While Alexander, Lord
Loughborough, Francis, Duke of Bedford and even
HRH George Augustus Frederick, Prince of Wales, all
had interests in Meldon it is the quarry to the east of
the river in Okehampton Park (dating from c.1793)
and the limekilns burning there that attract attention.

Mines, kilns and quarries helped the hamlet of
Meldon become established but the tide of industrial
development was to roll out of Meldon as well as in.
For the ensuing century the production of limestone
was almost king, despite the fact that the first kiln
was abandoned within 15 years, by 1808.

Parts of the area continued to change hands
frequently and in December 1816, an 'Indenture of
Lease and Release' by Richard Millman provided
Albany Savile of Sweetlands, near Okehampton,
with an eighth part of Meldon North and South
Downs. Five shillings was paid for the lease, and a
peppercorn at end of the year, by force of Statute for
transferring use into possession. The price, £250, was
little more than £1.14s.0d. per acre for the estimated
236 acres of land. ('Sweetlands' became better
known as 'Oaklands'.) While the early lime production didn't last long other quarries would be worked
and other kilns fired.

Inspection train and crew working on
Meldon viaduct in the late 1800s.

Meldon

Top: *Much of Meldon, old and new, from the air.*

Right: *Meldon viaduct and part of the 'industrial' area in the early 1900s.*

Above: *Mrs Hawking and her children dwarfed by the Meldon dam before the valley was flooded.*

Stand now by Meldon Pool, with its silent sinister waters, and consider the area where once an outcrop of limestone was worked, to a depth of near 140 feet, until the site was exhausted. Farmers and landowners increasingly demanded burnt limestone during the nineteenth century for spreading on their fields to reduce acidity or for using as a fertiliser. Carriers competed to transport lime from the quarry to the farm but they often wasted many hours waiting for the production process to be completed.

Layers of coal and limestone filling the kiln to the top was set alight through a grate at the bottom, burned at a high temperature and then cooled. The resulting lime was shovelled out onto carts of the often non-too-patiently waiting lime carriers for weighing and despatch.

In the shadow of the viaduct a kiln can still be seen and nearby part of an old weighbridge can be found, with the maker's name, Bartlett and Son, Bristol, still visible. Wheelpit remains can also still be found, reminders of the days when water was pumped from the limestone quarries, into the river through pumps powered by water-wheels. Leat channels and a storage reservoir that was once fed by leats from Red-a-Ven Brook and the West Okement river await those who take the time to search out evidence of Meldon's past.

The arrival of the railway at Meldon brought shadows with it. The first came in the form of competition from distant quarries whose output could reach Okehampton quickly; the second was that of transport progress, with the trains encroaching on the stagecoaches, carriers and turnpike roads. This was powerfully symbolised at 956 feet above sea level by the 541 feet of intricate ironwork that straddled the valley in which the quarrymen worked, carrying the line of the London and South Western Railway Co. onwards from Okehampton to Lydford. Its spider's web of wrought-iron riveted girders remains a testimony to the skills of iron-workers, engineers and construction workers of a bygone age and is one of only two surviving examples of this type of construction in the country. Built in 1874, widened with welded steel girders five years later to accommodate twin tracks when a railway line was added to Tavistock, it survives today as a cycle and walking route. When its shadow first fell on the floor of the valley below the fires of the last of the limekilns were already condemned to extinction.

But a new industry was struggling to emerge from the quarries. In the 1880s Charles Geen was leasing the quarries and he turned the attention of his quarrymen to a mineral called granulite, a form of aplite, the high silica content of which made it valuable for enamelling, abrasives and also in the manufacture of stoneware and glass.

By 1890, a Mr Lindsay Bucknall is known to have been intending to open a glass and china works at Meldon. Little is known of his early enterprise.

Notes in books of the period refer to there being 'masses of fine white granite, known as granulite' on and around the railway workings. There is also mention of a siding at Meldon used only for the transport of aplite. Whether or not Mr Bucknall fully achieved his aspirations has yet to be confirmed, but it was in 1920 that the *Western Morning News* reported that a new syndicate from London was by then in charge and had ambitious plans to make Meldon an important centre for the production of glass. The newcomers expected soon to be able to push 'the foreigner from the home market' and their plans must have had some substance since 100 men are said to have been employed and the construction of two 120-ton capacity furnaces was said to have been almost complete.

The company plans included 12 such furnaces and the employment of 500 men within 12 months. By February 1921 ambitious plans had obviously been thwarted because new purchasers were being sought to take over the business. A granulite quarry, opened in 1920, continued working until the 1970s, but not to supply the glass-manufacturing trade. Despite its useful qualities, most of the granulite produced was sold for road-stone.

Glass, however, was undoubtedly produced at Meldon, as evidenced by the large amount of broken glass found in the area which indicates that medicine and cosmetic bottles were produced there. Examples of the green tinted-glass bottles produced there and a decorative glass walking stick are to be found in the Museum of Dartmoor Life in Okehampton.

As far as the site of glass manufacturing is concerned, two theories exist. The first suggests that it is now buried beneath the huge spoil heap of today's quarry, while the other points to an area near the present quarry entrance; budding archaeologists take note.

Meldon gave birth to its most important industrial link with the present day 16 years before Mr Bucknall dreamed of turning it into a glass-making centre. Thanks to the viaduct, in 1874, the LSWR's Devon & Cornwall railway was heading westward to Lydford on a track supported by Meldon ballast; before later turning south towards Tavistock and, eventually, Plymouth. As ground was being cleared and levelled around the moor in preparation for track-laying the hard rock caused problem enough for examples to be sent to the company engineers, who recognised its value. They convinced the directors to install a siding to cope with the first removal of stone, and, though no one at that time considered a quarry, Meldon stone was soon to prove itself to be of a better quality than others used by the company; the Hornfels quarry opened in 1895, with the quarrymen using small explosive charges. Men shovelled the stone onto horse-drawn wagons to be slowly carted off, but as demand increased company directors awoke to the fact that Meldon might play an

Meldon Village Hall

Left: *The annual children's Christmas Party at Meldon in 1970 was enjoyed by members of the Littlejohn, Heard, Claydon and Lee families.*

Below: *'Farewell old friend, you've served us well.' The final fling at Meldon's old village hall, September 8th 2001, was enjoyed and the sentiment shared by Leonard Heard's family, Courtenay Heard's family, Trish and Christopher Wilson, the Littlejohns, John Heard's family, Philip Heard's family, Tina Vallance and her family, the Bennetts, David and Jane Heard, Derek and Ruby Webber, Mike and Chris Mew, John and Daphne Martin, and Colin and Jean Hutchings.*

Below left: *A 'duck race' at Meldon attracted many to join the ducks during the new hall celebrations, August 11th 2002.*

Below centre: *Piggy-back racing at the Meldon celebrations, August 11th 2002.*

Below right: *Mrs Heard* (left) *and Mrs Kelly at the Meldon 'new parish hall' celebrations August 11th 2002.*

Above: *India Martin putting style into bowling, August 11th 2002.*

Right: *On August 11th 2000 the millennium commemorative stone was put into place at Meldon.*

important role in the financial future of railway companies; others as well as their own.

Within three years continually increasing demands exposed a problem; water supplies were inadequate to clean the aggregate. In June 1900 the company engineer put forward his proposal to build a million-gallon open reservoir at Meldon to supply the water that was needed at Okehampton Station at a cost of £1,170; for an added £405, he noted, the reservoir could be covered. Approving the spring-fed reservoir, the company decided to save on expenditure.

The following year the engineer recommended the purchase of a steam crane to help speed up the excavation of ballast at Meldon and as the area of workings grew he supported proposals in 1902 that the company acquire more land adjoining the quarry. In consequence, eight acres were bought from the Luxmoor estate for £500 and, in the same year, to cope with output, 12 new 40-ton hopper ballast wagons were purchased.

By 1905 over 107,000 tons of rock were being taken from Meldon each year, three-quarters of the railway's requirements, and more houses were need-ed on the site for quarry workers. A second block of four cottages was approved for building at £890. Two years later the engineer was again asking for further water supplies for steaming purposes at the quarry. He requested approval to negotiate with a neighbouring landowner who, he believed, would permit the company to take up to 10,000 gallons of water daily from a stream on his land, for a fee of £5 annually. The need for yet more workers' cottages in 1907 saw a further four being erected at a cost of £960, while quarry modernisation introduced workers to pneumatic drills.

Rock blasting brought hazards with it and with the rock face near the railway line in these early days it was not only men on the footplate who came into firing range. On July 6th 1907, the quarry signal-box suffered 'slight damage' and the signalman was hit by a piece of stone. The engineer decided that the foreman was to blame and the man, found guilty of neglect, was fined a week's wages. Signalmen soon learned to take cover in their boxes when the blasting warnings were sounded but they weren't the only ones that could suffer injury, or worse. There were a great many horses in use at the quarry, pulling stone-filled wagons around the yards. In October 1907 the engineer reported that a horse belonging to the com-pany had fallen and broken its leg while hauling a wagon-load of stone and had to be shot.

Money-saving suggestions were made in an engineer's report in 1913 where it was noted that engines often returned to Exeter 'light', without wagons, and similarly returned to the quarry the next day. To avoid such uneconomic journeys the engineer suggested that sheds at Okehampton be rebuilt and renovated to house such 'light' engines as

and when required. When approved, his idea saved the company £500 per annum and provided today's Okehampton with visitor accommodation after the sheds were converted.

Time was beginning to run out for the old South Western but the Southern Railway, arriving in 1923, inherited a quarry company that possessed yet more potential. As demand for ballast and chippings increased, the need for labour also rose; especially during wartime when the maintenance of railway track using Meldon's hard rock was vital to the country's war effort. The cessation of hostilities brought no respite but in 1946 the company was able to purchase eight surplus road vehicles from the Ministry of Supply; five 4-ton Thornycroft lorries costing £450 each and three Austin ambulances at the bargain price of £230 each.

The company wasn't anticipating increased accidents but its engineers could see the value of ambulances being converted for passenger carrying since the company needed to bring workers in from a wide area around Okehampton and between Hatherleigh and Lydford. Less than seven years later quarry production was up to 340,000 tons a year, with the majority of it being ballast, 70 per cent in 1953, used by permanent way departments through-out the 'Southern Region'. By the mid 1950s the quarrymen had created the largest quarry owned by the railway in Britain.

But then came Beeching. Railways across the county and country were decimated as the butcher wielded the axe and Okehampton's line was cut, save for the use by Meldon – a use that might yet offer the town a rail-bright future if political will real-ly prefers rail to road and recognises again the value of inland rather than coastal routes. But times they were a 'changing in the 1960s. The sale of the quarry to the English China Clay company was expected. The 'Western Region' was inheriting the railway tracks, rolling stock and sidings of Southern Railway and handed a life-line to the quarry as it directed ballast to its own needs.

Wrestling hard rock from the moor has never been less than a very dangerous occupation which, at its peak, employed the hands of hundreds of experi-enced men, dozens of horses, and mighty machines. Specialists drilled the rock and set explosives that brought 40,000 tons and more crashing to the ground to be hauled to a conveyor belt that transported it to the 72-inch gyratory crushers that reduced chunks of granite down to manageable lumps for a secondary crusher to reduce yet further as it was turned into permanent way ballast or concrete aggregate; then conveyed by belt again to storage areas. Trains drawing 40-ton wagons still leave Meldon's quarry regularly (though far less frequently), yet rock suffi-cient for another century remains to fall to the talent of explosives experts and quarrymen as yet unborn, for such is the heritage of Meldon.

Blizzard Conditions

Left: *Jean Worden at the family shoe shop in the Arcade, 1963.*

Above: *During the winter of 1962/63 it was necessary to dig out abandoned cars, although some were pushed aside by snowploughs in the rush to rescue people.*

February's weather in 1978 made Fore Street a traffic-free zone.

Above: *There was at least some warmth and refuge in Charter Hall for those rescued from their stranded cars.*

Right: *The scene is hardly recognisable but this was Chichacott Cross in February 1978 when drifts there were recorded as 25ft deep.*

6

The Winter Years & Heritage Anew

For most born after 1970, the heritage of Okehampton's weather is hardly considered, unless 'Soakhampton' is referred to, in which case they might heartily agree; with little foundation it must be added. There are tales and legends of winters past that we could have included but in selecting a report by David France, and other extracts from the *Okehampton Times*, Friday February 24th 1978, the close proximity in time confirms that such a heritage may reappear once again in the not too far distant future. 'We made it – alone !' was the reporter's exclamatory headline. 'OKEHAMPTON made it – alone.' That was the feeling of exhausted officials after eight days of horror, tragedy, drama and discomfort in blizzards accompanied by hurricane-force winds which cut off the town from the rest of the world, isolated villages, marooned cottages and farms and overnight transformed West Devon into a desolate Arctic wasteland. But a sense of triumph and companionship prevailed as good neighbourliness stepped in where helicopter-aided rescue services failed. The report continues:

Shortages of important foodstuffs such as bread and milk were met with a rationing scheme introduced by an emergency committee set up by the police and including town councillors, rescue and welfare groups.

As flour stocks ran low at the town's bakers the committee requested batches of 500 loaves to be baked which were distributed on a 'one-per-family' basis with 100 loaves kept in reserve for emergencies. It was the same with milk. Ironically, as farms in outlying areas poured thousands of gallons of milk away because tankers could not get through, the town itself faced a severe shortage. Eventually a daily supply of 400 gallons was found at Pudson Farm and distribution organised by the committee.

But these were the administrative details of what was an epic event in the history of the town. And in the history books it will be recorded as a chapter in which the community welded itself together in a joint effort to overcome disaster.

On Tuesday night, shortly after leaving one of the nightly meetings of the emergency committee at the police station, the Mayor, Peter Woodgate, told of the courage of individuals who had turned out to rescue stranded travellers, to take life-saving drugs to the sick. He talked of the untiring efforts of paid and unpaid helpers who worked almost round the clock clearing roads, checking that elderly residents were being cared for...

Said Mr. Woodgate: 'The people of Okehampton and the surrounding area have stretched the limits of human endeavour beyond the impossible. At the height of the storm they faced the impossible and overcame it.

I cannot praise too highly those who have worked through it all, the people who unstintingly offered their services, the traders who stayed open or donated food, the welfare and rescue services, the Army, Navy and Air Force, and most of all, the people themselves who refused to be beaten.' But the Mayor's words concealed feelings of bitterness amongst council and emergency chiefs who believe the County Council and the Government let them down.

Top of the list of unspoken complaints was the lack of attention given to the task of clearing the vital arteries. The A30 remained blocked by mile after mile of unbelievable snow drifts whilst other main roads in the county were quickly cleared. Exactly a week after being closed it looked as though the A30 might be opened to Exeter by Devon County Council gangs. But in the opposite direction Cornwall County Council men had cleared a path through as far as Bridestowe two whole days earlier. Other roads remained untouched. The A386 to Tavistock may not be cleared by this weekend, and its extension to Folly Gate is not listed as a 'priority route'. Hatherleigh was still cut off from all other towns on Wednesday.

Another artery, the railway, remained closed and the capillary network of lanes could be blocked for several more days given even reasonably favourable weather conditions.

But over all it was an experience not to be missed just once in a lifetime. Strangers in the streets of Okehampton could not have failed to notice that people were actually smiling. The children played happily on 'Sunshine Fields' at Klondyke. They improvised with plastic sacks for sledges and chucked feather-light snowballs from behind skilfully sculpted snowmen. Neighbours who previously had exchanged hardly a greeting became firm friends. People discovered they had legs instead of wheels. And it all came out of adversity.

THE RESCUERS

DOZENS of people owe their lives to prompt action by rescue teams. Most of them were the hundreds of lorry drivers and car drivers marooned – often buried – in deep snow. As early as Thursday morning reports were being received of people who had spent the night in vehicles praying for relief.

Sixty people were marooned at the Rising Sun at Sticklepath, another 50 were received in the village hall – all attended by publicity-shy villagers.

And in Okehampton 35 people were billeted in the Charter Hall after their vehicles came to grief in atrocious road conditions. The proprietor of the Okehampton Café stepped in with two urns of soup to feed them.

Those same people were still unwilling visitors to Okehampton five days later! But they were moved into more comfortable accommodation at Tenby House later in the weekend and WRVS volunteers took over feeding arrangements whilst blankets and even a portable television were found for warmth and entertainment.

Their move came as a result of a decision to billet soldiers of the Junior Leaders Regiment in the Charter Hall whilst they helped with various tasks in the town. But as a bad snowstorm turned into disaster the rescues became more heroic, the margin between life and death became a hairstring.

One man who owes his life to others is Mr S. King of Folly Gate who became stranded whilst walking from Okehampton to Folly Gate at the height of the storm. And another is an asthma sufferer at Exbourne who received a consignment of drugs from the Dartmoor Rescue Group.

More spectacular was the trip by sport shop proprietor Rod Crabtree and businessman Adrian Thomas – both of Brandize Park – who journeyed nine miles on skis over 15–20ft drifts to reach Belstone with insulin for a 7-year-old girl. And then they went on to Sticklepath with drugs for an elderly woman. At one stage, said Rod, they were literally ski-ing above house rooftops.

When we spoke of these events to Ray Balkwill, now an internationally renowned artist, they triggered even earlier memories:

'My parents moved to Okehampton in 1949 (when food rationing was still in existence) and I was one year old. My father, Jim, was a popular figure in the town, and manager of Eastmans, the butchers (originally in East Street and then in Fore Street). He worked for the firm

for fifty years altogether – 33 years in the Okehampton branch. I have many happy memories of my childhood, but the most vivid must be of the winter of '63. As a boy I kept a diary of the events of the 'Little Ice Age' as it became known, from the start with the blizzards on 26th December 1962, to the thaw on 13th March 1963.

February 4th 1963; *Today it snowed continuously, thick at times. It snowed all last night and a blanket of snow was left all over Devon and South East England. Many thousands of children have not been able to get to school. Many roads are ~~cold~~ closed and many towns and villages cut off from civilization. The wind is drifting the snow, and it is very cold out. There are many snowploughs going through Okehampton from everywhere.*

(Ray still gets lost finding Exmouth, but he's an exceptional artist.)

'Now, that really was a winter. We lived on Prospect Hill to the west of the town and because the school was closed for long periods, much of my time was spent outside in the snow, of course. Simmons Park and the playing fields were one favourite haunt, as there was much activity there – particularly with the RAF and Navy helicopters collecting fodder to be dropped to farm stock on Dartmoor. I remember on many occasions enthusiastically helping to load bales of hay alongside other children and RSPCA officers. Watching the helicopters land and take off at close quarters was very exciting for a young lad in a normally 'sleepy' town. My other lasting impression of the winter was walking the fields behind our house toward Old Road and Church Lane and finding the fields and roads the same level. The roads and fields being so deep with snow that the only clue to a road being there at all were the row of trees and telegraph poles.'

December 1962 and it was not unusual for people, especially the elderly, to be trapped in their homes, unable to open their doors.

A Heritage Lost

Rural decline was being experienced around 1720, for as the wool trade declined so did Okehampton's prosperity. To protect its own interests the town petitioned against the construction of the new road across Dartmoor, linking Moretonhampstead with Tavistock.

Until 1826, the Old Market House stood in the Middle Row, stretching down the main street from St James' and the butchers' stalls in the main street until 1826 when the new market (since enlarged) was built. Mr Solon Luxmore, then Town Clerk, lent £500 on the security of the tolls. The loan was paid off in 1839.

By the mid 1800s, the area's population was declining, many abandoning agriculture for work in the towns while others emigrated; some to Australia to found a new Okehampton.

In 1851, 38 houses were unoccupied in the parish. In the town there were nearly 100 paupers, in addition to 180 in the workhouse.

The railway was pushing its way to all parts of the county, for which W.G. Hoskins attributes the destruction of markets that had existed since the twelfth century; but Okehampton's was not one of them. The railway arrived in the town in October 1871, 14 years before electricity – a gas company formed in 1858 with a capital of £1,200, having first brought 'modern' lighting and cooking facilities to the town. If anything, the railway brought new buyers to the market and a boost to the town

White's Directory in 1878/9 refers to Okehampton, a town formerly engaged in the manufacture of serges and other coarse woollens, as being:

... much improved during the last fifty years. The present commodious market buildings were erected in 1826, when the old shambles were removed from the street. The market, held every Saturday, is extensively supplied, and great quantities of agricultural produce are bought here for the markets of Exeter and Plymouth, and there are large cattle fairs on the second Tuesday after March 11; on the second Thursday in May; on the Thursday after July 5 and August 5; on the Tuesday after September 11; and on the Wednesday after October 11.

Here is a great market on the Saturday before and a giglet or pleasure fair, on the Saturday after Christmas day.

Giglet fairs were common across the South West and were commonly seen as wife markets, taking place on the first Saturday after Christmas, when young people came to the market town from the farming community to select their partners. Parents and older people traditionally stayed at home that day to allow the young men and women to get together without fear of being watched. Many will know from Hardy's *The Mayor of Casterbridge* of the sale of

wives like cattle and readers can find a drama-filled giglet market described in Trevena's novel *Arminel of the West*. The giglet market was not the only one associated with sexual relationships since marriage banns were often proclaimed in the market-place from the mid 1600s until the late-nineteenth century.

The fairs were regularly visited by white witches, as testified by E.H. Young in 1925:

When I first came to Okehampton, in 1887, the 'white witch', a man called Snow from Exeter, came weekly to the market, but I think he ceased coming about 1890. He had a great following. The isolated region of Broadbury provided a large percentage of his 'practice', which mainly consisted of charms, but with a substratum of herbal treatment. In addition to his weekly visits to Okehampton, a great many people told me they used to go up and see him professionally at his house in Exeter. One good lady told me that she paid him regular visits for years.

Okehampton's market, a prized heritage, had a chequered career but down the centuries it was never regarded as anything less than vital to the prosperity of the town and many of the older generation that used the market still speak of it in those terms.

In 1914 it was reported in *Kelly's Directory* as being the 'principal support of the town, large quantities of agricultural produce being forwarded to all parts. The market tolls are let for three years for £413.' A quarter of a century later, on the eve of war, the market still held its position.

Charles Westlake's memories of the indoor market in the 1950s are of a market hall that is now the Charter Hall:

In those days it was a food and flower market on Saturday... and all the traders there were local people, but the exception of one person who had come down from up-country.

They were mainly small-holders who brought in fresh farm produce and home-made butter, and cream and flowers (set out) on little tiny stalls which they rented for a very small amount of money... and there was a big stall down the middle. Mrs Rundle and her son-in-law, Brian Hodge, came from Ferry Farm, Bere Alston, with Tamar Valley produce and flowers... and up 'til the 1960s the Tamar Valley was still a very busy market gardening area... and fruit and vegetables from the Tamar Valley were very sought after, and there wasn't the same availability as there is today with fruit and vegetables; it was much more seasonal and much more difficult to obtain and they came up every week with a long stall and they were assisted by Mr Rundle's sister, Mrs Hilda Rowe, who lived at North Lew.

Holman's bakery, from South Zeal, had a long stall selling cake, and the only shop in the town that had a stall in the market was Shobrooke, the fruit and vegetable and seeds and grocery and provisions... Mr

Shobrooke's sister, Mrs Petvin, and Mrs Shobrooke's sister, who married my uncle, used to go down to help them with their stall. Some people that had stalls lived in houses and cottages in Okehampton and in the villages around. They used to grow extra vegetables and flowers and fruit in their garden and have a foot of stall and sell it. Mrs Lily Barrett who lived in Beare Farm Cottages, Oaklands, did this; she was a 'Colwill' from Jacobstowe and had a market stall for several years. The Market Hall, as it is now, was the lower market and had previously been the butcher's market... that was all full of stalls and lock-up units selling... non-food items and it included Maunders' ironmongers from Holsworthy, a china shop from Wolborough Street in Newton Abbot, with china, Mr Button, colporteur from North Tawton selling bibles and Christian books, and a clothes stall.

They all came in with their stalls every week... the market was packed. The town was hectic on Saturdays from early in the morning 'til early evening... and, of course, in the fifties we had over eighty shops in the town.

Joe Gordon Vick, qualified with auctioneers Pearce Pope of Gloucester, went to work in Launceston in 1934 and two years later joined Frank Ward of Ward and Chowen of Tavistock to take charge of the Okehampton office; and also bought out Mr May who ran Hatherleigh's market in 1936; the turnover was about £16,000 per year and in the 1950s and '60s rose to about £12m. annual turnover.

During the war Mr Vick was seconded by Sir Winston Churchill to assist three other West Country valuers to requisition farm land for airfields so he left Hedley G. Stanbury in charge of the office until 1945 when he returned.

The Waitrose supermarket now operates where some 2,000 sheep were regularly penned and sold at the Saturday market and the cattle pens were placed where the Somerfield supermarket is sited.

George Gratton, from Oaklands House, would regularly be seen driving his Rover car in front of some 50–100 sheep with boy, stick and dog at the rear to pen his sheep at 7.00a.m. or earlier on a busy fair day at the charter markets. And 300–400 store and fat cattle would be penned early too.

David Vick, who joined the family firm in 1955 also remembers Mr Wildblood, who caught a train in Leeds and would be in Okehampton by 11.00a.m. starting time:

He would buy his usual 400–800 heavy hogs, ideal for the Leeds trade, leave us his signed blank cheque, and we would pop him back on the 2.00p.m. train back to Leeds, whilst we loaded his sheep on to his own lorry and hoped to see him again next Saturday.

Bob Ketley, of Essex, whose grandson still came down until foot and mouth affected matters in 2001, would buy cattle in the autumn of the year:

We would run the cattle on foot (Ginger Hawkins, drover, in charge and in full cry) up to Okehampton Station where a pre-arranged train with reserved cattle wagons was loaded.

Hedley J. Stanbury had already set up in opposition to J. Gordon Vick, as joint market auctioneer with Messrs Harris & Co. in 1957 when the Council invited tenders for market rights from interested parties. The Council received tenders from both Mr Vick and the joint auctioneers.

What followed has been a source of speculation ever since but in working our way through a nine-month problem period we were able to look at Borough Council records and also copies of correspondence between Mr Vick and the Council and joint Stanbury/Harris Co. correspondence with the authority. A resolution passed by Council on December 16th reads:

That negotiations be entered into with Mr. J. Gordon Vick, Auctioneer, Okehampton for granting to him the exclusive use of the Rostrum and Rings in the markets and a certain number of pens for a term of years.

Mr Vick, when learning of the resolution from a newspaper report, called to see the Assistant Town Clerk, Mr William J.Q. Yeo, on December 21st, who could tell him nothing and referred him to Town Clerk Mr J.J. Newcombe who was dealing with the matter. Mr Newcombe, later the same day, was unable to tell Mr Vick anything about any negotiations. Mr Vick wrote to the Council on December 24th suggesting that he should meet with the relevant committee. Members of the Council did visit Mr Vick, but explained that on no account could they negotiate or offer anything. By 30 January 1958, without negotiations commencing, matters took another turn when the Council allowed the Fatstock Marketing Corporation to come to market.

Mr Vick wrote again, reminding the Town Clerk of the awaited negotiations adding:

I am most concerned about the fact that you will be splitting up your Market, and this can cause a complete dislocation of the Auction Market, just when we have been working hard for some time to get it right. This will take stock from the Auction Market...

At the F.M.C. collection you will not get a lot of people to town as with the Auction... buyers will not think it worth coming and you will kill what has been a difficult Market.

A reply from the Council, dated February 7th, advised him that legal advice regarding the market was being sought.

Mr Vick's notes state that a Council deputation later visited him and suggested that, with time passing, it was not expected that he should stick to his previous offer (£500 or 10 per cent whichever was greater). Mr Vick's response was to offer a straight 15 per cent gross commission but Mr J.J. Newcombe considered this a second tender, which he ruled 'out of time'. On April 28th Mr Vick wrote again to the Council expressing his concern about the position with regard to the market, pointing out the reduction of business; practically nothing in Okehampton against £20,000 in Hatherleigh:

The Fat Stock market is also getting smaller and people are fast losing interest. Something must be done immediately if you wish me to proceed according to my offer, otherwise I must withdraw.

A resolution was passed at a meeting of the Council in a committee held in the Town Hall on Tuesday May 6th 1958, that subject to the rights of others, the exclusive right would be:

Saturdays and March Fair Days to sell Cattle, Sheep, Pigs and Animals in the Okehampton Cattle Sheep, Pig and Animal Markets and to collect and receive the tolls therein offered to Mr. J. Gordon Vick, Auctioneer &c., of Fore Street, Okehampton for a term of 21 years, determinable by either party at the end of the 7th or 14th year of the said term, subject to a Lease to contain such terms and conditions as shall be mutually agreed on being entered into; and that a Committee consisting of His Worship the Mayor (Councillor H.R. Horne), Alderman Passmore and Councillor White with the Town Clerk be appointed to interview Mr. Vick on the matter.

Bidders had originally been invited to tender for 'exclusive use' but now this was reduced to Saturdays and March Fair Days only. Even so, the terms offered included a fixed fee of £750p.a. for the first three years and £1,000 annually thereafter. Lengthy clauses were generally acceptable bar one, that Mr Vick should 'leave a sufficient number of pens for use by the public and other Auctioneers.'

When those delegated interviewed Mr Vick they had no powers to negotiate so, feeling time was being wasted, he drew up a draft agreement that included all terms which the Council wanted, except the one, and left the question of rent open. He asked for the matter to be dealt with by a specific time but this doesn't appear to have been achieved.

In his article for the *Western Times and Gazette*, May 16th 1958, headed 'Domesday market ready for battle of the fittest', Mr Jack Hellier reported that: 'The farmer demands a good distributive centre for his product, a fair price for it when he gets it there, and his wife fair treatment from the shopkeeper,' adding that Okehampton met all requirements and threw in, as good measure, civility and courtesy.

The same article quotes turnover figures at Okehampton:

1955	15,312	animals' value	£215,000
1956	18,672	" "	£280,000
1957	21,744	" "	£370,000

The same newspaper's market reports included:

May 10th Okehampton market auctioneers J.Gordon Vick, H.G. Stanbury, and Harris & Co. sold between them only 15 Cattle, – 54 Sheep, – and 30 Pigs.
May 13th Hatherleigh market J. Gordon Vick reports sales of 449 Cattle (290 attested), – 35 Dairy Cattle, – 135 Calves, – 1068 Sheep, – and 575 Pigs.

The farmers were already voting with their feet.

Okehampton's market in the 1920s brought people and money into town.'

Since 1946 market modernisation in Okehampton had been held back by Government restrictions on capital expenditure. In Hatherleigh, private enterprise had been upgrading and enlarging the market. On June 3rd Mr Vick wrote to the Town Clerk, saying that he gathered his offer had not been accepted:

There appears to be considerable disagreement amongst members of your council and under these circumstances (without the whole council behind it) I think it best to drop the whole matter of Letting the Market to my firm, and we will carry on as best we can, as we have been doing.

On June 14th Mr Vick received three clauses considered essential in any lease. These he included, as nearly as possible, in another draft lease and returned it in time for the Council meeting on the 16th, exactly six months after the original resolution. He asked for an immediate conclusion to the matter as it had been left too long.

The conclusion was that the resolution of December 16th be rescinded and that each Auctioneer should have alternative 'first terms', J. Gordon Vick and H.G. Stanbury to each have only 26 weeks out of 52 weeks, i.e. half the income; for what it was worth. The proposal, however, was not the end of the matter. Market business was in recession, the Chamber of Trade was not entirely happy as to the future of the market and a concerned Mr W.J. Passmore was quoted by reporter Mr Jack Hellier in the *Express and Echo*, July 22nd, as addressing the Town Council, saying:

The market situation is a farce, and something must be done if we are to keep a market here at all. The position is really grave. The council must decide on some definite plan quickly or else we can write off our market.

By August 30th G.D. Cann & Hallet, Solicitors, Exeter were writing to the Town Clerk:

We understand from Mr Vick that your council has now offered the Market to Messrs Kivell and Sons and that Mr Vick has given notice to our clients Messrs Harris & Co. and Mr H.G. Stanbury that all three firms will, as from 1st September, be back on the rota system arranged by your council.

The letter continued, asking for clarification of the situation.

A letter from Kivell & Sons, dated September 3rd, advised the Town Clerk that:

... after profound and prolonged deliberation... reluctantly... and with due regard to their... long and cordial relationship with Messrs Harris & Co. who are at present operating the market, we must turn the matter down.

On the same day, Messrs Harris & Co., with H.G. Stanbury, wrote to the Town Clerk about the market:

With reference to the above no doubt you are aware that Mr. J.G. Vick has broken off all business negotiations

Some of the county's finest on parade at the Okehampton Show at Oaklands in 1955.

The public weighbridge in Market Street. The town's fire engine used to be garaged in the centre building.

June 1966 and the market pens are empty. The loss of the town's market was a serious blow to the town, as well as to local farmers.

with us in connection with the above and advertised the fact and advised the Producers of the above Market accordingly.

We beg to advise you that Mr. H.G. Stanbury and ourselves still hope to continue to do business in Okehampton Market and therefore we are prepared to negotiate with your Council on terms for the first use of the Auction Rings and Rostrums and would be pleased to discuss terms with your Council on this matter when we will assure you that we will do our best to improve the above Market with the help of your Council.

Had we known Mr. Vick was going to break off his working arrangements with us we should have made your Council an offer when you invited us to do so.

Thanking you for an early reply...

On September 4th, Mr M.R. Gloyn wrote to the Town Clerk as chairman of a newly formed 'Okehampton (J.G. Vick) Market Committee', the members of which included Mr A.J. Knapman (vice-chairman) and Messrs A.S. Hodge, T. Hodge, J.A.T. Hodge, L. Heard, K. Heard, C. Heard, K. Watts, A.W. Knapman, N. Knapman, S. Wooldridge, J.B. Hill, G.H. Drew, W.G. Clark, J. White, W.J. Wedlake, A.P. Squire, T.W. Horn, F.J. Sampson, D.O. Soby, R. Trerise, P.I. Pellow, J. Morris and T. Squire. The letter expressed the concern of those listed, representing the main vendors who support the market, on hearing that the Council was negotiating to let Okehampton market to a firm of auctioneers not at that time selling in the market. It was considered that the Council should immediately cease any such negotiations, and continued:

We further consider that you should now revert immediately to the system which existed prior to 1950, whereby the firm of J. Gordon Vick shall sell all stock sent to him before anyone else, and that following this, as soon as possible, you should let the market on lease to the firm of J. Gordon Vick, as we are quite convinced that this would be in the best interests of all concerned.

We wish to make it quite clear that we are not prepared to support another firm as we consider we have the best firm available to sell for us.

We have formed this Committee in order to get the best co-ordinated management of the market and we ask for your Council's full co-operation.

We shall be glad to know from your Council as soon as convenient that you are meeting the firm of J. Gordon Vick, and if it is of any help, this Committee will be pleased to meet you with the firm.

The letter continued but the wishes of local farmers and their offer to assist could hardly have been made more clearly.

Despite the support, the future of Okehampton's market (at least in the short term) was sealed at or about this time. J. Gordon Vick withdrew his personal association with it and continued his work in Hatherleigh. The company he founded in Okehampton continues as estate agents, and still thrives. Mr Stanbury was associated with Okehampton market until its end. When the auction market closed for the last time, over 1,000 years of Okehampton's heritage came to an end.

A Young Heritage to be Proud Of

In 1967 two young cadets, participating in a military exercise, tragically died, near Fernworthy, but their untimely passing was to introduce another strand to the cloak of heritage worn by the town. It is a story Mr Fred Barlow, a voluntary warden for the North Moor at the time, was pleased to relate:

Dr Jones was the doctor in town called out that day... as the army camp's doctor, when the cadets were found. He was also the local MOH and County Youth Officer.

Dartmoor Rescue Group

Dartmoor Rescue Group, at Hound Tor in 1975, trained for all emergencies.

Above left: *Jim Hannaford* (right) *and Fred Barlow hold the tape for Mr Bernard Whitehead to cut to gain entry to the new DRG HQ, February 26th 1983.*

Above right: *Chief Inspector Rachel James gets the message across for the Dartmoor Rescue Group on February 26th 1983 at the opening of the group's new HQ behind the Natwest Bank.*

DRG training with a dog that has obviously found something.

Blizzard heroes praised for 1978 rescues. Mr J. Alderson (Chief Constable for Devon and Cornwall), Mr F. Barlow (DRG North Group Controller), Lt/Col Hodgson.

DRG members 'stretchering' and fund-raising between Ivybridge and Okehampton, c.1982.

Dr Jones in turn advised Mr Barlow of the unfortunate situation and he accompanied the doctor to the site where the doctor certified the deaths as being caused by hypothermia. If only we could have got to them earlier, was perhaps uppermost in the men's minds as they returned to Okehampton.

A Court of Enquiry was conducted and from that came a suggestion that the army might consider forming some sort of rescue association which could assist when army personnel were believed to be in trouble on the moor.

The 43rd Wessex Field Ambulance was based at Tavistock, but was on the point of closing down and it fell to Dr Jones to call a meeting in Tavistock attended by senior officers of the 43rd (both medically trained and representatives from the police and the youth services, and Fred as a moorland warden) that was to extend the suggestion considerably further. [It was] A voluntary civilian organisation made up of people with a good knowledge of Dartmoor, in all areas, that could liaison with the armed services, area police and local fire officers, and that could be called upon day and night was what was needed.

That all encompassing but brief description may have been a vision of some future super-team in 1968 but it reflects quite accurately what was to become the Dartmoor Rescue Group.

The army officers were able to offer medical supplies, stretchers and bandages and Fred believed that it would be possible to find the right people with the knowledge and the interest in the new project to get it started:

I was co-ordinator of Dartmoor's cave and mine rescue group and had men in mind. Bill Aymes became the group's first secretary and Eddie Haines let us use his works garage in Mill Road as a base.

Such was the initial establishment of the Dartmoor Rescue Group but it soon had nine members on call at a Tavistock base and ten in Okehampton. Fred continues:

When we got called out to begin with, the team setting off onto the moor always had to include a fit runner who could search the moor with the others looking for people in trouble. Then... they had to run back to the starting out point to report to a waiting team member, sitting in a car probably, who would hurry off to the nearest telephone box to call out medical help or what was needed.

Ten Tors used to start at Hay Tor and end at Willsworthy but it came to Okehampton about 1969 and I was safety officer for thirty years.

The introduction of radio communication was appreciated, but the moor being what it is, wasn't exactly helpful:

... we'd put a radio call-out and it was picked up by the

South Wales Rescue team who could then contact Tavistock to pass on a message. Back the same way an answer would come. Up at OP 15 (a moorland observation point) you could see Hanging Stone Rock but not be able to communicate with a team there. It was quicker to flash a torch.

With many moorland mines, the increasing interest in Dartmoor by walkers had made even more valuable the formation of a voluntary group to be ready and on hand to deal with any underground (as well as overground) emergency:

There was Caves and Mining Rescue... lots of caves... I was a controller... at Buckfast... and it's still going. This was where a lot of the original volunteers came from for Dartmoor Rescue.

Nowadays we search the levels as much as the moor. [We] often get called out to Torquay. An elderly person roaming off and getting lost perhaps. I have a friend up in the North of England, who got called out and eventually found a man behind a fridge in... (a well-known supermarket). He'd been lost three days... but he was alright.

Communication problems were eased, to a degree, when the police were permitted to provide equipment to rescue groups, but there were still some problems:

In our base you just couldn't get a [phone] signal all the time. Then we found out that they worked all right in the toilet. I've spent many a time sending messages and receiving information sitting in there.

The valued initial DRG base in Mr Haines' garage in Mill Road could only be a temporary arrangement and the group moved to a room above the market hall for a while until some derelict stables in George Street were noticed.

A friend of the group was also a friend of a senior executive at Natwest, the owners of the stables, and acted as intermediary. The serious state of dereliction was a cause for concern but DRG members, with a multitude of talents between them, assured the bank that if agreement could be reached for the long-term use of the old building, they would invest their time and personal funds into restoring it to a safe and useable condition.

This offer, made by volunteers, the bank was pleased to accept and, wishing also to assist Dartmoor Rescue Group, the local community and visitors to the region, it generously offered to permit use of the premises to be established solely upon the basis of a peppercorn rent payment annually.

The DRG members were as good as their word. The building was treated by them to a new roof and once protected from the weather the inside was cleaned and restored. Toilets and showers were installed, special windows called for by building regulations were introduced, and a radio control room established. Over the years, when volunteers could be on duty for many more hours than six, bunks were brought in, a computer room developed, and more facilities added as the work of the group expanded. In all the DRG believe that over £18,000 has been spent and endless man hours and woman hours given to create an important base in Okehampton.

Over the years DRG has grown from those original 19 volunteers to a highly efficient force of over 140; with bases in Plymouth, Ashburton and Tavistock as well. Its members attended and helped in Locherbie when the community there was devastated by the airline bombing that shook the world. During the daily search-and-recovery programme that extended 60 or 80 miles or more around the area the value of radio communication was obvious. Few people throughout the UK who watched those horrors unfold, and appreciated the assistance given, realised that each group of volunteers pay a licence fee of £800 annually for the privilege of using their radios; and £2,000 a year to keep them maintained.

Communication had a lighter side when the DRG members were in Switzerland, training with alpine teams. The use of a mountain horn that could be heard for miles appealed to the Okehampton people. The horn, incidentally, was a small brass one. Intent on acquiring one or two the group members wondered if their hosts would help with translations for orders, and so on, but, when asked, their hosts assured them that translations would not be necessary. 'We get our alpine horns from the Acme Whistle Company of Birmingham, England,' they were laughingly advised.

A valuable piece of equipment carried by the DRG 25 years ago was a survival bag that can best be visualised as a big sleeping bag. Instructions on a course for dealing with cases of hypothermia, suggested that in the event of there being no means of warming a person, one should loosen their clothing and get them into a warm sleeping bag. One of the rescuers was then also to 'divest [him/herself] of [their] clothes, get into the bag, clasp the person to [their own] body and transfer body heat to him or her.' A team was out one winter's night, up behind Cranmere Pool looking for a couple of missing people. It had been raining but, by two in the morning, it turned to snow and was growing bitterly cold when one of the team had an idea: 'Charlie Hodge's sheep always used to get down in the hollow when the weather got like this. Perhaps we should go and have look down there.'

A tent was soon found but one of the two girls in it was already suffering from hypothermia so the instructions were put into practice. The unconscious girl was put into the bag and 'Charlie' volunteered to climb in with her. Undressed down to his Y-fronts he also, with his arms clasped around the girl, was

zipped into the bag and off went the team, pushing and carrying them on a wheeled stretcher. Two days later Fred visited the girls in hospital and asked how they were. 'I remember,' said one:

... there was a lot of noise and someone saying 'Here the buggers be,' then I passed out. Then next thing I knew was the bumping, bumping, bumping. I put my hands up and I felt this hair... and a voice said, 'Don't you worry my dear, its only Charlie,' so I went to sleep again only to wake with a start and shouted, 'Who the hell's Charlie?' I put my hands up and Charlie said 'That's far enough my dear.' 'Who are you?' 'I'm just one of the rescue blokes.' 'Well what are you doing in my bed?' 'I'm not in your bed my dear, you're in my bed and I'm keeping you warm.' We stopped and they gave me a hot drink; I was sick. Then I felt better and had another drink, and Charlie had a drink and said, 'Snuggle down and be a dear, 'cos' we got another three mile to go yet.' And before we got back to the road, Charlie was enjoying it and so was I.

Since the DRG is ever in need of funds, Fred said he never refused an invitation to give a talk to help raise the necessary money. He recalled being asked at short notice to stand in for a speaker at an elderly persons' residential home, to give a talk, and bring his sleeping bag with him. Off he went and was telling the ladies all about the DRG when 'Emma' asked if he had brought his big sleeping bag with him. He got it out and showed the ladies how it opened up and how it worked. 'Right', said Emma, and she was gone. Fred was bringing his talk to a close when Emma reappeared, in her nightie. Fred asked 'So, what now then Emma ?' 'Well, I'm getting in that sleeping bag... and so be you.' Fred looked at the matron, who shrugged and replied, 'Well... all right,' and started to get into the bag. 'Oh no,' said Emma, 'You told us afore that Charlie got down to his Y-fronts.'

The elderly ladies in the audience started clapping, the matron responded to Fred's wide-eyed look with 'I'll bet you don't,' and Fred asked if she would be offended. 'Oh no', she said, 'we've been looking forward to it.' Fred stripped down to his Y fronts and got into the bag with Emma. He was zipping the bag up when she said, 'Do you know, my man's been gone 37 years, I'm nearly 90, and this is the first time I've been in bed with a man for 37 years, and I'm loving it.'

The heritage of the DRG and all the other voluntary organisations in the town, be it the WI, the Otters, Scouts or many more that we have met, but have been unable to include, deserve to be revealed in full. During trying times, hard work, humorous episodes and through all the trials and tribulations of life experienced on this corner of Dartmoor, it has always been the people of the community that have preserved Okehampton's rich heritage.

7

Sporting Life & The Great Outdoors

Rugby

It is believed that a rugby team existed in Okehampton as early as 1884. Games would obviously have been local ones, and probably played on an irregular basis. By 1890, however, a more regular pattern had been established, largely through the influence of Dr Knott who captained the side. This team included two brothers, R. and W. Furse, and it is especially pleasing to know that Alan Furse, a direct descendant, still maintains an active interest in the club to this day, in 2002.

A century ago, in 1902, the club became a member of the Devon Rugby Football Union, confirming that by that time the Okehampton team was fully established and able to undertake a programme of regular fixtures. Records show that the ground off High Street known as Northams Meadows was the scene for home games between 1902–12. From 1912 until the 1920s home games were played on a very wet ground in North Road, except during the First World War. Playing conditions improved in the 1920s when land known locally as 'Cawlands Fields' became available off Mill Road; this became the club's home ground until the onset of the Second World War.

The status of the club during that period had climbed sufficiently for a social visit to Okehampton to be included by the All Blacks in their 1936 itinerary. On their way to Redruth, the All Blacks stayed at the White Hart and entertained the Mayor, Mr Samuel Rich, and some club representatives to a meal.

The increasing skill shown by the players was recognised through regular fixtures against the Devon Barbarians, providing a means by which some of the larger clubs, such as Plymouth Albion, could see at first hand what Okehampton players were capable of; and indeed they were encouraged to go into the senior club. The outbreak of war in 1939 caused the club to close, and most of the players were called into the Armed Forces.

By 1946 several players had returned from active service and were ready and eager to re-establish the club. This was to prove no easy task, however, as the pre-war ground had by then been purchased by the Town Council for housing development. Saville Mead and Wardhayes were constructed on the site.

A newspaper report covering the first match to be played after the Second World War, in September 1946, reads as follows:

OKEHAMPTON HANDICAPPED
Despite a 13pts.–4 reverse in their opening game at home to Buckfastleigh, writes 'J.H.', Okehampton showed flashes of the things to come when the side settled down and developed a tactical understanding. Therein lay the fault if fault there were. Okehampton have spent weeks in finding a ground, and having found one, getting it in readiness. This has meant a loss of practice time, and Buckfastleigh were quick to fasten on the errors and misunderstandings.

They crossed over at half-time leading by an uncovered try (J. Harvey) to nil. L. Moore raised hopes of an Okehampton revival with a drop goal, but Buckfast added to their advantage through F. Harper (drop goal) and tries by Ford and Miller.

WELHAM INJURED
Okehampton's chances were not improved when A. Welham sustained a head injury which put him out of the game midway through the second half.

The 'Old Brigade' – Bert Cockwill, Harold Westlake, Jack Moore, W. Kelly – again did well, but none did better than Guy Wright playing his first game.

Other newcomers to catch the eye were Knapman (threequarter) and E. Cann (forward). Club president (Mr. H.M. Brooking) kicked off.

The club was honoured this week by the selection of Moore and Westlake for the team representing Devon Regt. Past and Present v a County XV at Barnstaple.

These post-war players were certainly not downhearted, despite having no ground, no changing facilities, no kit, no money, and nothing other than a determination to rebuild the club. But it was that determination which was to provide a firm foundation for the future.

Discussions with other sportsmen in the town facing similar difficulties, and negotiations with the Town Council, brought about an agreement that provided for the Rugby Club and Okehampton Argyle Football Club to try sharing a very good surfaced ground in Simmons Park – two sports, two teams and the arrangement was soon beset with problems but the Argyle Club, which was very strong at that time, fortunately found a ground of their own in North Road.

With the ground-sharing problem behind them the Rugby Club players still faced another problem; they had no changing facilities on their ground. Undaunted, the club obtained the use of a disused store at the Fountain Hotel. This was primitive; in as much as there was no lighting, or windows, and the only way to let light in was to leave the door ajar. All players, including the opposition and referee, shared the same room and the bath, which was built into a corner and was heated by a ten-gallon gas boiler. Washing was not taken too seriously though, as it interfered with drinking time; some players are remembered as being still in their rugby kit at closing time. The spirit of the players at that time can hardly be imagined now.

The absence of facilities was sometimes trumped by the absence of a pitch. Whenever the park pitch was declared unfit for use by the Council's permanent park keeper, those players who did not work on Saturday morning would take up the posts and crossbars, etc. and transport them to a field on the outskirts of town, which is now part of Exeter Road Industrial Estate, and put the posts up and mark out a pitch, rather than miss a game.

The team had a hard core of senior players who had survived the war, but it was forced to rely on a large contingent of boys who were still at the grammar school. Fortunately, rugby had been introduced there by a new headmaster, Mr H.J. Mills, in 1945 and such was the boys' enthusiasm for the sport that it was not unknown for them to play a school match in the morning followed by a club game in the afternoon.

Another source of players at times was the Army camp, and the club was able to call on players who were stationed there, including those who were attending the Officer Cadet Training Unit. These were generally sportsmen of high quality, some of whom are remembered as having progressed to becoming international players.

By 1950 rugby football had also been introduced to the secondary modern school under the headmaster Mr Burgess, himself a former county player. This triggered a new enthusiasm among young players and brought about the formation of the Colts XV in the early 1950s.

For over half a century this has been the very life-blood of the club and is largely responsible for a long-lasting love of rugby amongst so many families. Ever improving standards of play by the 1st XV raised enthusiasm and a new determined attitude towards the winning of games – so much so that dur-

ing the 1951–53 period the 1st XV played 32 games without defeat (26 games won with 6 drawn).

By the 1955–56 season, though, many of the players had retired or left the area, the playing strength declined and a couple of seasons with poor results followed. This decline was brought to a halt in 1958, with the arrival of Frank Webb, a former captain of Oxfordshire, and Dr David Shields, a former Middlesex player. This pair not only breathed new life into the playing side; they were instrumental in moving the club forward and into purchasing its own ground. At the time teams were using a former stable at the White Hart Hotel. Converted by club members, this accommodation boasted three rose-head showers on severely limited water supply. Nevertheless, it was an improvement and the envy of many other clubs.

Through the determination of Frank Webb, David Shields, Roger Vick, David Brough and chairman Derek Brown, the club purchased its present ground from the local Agricultural Association in 1961 and opened up a sporting chapter hitherto undreamed of. The showground boasted a none-too-clever grandstand, into which bathing facilities were quickly installed and games were first played on the ground in the 1963–64 season. With a former office building placed nearby, the club now possessed four changing rooms – which were essential as more and more players came into the club. Very soon a second XV was formed, shortly followed by the Acorn XV. Going from strength to strength, the club was fielding four sides on most Saturdays, having gained the use of former school pitches adjoining its new property.

Purchasing the showground was a gigantic step for the club to take at that time but, with the passing of the years, it has proved to be the best investment they ever made except for one thing; their early resolution to foster young talent. Over the years, certain sections of the ground not required for the playing of rugby have been sold off in stages to enable the club to improve and extend its facilities; today they rank as a benchmark for all clubs.

From 1963 the teams continued their normal run of fixtures and confidence in the club's future increased with every passing season. A strong social and family side of club activities developed and in 1972 it was decided to enhance this aspect of club life with new bar facilities in a purpose-built extension to the grandstand. This welcome addition was opened on December 7th 1975 and new kitchen arrangements also helped the club ladies who were doing wonderful work for the social side of activities.

On the pitch, the reasonable results of past years were built upon with every passing season until, due to the influence of a strong schools side, playing results became consistently good. In 1979 the club not only entered the Devon County Havill Plate competition, it came home with the prized trophy. This success set the pace for a prolonged period of very good seasons for the club during which time their Okehampton ground became a fortress where few sides could come expecting to win.

There were occasional disruptions though. During a heavy storm at Christmas 1981 the original grandstand was so extensively damaged that it became dangerous. Thankfully it was insured, permitting the building of a larger, improved grandstand, which was opened three years later incorporating changing rooms on the first floor. It became the envy of clubs everywhere.

In the early 1980s Devon RFU introduced a merit table system, as a result of clubs requesting more competitive rugby. Entering into the system, Okehampton won Merit Table B in 1982–83 and immediately followed this up by winning Merit Table A in 1983–84. When league rugby began in the season of 1987–88, Okehampton was placed into a very prestigious Western Counties set-up, confirming tremendous regional respect and regard for the club, as the league extended from Penzance to the Forest of Dean.

Distances between clubs began to cause serious travel problems for clubs and eventually it was decided that the geographical area should be split in two but, to the present day, ORFC has maintained its place in the league.

In 1990 the club obtained grants for the draining and levelling of the back pitch. The landowner, Mr Eddie Hawkins, agreed a 99-year lease on this ground, at a peppercorn rent, thus making the club very secure. At the same time the bold decision was taken to build a functions/dining-room by extending the bar area. With the help of a great many voluntary labourers assisting the professional builders, the very fine facility, which included a new kitchen and toilets, was ready to be opened in December 1991. This added a completely new dimension to the social side of the club, helping it to keep faith with the many people and companies who had so generously sponsored it since the early 1980s. The sponsorship scheme is absolutely vital to the club's continued existence and it is always a pleasure when members are able to entertain their guests, in what they might rightly call 'our club'.

Quite apart from the league rugby, a large measure of success in the Devon Senior Cup enabled the club to host Plymouth Albion in 1987–88, followed later by Barnstaple in 1996–7, both in the final. These games were lost, but Okehampton rose above its lower-league status and pleased large crowds in 1996–7 by winning the Western Counties (West) title,

Julian White in action in Okehampton before his talent took him on to play for England.

and gaining well-earned promotion to SW II the following season.

For half a century the club has continued to introduce young players to the game of rugby and nurture their talents. Over the years, and not to be outdone by any senior team, the Colts XV have earned their own trophies, winning the Devon Colts Cup at Barnstaple in 1982, and always performing well at the Tiverton 7s against sides from all over the West of England and occasional sides from Wales.

Much of the groundwork for this success began midway through the Colts' history in 1978 when under-14s and under-16s were established. The younger ones' interest in the game waned in the early 1980s and there was almost a struggle for survival until it came roaring back to life by 1985/86 – so much so that it became difficult to keep pace with the demand by young people for rugby and in 1992 the decision was made that for the following year a completely separate section for juniors would be established.

Today this section is vibrant, ambitious and forward-looking with the club thronged with young people each Sunday. It is a section that has become a club within a club in its own right, requiring a massive organisation and the total cooperation of parents and friends. For the 2001–02 season the sheer scale of activity can be gauged by the fact that over 100 junior players paid their subscription to become members. They are the very lifeblood of the club; the future is theirs and the club is there to help them go forward.

Starting at eight years old, remaining as juniors until 16, there are eight stages of progress each one becoming more demanding; and at each stage the young ones prove their worth. Among those taking to the game there will be players who will represent their club, their county, and even their country in future years.

Possibly the best recognition for Okehampton Rugby Club came in 2000 when Julian White was capped for England 'A' versus Ireland, whilst playing for the premiership side Saracens. Since that time Julian has played for the full England side on a regular basis. It is a great source of pride to the club to think that much of the early stages of his very successful career began here. In honour of Julian's achievements a fitness room was created in the clubhouse. Opened in 2001 this facility represents the latest stage of the ever-ongoing development of a progressive club. Rugby, many local players have found, has much to offer as a game, and as a career.

Okehampton Rugby Football Club

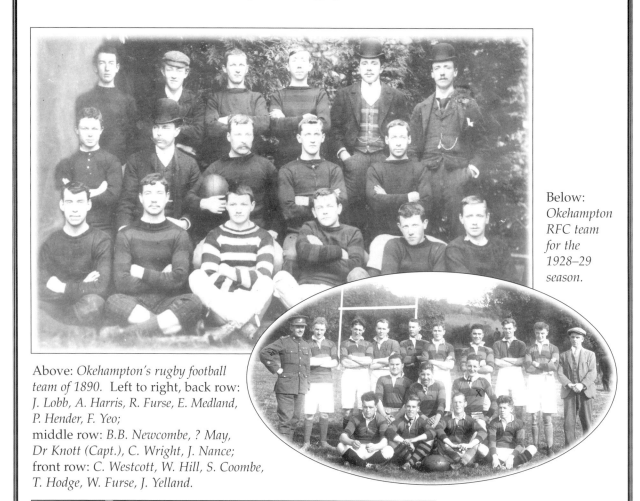

Below:
*Okehampton
RFC team
for the
1928–29
season.*

Above: *Okehampton's rugby football
team of 1890.* Left to right, back row:
*J. Lobb, A. Harris, R. Furse, E. Medland,
P. Hender, F. Yeo;*
middle row: *B.B. Newcombe, ? May,
Dr Knott (Capt.), C. Wright, J. Nance;*
front row: *C. Westcott, W. Hill, S. Coombe,
T. Hodge, W. Furse, J. Yelland.*

Below: *Okehampton Rugby
Football Club – Devon
Representatives, 1980–81 sea-
son.* Left to right, back row:
*Alan King, Nick Bassett,
Graham Phenna, Martyn Cox,
Steve Friend, Bryan Hain,
Kevin Cornwall;*
front: *Andy Dennis, David
Hawkins, Justin Hard.*

Above: *Okehampton Rugby Football Club XV,
1952–53. They played 28, won 26, drew 2 and lost 0
in an unbeaten sequence of 34 games.* Left to right,
back row: *A. Welham, O. Parker, A. Studden,
M. Palmer, W. Fanning, R. Balsdon, E. Hawkins,
A. Vanstone, P. Hayes, R. Furse, J. Cornish;*
seated: *G. Stewart, G. Westaway, L. Turner (Capt.),
D.F. Brown, H. Westlake, P. Moore, S. Mead;*
front: *V. Lancaster, T. Cann, T. Coombe.*

Okehampton Rugby Football Club

Below: *Okehampton Rugby Football Club XV, Western Counties Champions, 1996–97. Left to right, back row: K. Pollard, I. Thomas, B. Blatchford, S. Collier, G. Vick, P. Davey, R. Appleyard, A. Searle, K. Lee, D. Mugliston, G. Sage, R. Burgoyne, A. Curtis, R. Westlake; seated, includes: P. Balsom (Courage's rep.), T. Cann, E. Chowings, E. Pengelly (President), M. Curtis (Capt.), D. Curtis, R. Wills, I. Hodge, P. Bryant, A. Jones, E. Hawkins; sitting: R. Barkwell, S. Francis, C. Ewen, M. Sansom, A. Dennis, D. Bickle, S. Penna, N. Folland, I. Langbridge.*

Above: *Colts XV, Devon Colts Cup winners, 1981–82. Left to right, back: T. Curtis (coach), N. Crocker, R. Davey, P. Leth-bridge, N. Cox, D. Chowings, D. Hawkins; centre: S. Theedom, M. White, D. Palmer, D. North (Capt.), P. Short, P. Heard, N. Bassett; sitting: P. Woodgate (President), I. Petheridge, A. Dennis, N. Abel, A. Curtis.*

Below: *First XV players and sponsors, 1998. Left to right, standing: M. Tomlinson (coach), R. Cunliffe, K. Lee, T. Donovan, I. Langbridge, C. Ewen, C. Yukov, A. Searle, G. Vick, J. Clarke, J. Thomas, R. Camies; seated: A. Dennis, R. Barkwell, E.G. Hawkins (sponsor), D. Mugliston (Capt.), E. Pengelly, M. Sansom (Sec.), P. Balsom (Treas.), S. Cook, A. Curtis.*

Above: *A new scoreboard in memory of talented player Neil Carman who tragically died in an accident. Neil's proud parents can be seen here with his friends.*

While compiling this part of our book we were fortunate in having the assistance of Mr and Mrs Eddie Hain who put us in touch with their son, Bryan, whose career in rugby has taken him to the other side of the world. His inspiration undoubtedly started when he first touched a rugby ball in Okehampton and, from Australia, Bryan was kind enough to write and inform us all of where that first touch-down had taken him. His achievements, like those of many players and coaches that have been associated with Okehampton rugby, can inspire others. In the 1970s, it seems, there was a small core of keen sports students all attending Okehampton Community College at the same time. In those days boys could look forward to a full rugby fixture list that saw them play over-15s school rugby fixtures nearly every Saturday morning in September, October and November; and keep fit after Christmas by playing soccer until March. Bryan recalls:

In 1976 and 1977 a group of local lads seemed to work well for each other and rarely lost, winning most of their matches against the more fancied schools in Exeter and Plymouth. Under the tutelage of PE teachers Jennison, Radnor and Stephens, Okehampton saw many of these boys go on to represent Devon at various age levels and play many seasons for Okehampton and a season or two at Plymouth Albion.

I was lucky to play many games with the likes of Kevin Cornwall and Ray Westlake who both learnt their skills in the town and yet always came back to play and coach at the Okehampton RFC.

The sport of rugby has taken me on a marvellous journey but a motivation for coaching probably started when I injured myself playing for Okehampton Colts v Exeter Colts in a Cup match. A tackle I can briefly remember twisted my right knee and tore both cartilages and snapped the anterior cruciate ligament. These days I'm sure a similar injury at 19 would mean instant micro surgery and one could expect to be back on the field for the following season.

That all sounds horrific enough to end the rugby-playing days of any young man but we do know that Bryan went on to play for another five years, captaining St Paul's Physical Education College in Cheltenham, playing for English and British colleges, representing Devon and captaining Plymouth Albion for two seasons. His knee was never quite the same and at the age of 25 – too young, he thought, to take up coaching – he left Okehampton to start a new teaching career in Hong Kong:

Soon after my arrival in Hong Kong I joined forces with a top Kiwi coach called George Simpkin, who was the ex-coach of Waikato in New Zealand and the coach of Fiji in two World Cup campaigns. George had just been appointed the Technical Director of Rugby in Hong Kong and I was later elected the Director of Coaching.

The main aim was to introduce the sport of rugby to the local Chinese so when the colony reverted back to Chinese rule in 1997 the sport would hopefully survive. This new coaching appointment meant that I was now in charge of developing coaching standards in Hong Kong (approximately 50 club teams) and setting up a new coaching award scheme. It was exciting work and because the Hong Kong Union was quite wealthy I could invite the world's top coaches into Hong Kong to run various coaching clinics. On many occasions I would then return as a guest of the invited coach back to their Union and participate in rugby seminars in Australia, Canada, USA, Britain and New Zealand.

Before leaving Okehampton Bryan knew nothing about rugby outside the Five Nations and yet Asia has an extensive history in the sport. He soon found himself involved in tournaments and coaching courses all over Asia, visiting countries like Korea, Japan, Thailand, Sri Lanka, Taiwan, Singapore and Malaysia, which left indelible memories. He continues:

A less than memorable tournament in Taiwan saw the Chinese groundsman mark out the oval in real lime. Not only were the wet and muddy conditions atrocious but the locally made rugby shirts shrank to half their original size. The lime burnt the players' skin so badly that many had weeks off from the sport. I also travelled to Fiji, which just happened to coincide with England's rugby tour down under. I think I forgot to mention this fact to my wife when suggesting the trip away from the crowded shores of Hong Kong.

Not only did Bryan get to work with George Simpkin and the Fijian national team, but he also flew out to a number of surrounding Fijian islands to help the Fijian development officer Navi Tucker. On one such trip he was honoured to meet the President of Fiji who was keen to strike up a long conversation about the Hong Kong Sevens and his views on Fiji's chances in the coming HK 7s' tournament.

As Bryan discovered, it is a small world:

The only white person I met on the outlying islands went to school in Plymouth and the first question he asked was did I know Nick Vosper the ex scrum-half of Plymouth Albion. There I was half-way round the world talking about my previous head of department and the current state of rugby in Devon.

Since retiring from competitive rugby Bryan says that his most memorable rugby trip was being part of a small team of coaches from the Hong Kong Rugby Football Union who conducted the first ever rugby coaches' seminar in China. Although the sport was introduced into China by a Taiwanese businessman a few years earlier, they were the first ever to try to develop the sport and put a coaching plan in place:

The course took place at the Beijing Agriculture University who boasted the best vegetable-growing programme in the whole of China. That might have been so but they did not have a blade of grass growing on their rugby pitch and on the half-way line there were two fully exposed metal manhole covers – not an ideal playing surface for the development of a new sport in Communist China. Since that first coaching course, the People's Liberation Army (PLA) established a team, and regional rugby centres from all over China have taken up the sport. They now compete regularly with cross-border teams in Hong Kong – the Chinese National rugby team was formed a few years later. China now competes in tournaments all over the world. I will never forget the coach from northern China who had somehow found a faded copy of a RFU laws booklet in his village. The book had been printed in 1938 and although he had never seen a game of rugby, he knew the laws of the game and could recite them in broken English.

In 1998 Bryan and his wife left Hong Kong and moved to The Southport School (TSS) in Australia. It is located close to the city of Brisbane on the Gold Coast of Queensland:

I suppose I am extremely lucky that the sport I learnt in Simmons Park and up the hill at Okehampton RFC has taken me all over the world. I am now the Director of Sport at a top private school in Australia which fields over 40 rugby teams in their winter sports season and employs over 60 coaches each weekend. The school is like a mini institute of sport and has a large number of full-time professional coaches in 11 different competitive sports programmes. These coaches do not have a similar curriculum teaching commitment like the PE teachers in the UK but start working with talented sports students in the school from an early age. Some of the students are even on reduced curriculum loads so that they can meet the long training hours in sports such as swimming, rowing, golf and tennis. Gone are the days when the coach just sits back and waits to see which students sign up for a new sports season. In Australia they are now out scouting the junior school PE programme, assisting teachers and working on the core sports skills. The aim is to develop a sound base for the more serious training sessions to come in the senior school. In 2001, The Southport School won the Queensland GPS Rugby Premiership, rated as one of the toughest competitions in Australia. It was the first time the school had won the title since 1938 and a proud moment in the school's history. The final school match of the season attracted over 6,000 spectators, which was a far cry from the few Mums and Dads that looked on as we played rugby back in 1977. I sometimes ask myself where will we go next and whether I will ever get tired of coaching rugby in the warm and sunny Queensland climate.

Of course as a family we miss many things about Okehampton, most of all Ed and Ann Hain, the grand-parents in Crediton Road, closely followed by a pint of warm beer with old friends. The snow on Dartmoor [the Hain boys Rory, 8, twins Sam and George, 6, have yet to see snow] and walks out and around Belstone still rate as my favourite. We also miss the long history of everyday buildings most folk in Okehampton would probably take for granted. Australia is a young country and has a lot going for it, but Okehampton and Devon will always be home.

Okehampton Rugby Football Club has a proud history, with highs and lows, and joys and disappointments. Its players, coaches, officials, staff, sponsors and supporters throughout the past century, while creating a valued inheritance, also made a tremendous contribution to the quality of life enjoyed by people of the district. That inheritance and those contributions continue to be increased by those that now follow in their footsteps.

A report in the *Okehampton Times* on May 9th 2002 confirmed that the future of rugby in the town is in safe hands:

GLITTERING PRIZES AT AWARDS EVENING
MORE than 150 youth players and parents enjoyed the annual awards presentation at Okehampton Rugby Club on Saturday week. Presenting the trophies was Jerry Ovens, club president. John Shields retired after seven years' loyal service as coach and youth treasurer and was presented with a signed photo of his team along with some malt whisky as a small reward for all his hard work. With ten youth teams from under 7s through to under 16s the club has gone from strength to strength in the last few seasons – finally seeing more than 100 signed-up players. The U8s were unbeaten, only drawing one game while winning the rest. The top points scorer for the mini section was Matthew Johns with 30 tries.

In the youth section Richard Bolt of the U14s won the top points award for the second year running with 136 points – 24 tries and eight conversions.

Awards: ORFC Youth top points scorer U14, Richard Bolt (136pts); U16 player of the year, Simon Bennett; U16 most improved player, Ben Woolams; U16 coaches award for endeavour and sportsmanship, Mark Shields; U15 player of the year, Tom Smith; U15 most improved player, Tristam Bedford; UI4 player of the year, Simon Cox; U14 most improved player, Sam Turner; U13 player of the year, Paul Frost; U13 most improved player, Josh Stevens; U12 clubman, John Radnor; U12 player of the year, Luke Wonnacott; U12 most improved player, Matthew Stratton; U11 clubman, William Heard; U11 most improved player, Mason Whittle; U10 player of the year, Darcy Heard; U10 most improved player, James Ewen; U9 player of the year, William Searle; U9 most improved player, Jordan Lee; Top points scorer minis (30 tries) Matthew Johns.

Training for next season will start in August. Any new players please contact John Herrod-Taylor.

67

Okehampton Football Club, 1904–05, who played 24, won 11, lost 7 and drew 6.
Goals for: 60, Goals against: 43.

Okehampton's Argyle Football Club

In 1926 a group of railway workers, including the late Claude Cockwill, met in the Plymouth Inn in West Street in the hope of forming just one football team in the town. At the time, there were three local sides competing for players, Okehampton Town, Ivyleaves and Devon Motor Transport. At a later meeting it was agreed that the name of the new team would be Okehampton Argyle.

Okehampton Argyle entered the West Devon League in 1926. In the 1931/32 season they won the league shield and start cup without losing a match. That same season it was decided to join the Exeter and District League where the team stayed until the 1993–94 season. In the 1946–47 season Argyle won the Devon Junior Cup by beating Astor United by 4–0. The match was played at St James' Park, the ground of Exeter City Football Club, with the club fielding probably the strongest side in its history.

There were several players capable of playing to league football standards, one of whom was schoolteacher, Denzil Mortimer, who had played as an amateur for Exeter City before the war. His skills earned him a successful trial for Arsenal, but the outbreak of war ended what might otherwise have been a successful career in big-time football. After the war Denzil taught at Okehampton Secondary Modern School, encouraging boys to enjoy football as a sport.

Later, he became headmaster at North Tawton but returned to Okehampton, to what was by then the town's comprehensive school, to take up the post of head of the lower school.

Another outstanding player in the trophy-taking team was Eric Furse, the captain, who was one of the founder members of the club and who went on to create a playing record of 40 years before retiring at the age of 55 years. Dennis and Eddie Guy, Maurice Sage, Ron Connor, George Crews, Dave Hearn, Bill Stewart, Bill Jarvis and Jack Roberts were the other team members who returned to Okehampton in triumph in 1947 bearing the Devon Junior Cup; and who extended their success the following year, with Eric and Denzil completing the team, by winning the Division Junior One title. Argyle had further success in the 1952–53 season when they won the Football Express Cup by beating Westexe Rovers at St James' Park, Exeter with a 2–1 win, with Bob Slee scoring both Argyle goals.

A lean time followed and it was not until the 1961–62 season that Okehampton Argyle found sufficient form to bring smiles to home-town faces by becoming Junior One League winners. Again, the years flowed by without trophies coming Argyle's way until the 1977–78 season when that year's team found success and won both the Intermediate One West League and the Okehampton Cup. It was a season of goals galore with Nigel Stephens scoring an incredible 60 and Ron Stagg finding the net for a very welcome further 50.

In the 1977–78 season the club lost only one league match while gaining promotion to senior football and on to the Premier Division. The season also saw one of the best finals in the Okehampton Cup with Argyle losing 1–4 at half time but coming blistering back in the second half to beat Hatherleigh by six goals to five. From 1993–94 the club played its football in the Jewson South Western League for three seasons but returned to the Devon and Exeter League for the 1996–97 season and the club has been playing in the Premier Division for the past seven years.

Committee members are Vic Jordon, Jim Burbas, Trevor Drew, Peter Carter, John Domaille, Chris Dearing, Nick Drew, Keith Smith and Mrs Jeane Bailey. Officials at the club at the last AGM before going to press included: president Mr John Burnett MP, chairman Mr Colin Maddax, secretary Mr Colin Beer and treasurer Mr Gordon Alexander. The club has had only five secretaries in the past 74 years. Its secretary at the time of writing is Colin Beer, who as player, manager and now secretary has been associated with the club for over 40 years. Colin's career started for his school team, and he quickly made his mark, at the age of 13, scoring all seven goals in a 7–2 win, after which he never lost his place as centre-forward. At the age of 16 he joined Exbourne, then in the Kingsley League. Colin was still with Exbourne, by now in Exeter and District League Junior II, in 1954–55 when the team won the Division only losing one game, and also won the Devon Junior Cup

The Okehampton Argyle Football Club, 1977.

beating Alphington 3–1 at St James' Park. His goal tally that season was an astonishing 87 goals, so it was no surprise the following year when he moved up a standard with Exeter City A. His career reached its pinnacle when he was signed by Exeter City as a part-time professional on a massive salary of £3 per week! He was good value for money though, scoring two goals on his full debut for the first team, against Southend Utd. One of the highlights of Colin's three years with Exeter was a match against Kettering when he found himself on the same pitch as Tommy Lawton. Colin eventually returned to Okehampton in 1962 at the age of 27 and carried on playing for the next 20 years. He was one of Okehampton's most successful goal scorers and was 42 when they won Intermediate Division One in 1977–78, finally hanging up the boots five years later.

The club has not always played on its present pitch. In 1946–47 Argyle played in Simmons Park, at the bottom end by the Bowling Green with the river on the other side. When the ball went in the river Argyle used a long pole with a net on the end to retrieve the ball from the river. They took it with them when they played in the Junior Cup Final at St James' Park, Exeter. There are now three senior sides: the 1st XI (Premier Division, managed by Paul Adams), the 2nd XI (Intermediate One Division, managed by Bob Reddington) and the 3rd XI (Intermediate Four Division, managed by Chris Drew).

Providing for the young ones in the town, the next generation of senior players, the club runs six youth sides playing in leagues from under-10s to under-17s, and the club has nearly 200 youth-team members. Children can join from the age of six years and we have teams for under-8s and under-9s playing 'friendlies'. There is also a ladies team so there is no excuse for any family not to be playing football in Okehampton.

Club Honours

1931–32	Winners West Devon League Champions
1931–32	Winners West Devon Start Cup
1946–47	Winners Devon Junior Cup
1947–48	Winners Junior One League Champions
1952–53	Winners Football Express Cup
1961–62	Winners Junior One League
1977–78	Winners Inter One West League
1977–78	Winners Okehampton Cup
1981–82	Winners Okehampton Cup
1990–91	Winners The Bill Rees Sportsman Trophy
1991–92	Winners The Bill Rees Sportsman Trophy
1994–95	Winners Jewson South Western League Sportsman Trophy
1995–96	Winners Jewson South Western League Sportsman Trophy
1995–96	2nd Eleven Winners Devon & Exeter Intermediate Three Division
1995–96	Runners-up Okehampton Cup
1996–97	Winners Okehampton Cup
1997–98	Winners Okehampton Cup
1997–98	Runners-up Devon & Exeter Intermediate Two
1997–98	Winners The Bill Rees Sportsman Trophy

Okehampton Argyle Football Club

Above: *Okehampton Argyle Football Club; Devon & Exeter Premier League, 1998–99 (sponsored by the Okehampton Times).* Left to right, back row: *Pete Goss (manager), Ian Gill, Kevin Gill, Neil Clift, Michael Vernon, Steve Ausden, Adam Mortimer, Peter Carter (physio.);* front row: *Simon Green, Stuart Cann, Neil Agnew, Danny Maddax (Capt.), Tony Pickering, Martin Taylor, Chris Drew.*

Above: *Okehampton Argyle Football Club, ladies team, 2001–02.* Left to right, back row: *Jim Burdus (asst coach), Hayley Vincent, Kate Shannon, Sarah Rew, Gina Burdus, Ceri Chapman, Karen Fuell, Lynda Cann, Gordon Alexander (coach);* front row: *Miki Burdus, Kelly Cooper, Sam Burdus, Becky Walker, Kerrie Drew, Michelle Burdus, Jessica Burdus.*

Left: *Okehampton Argyle Reserves, 1995–96 season – Intermediate III winners.* Left to right, back row: *C. Maddax, I. Wilson, S. Ausden, P. Adams, N. Clift, C. Drew, M. Taylor, R. Voaden, S. Letchford;* front row: *P. Blatchford, D. Grimes, N. Jones, D. Wooldridge, T. Pickering, S. Harris, R. Wooldridge (mascot).*

Cricket & Hockey

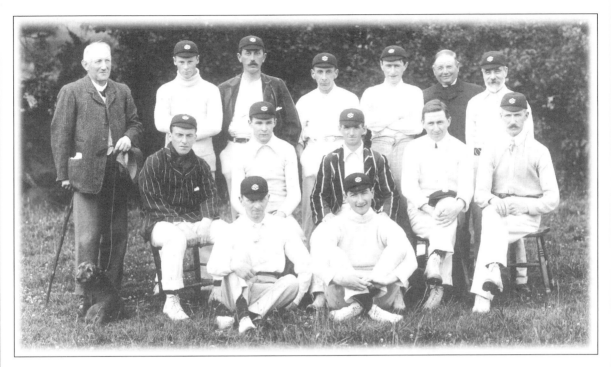

The Okehampton cricket team of 1908.

*The Okehampton Columbines Hockey Club's history goes back to 1918 when Grace Holley
first set the ball rolling.*

Bowls, Putting & Golf

Right: *It is a tradition that the serving Mayor opens each season for Simmons Bowling Club. Here Cllr W.F. Brock performs the honourable duty.*

Below: *Okehampton has a considerable sporting heritage and bowls has long been popular in the town.*

Right: *Okehampton Ladies Putting Club annual dinner at the Dovecote, Red Lion Yard, October 15th 1999.*

Below: *Garage owner Mr T. Day (centre standing) with friends at Okehampton Golf Club in the mid 1920s.*

Above: *Cllr Jeffe Cunliffe presents a trophy to Okehampton's young netball team.*

Right: *Arcade shopkeeper tobacconist Brian Weaver was the town's snooker and billiards champion on December 19th 1958.*

Ten Tors

One totally unique event which contributes to the heritage of Okehampton was not born of political minds nor those of local enthusiasts. For an outstanding event for the youth of the United Kingdom and beyond, that blazons the name Okehampton around the world, the town must be grateful to three Army officers enjoying an evening meal on the moor after an exercise over four decades ago.

Doing much to meet the needs of youth organisations across the South West the first Ten Tors was held in September 1960, a mild success with 203 young people participating. Repeated in following years, over Whit bank-holiday weekends, its popularity grew and, even with responsible controls being adopted, by 1980 a record 2,670 participated.

In 1960 there were ten manned checkpoints only, along routes of about 50 miles. The following year 35-mile routes were added, and for 1962 a long-distance route of 60 miles. From 1965 any element of route choice was removed, and teams had to walk the route specified on their route card.

From 1961 girls of all ages (14–19) were restricted to 35 miles, and until 1967 they had to sleep overnight at a fixed camp prepared for them first at Rundlestone and later at Holming Beam.

From 1960 to 1967 Ten Tors assembly was at Denbury Camp, with a start at Hay Tor and various finishing points, but in 1968 the camp closed and Okehampton Camp was chosen not only as the new assembly point but also as the start for the expedition. The finish that year remained at Willsworthy, but in 1969 this too was switched to Okehampton.

The North Moor, however, is high, very exposed, not easy to walk and made Ten Tors harder because teams had to cross it on both their outward and return journeys. For safety reasons, the medium- and long-distance routes were shortened to 45 and 55

miles respectively and the finishing time on Sunday reduced by two hours, to 5p.m.

From 1975 there was a gradual movement towards equality of the sexes – the girls' fixed camp was abolished, all girls' teams carried their own tentage and, like the boys, camped at tors along their route. That year also saw the first girls' team tackling a 45-mile route and the following year the first doing 55 miles.

Jubilee Year, 1977, saw the introduction of a very welcome one-day special event for handicapped youngsters. This instantly proved popular and successful. Today well over 200 individuals participate, and the finish scenes are always highly emotional. In 1996 the event was renamed the Jubilee Challenge.

In the Ten Tors of 1984, mixed teams had been permitted, restricted to those on the 55-mile expedition, and there had to be an even split between males and females. By 1988 complete equality was achieved as unisex teams of any composition were permitted over all ages and distances.

Although the Ten Tors Policy Committee has been keen always to maintain the traditional atmosphere of the event, its participants today are far better equipped than their predecessors of the 1960s.

From 1960 to 1967 Ten Tors was organised by the Junior Leaders Regiment, Royal Corps of Signals. From 1968 to 1985 responsibility lay with South West District, organising the event from its headquarters first at Sherford Camp, Taunton and then, from 1978, at Bulford Camp near Salisbury.

In 1986 43 (Wessex) Brigade assumed responsibility from its HQ at Wyvern Barracks at Exeter but in 1999 this too moved to Bulford Camp. Assistance in staging the event is given by all three Services together with civilian organisations such as the Dartmoor Rescue Group.

The intervening years have seen a blossoming of outdoor activities and a growing consciousness

Ten Tors

Ten Tors entrants need a camp to begin with.

Left: *A few words from the Padre and the Ten Tors will begin for a few thousand more eager young people.*

Background: *Off and away they go as another Ten Tors sends young people forward to become even better prepared for future steps through life.*

of the need to treat wilderness areas with respect.

In 1996 Ten Tors experienced the worst single day's weather in its history, having experienced bad weather in 1967 (still the worst two days in its history) and again in 1973, 1981, 1986 and 1993. After each storm-battered event the safety rules, especially those regarding dress and equipment, were further refined. Since the mid 1970s kit scrutineering has been an important feature of the event: the dress and equipment of every person participating is inspected beforehand, and spot checks are conducted during the expedition.

Ten Tors presents a challenge to its participants while ensuring a more than adequate safety cover. During the prior training, however, the manager who brings his team to Dartmoor is unable to call upon the same level of resources as available during the event itself. Since 1982, it has been mandatory for managers (and recommended for trainers) to attend a special weekend on the moor in January or February during which safety, and more recently environmental, considerations are at the forefront of all discussions.

Although challenge walks are plentiful in Britain today, Ten Tors remains unique in that it caters solely for young people. It has not been without its critics over the years, but one wonders how many of those

who criticise have actually seen the event close up. The immense pride and joy (and not a little relief!) so obvious on the young participants' faces as they receive their certificates and medals are but the first rewards of a unique experience that will stay with them for the remainder of their lives.

In recent years architect Peter Woodgate has been capturing Okehampton's past in scenes around town but his recently revealed 'Walker' on the wall looks to the future also.

8

Heritage of Churches & Chapels

All Saints & St James'

'At Oc mund tune' one midsummer evening a priest named Brown witnessed the freeing of slaves which took place at a crossroads, to symbolise the fact that they were at liberty to choose their own path in future. This note from the missal of Leofric, last Saxon Bishop of Exeter, is the first known mention of Okehampton. Any trace of a Saxon church has long since vanished, but its successors have occupied the same, consecrated site ever since – 'on the top of a toilsome hill... it pays no compliment to the people of the town by leaving them at half a mile distance.' In 1086 'Oc mund tune' had perhaps a population of some 500 souls whose descendants ensured that by 1261 there was a fine new church on the old Saxon site for Bishop Bronescombe, a man of fiery energy, to consecrate.

In 1239 it had been appropriated to the Benedictine priory of Cowick at Exeter, and Robert de Denvorn is named as vicar in 1233. In 1267 six Okehampton men were heavily fined for converting to their own use bequests made to the Parish Church. At another time two priests were found poaching deer in the lord's park of Okehampton, and added to their offence by assaulting the keepers. As for the church, a Visitation report of 1342 described the chancel as 'dark and inadequate', also noting that service books were 'defective', a psalter was 'lost', and that the vicar's house was 'vile and inadequate' to the extent that it could 'scarcely be repaired for ten pounds'.

When the Black Death struck in 1348 priests were as vulnerable as any. Between April 1349 and September 1350 the church had as many as four vicars. In 1365 the townsfolk were petitioning the Pope to grant the right to regular celebration of divine service in St James', citing the church's distance from town as a problem, especially when there was flooding, in which event they could not even attempt to get to church. Moreover, they claimed, it was necessary to provide for travellers on the great road through the town, 'by which many caravans enter and pass'. Their petition was granted.

The Parish Church obviously passed into a serious state of disrepair because in 1447 the vicar, John Newecum (1413–51) is recorded as having rebuilt it 'handsomely', after some dispute with the

Okehampton's All Saints Church in 1908.

prior and monks of Cowick on the matter. Only the tower of Newecum's church still stands today, the rest having been destroyed in a fire in 1842. It is said, however, that the old church looked much like the present one, although the interior layout of a medieval church would look odd to us. Parishioners maintained parts of it; those from Kigbeare kept the north aisle named after their hamlet. A great gilt screen divided the nave from chancel and the church furnishings were, obviously, those of the 'old' religion; the Lenten veil, the pyx with a lock for the sacrament, the chrysomatory for oils, a great candlestick for 25 candles, a pax pole for the kiss of peace. There was the great cross, carried around the parish in solemn procession on festive days, while collections were made for the maintenance of the church, and, importantly, the image of the Blessed Virgin Mary. There were two altars, one of Our Lady and the second of Saint John. Churchwardens kept the accounts and during two seasons of merrymaking, when money was collected for the church, hoganers were responsible for sports at Hocktide, the second Monday and Tuesday after Easter, and wardens took responsibility for the 'Summer Plays'.

An artist's impression of Middle Row and St James' Church in its former glory.

The church had a profitable flock of sheep and sold the grass growing in the churchyard. Richard Estebroke, vicar from 1375–1413, left £13 in silver for Masses to be said daily for his soul for three years but, more importantly at the time, Thomas Estebroke received his best brass pot, Edith Wyke his third best and a saucepan, and he left 40 measures of wheat to be distributed among the poor of the parish.

The churchwardens' accounts reveal a great deal. In 1548, there were obviously concerns about the costs of re-leading the roof of the church, repairing windows and replacing bell ropes, and a note also adds that expenditure on a 'rope for use on the organ bellows' amounted to 1s.0d.

Sir John Jurden, the priest, had 'singing bread' provided for him and consecrated wafers were used at Mass. Also in that year certain men had to appear 'at hollysworthy before the kyngs comysseners', to be questioned about lands left for 'superstitious uses' in the maintenance of chantries for the souls of the dead.

Unpopular religious changes soon followed, with the introduction of the first prayer book of Edward VI (1547–53) that led to the 'Prayerbook Rebellion'. The men of Sampford Courtenay, objecting forcibly to the new Protestant services, joined with others from Devon and Cornwall and marched to the Siege of Exeter. There was fighting at Okehampton when the rebels, retreating in defeat, made a stand here before the remnants were driven back to their village on Saturday, August 17th 1549, and slaughtered in the streets. In 1553 the rood-loft in Okehampton's church was taken down at a cost of 6d.; the change in religion had been accomplished. By the time the beacon fires blazed warning of the Armada, the old religion was forgotten.

On the eve of the seventeenth century the growth of Puritanism was being witnessed by magistrates prohibiting church ales and other parish entertainments, ostensibly because 'many inconveniences, which with modesty cannot be expressed, have heretofore grown and happened.' At Visitations, one of the churchwardens' duties was to bring forward offenders, who might be excommunicated; but sometimes the churchwardens resisted. In 1608, Thomas Peter of Okehampton complained that the chancellor of the diocese tried to terrify churchwardens into presenting John Alford 'for living a naughty and adulterous life' with Peter's wife, Thomasine. The chancellor claimed that Peter was 'of greedy and malicious disposition' and hoping for a bribe. As for Thomasine, she fell sick, 'and most grievously languishing, within one month next after died with sorrow.' Alford was excommunicated.

At Okehampton in the 1620s visiting ministers preached every Saturday, for 2s.0d. A charter from James I in 1623 turned the portreeve and his brethren into the Mayor and Common Council, and Quarter Sessions and a court for the recovery of small debts were established. There was also one fair, of St James. The Chapel of St James was completely reseated, to be used thereafter as the Corporation chapel, and new seats for the town's dignitaries were installed in the Parish Church – all at the cost of the Corporation. Within a year or so alterations in the church included the building of an organ loft, repairs to the organ, the new casting of four bells and the addition of a fifth.

While James I detested Puritanism he could not suppress it and, after his death in 1625, the High Church policy of his son Charles became one of the principal causes of the Civil War; the Okehampton Corporation contained a strong Puritan element.

In 1631 the Bishop complained that the liturgy was:

... much neglected in your chapel of Okehampton, being not fully read at any time by the curate there and not at all by the lecturer, and not well frequented by the people when it is imperfectly read.

The Corporation, however, were satisfied to hear their lecturer, only requiring that the bell be rung half an hour after eight and the sermon ended by ten 'in respect to the market'. Church attendance was now becoming strictly enforced, drunkenness and immorality severely checked. In 1632, still a prosperous enough time, the ordinary expenses for St James included ropes for the bell, candles, payment 'for righting the surplice' and frequent payments 'for keeping the clock in order'. Evidence of public unrest may be gleaned from this, and from entries in the records showing that the glass often wanted 'amending' – so regularly it seems that in 1634 the Corporation arranged for a glazier to take up residence in the town, on favourable terms. In a 12-month period, from 1633 to 1634, 21 people paid fines totalling £1.18s.0d. 'for swearing several profane oaths', and eight men, 'drunk at several times', paid £2. During the same period 14 sellers of ale were fined for selling less than a full quart of the best ale for 1d.

Churchwardens distributed the fines (including those imposed for non-attendance at church) to the poor and needy. In December 1634 six men were hauled in for questioning, 'for playing at cards the last Sabbath day, for money and farthings.' Puritanism gained ground as 'lecturers' of that leaning preached in town and country. As war clouds gathered there were divisions in the town; not everyone was Puritan, and it was to be a bitter and confused war with not all Puritans toeing the line.

Okehampton's Mayor, Lewes Parker, a Puritan of strong principle and quarrelsome nature, was gaoled in Exeter in 1643 for refusing to give money to the servants of Queen Henrietta Maria. Okehampton, generally welcoming to both sides as occasion offered, prospered during the war while escaping the fighting, other than a battle at Meldon, which only recently was recognised as being of great historical import. Two troops of Parliamentary horse are reported to have been quartered in the church afterwards, where they damaged monuments, ripped up brasses and ruined an organ.

Peace, when it came, was bitter, and attempts made by Parliament to establish a Presbyterian form of worship proved too much for the Revd Richard Mervin to stomach. On June 4th 1646, five weeks after Charles I surrendered to the Scottish army on May 5th, he used the new Directory of Public Worship; it was not accepted. Two weeks on and 'some few were at Okehampton church' but here was 'no service or exercise, only the bread distributed.' A week later there was 'no minister or preacher at Okehampton church or chapel.'

Revd Mervin was succeeded by Jonas Ware, who is reported to have turned Papist and fled abroad c.1650; he was later reported to have been buried alive by the Inquisition. While the puritanical Corporation made a determined onslaught on backsliders and the ungodly, we can be assured that they also accepted their responsibility to the aged, poor and infirm by making unusual efforts to get them up the hill to Divine Service. In 1651 they had to pay fourpence for the repair of a hand barrow 'borrowed and broken in carrying poor people to church.'

Jonas Ware had been followed in the parish by John Hussey, son of a former vicar, and in 1655 Hussey participated in an attempt to organise a Presbyterian church system in the county, with district groups and an Assembly of Divines in Exeter. The Exeter Assembly, while being both divided internally and opposed by many from without, defended parochial organisation at a time when others wished it gone and in 1657 it voted also 'that our parish churches are true churches of Christ'. They were also becoming sources of temporal information following the commencement of the civil registration of births and deaths in 1653. Marriages were to be conducted by a Justice of the Peace, following the calling of the banns on three successive Saturdays... in the marketplace. That didn't last long, some couples were soon having the banns called in church and by 1657 the vicar, Revd Hussey, was conducting marriages there also; as closely as possible to the old way. He also thankfully noted the return of Charles II in 1660: 'the first year of his happy Restoration, whom God grant long to reign. Laudes Deo.' The town welcomed the return of the monarch by removing Lewes Parker from the Corporation. The vicar urged the churchwardens to repair church seats and, it is claimed, took upon himself the costs of pointing the tower and maintaining the clapper of the great bell; as well as having 50 elm trees planted in the churchyard at his own expense. Hussey was renowned for his marathon sermons, and in 1662 an hourglass was placed in the pulpit.

Around this time, occasional collections were made in church for donations to worthy causes: £6.9s.5½d. was raised to help victims of the plague in London and five years later, in 1670, £10.0s.7d. was raised for the redemption of English captives in Turkey. The reaction against Puritanism, however, included a ban on any religious meetings, other than those in the established church. The chaplain found times difficult and was sacked 'for refusing to read public prayers', and in 1671 seven parishioners were excommunicated.

The pro-Catholic policies of James II were opposed in Okehampton and throughout the country, as fervently as the Glorious Revolution of 1688/89 and the proclamation of William and Mary were enthusiastically celebrated. Effigies of the Pope were burned in the town and a Mr Edward Reddaway, who celebrated too well, was drowned in the Okement; accidentally it is assumed.

With the Church of England firmly established a period of relative tranquillity followed, until parishioners decided that changes to their church were overdue and set about gaining a gallery; to meet the

Church Features

Above: *The reredos, a fine piece of work in Caen stone and marble by Hems of Exeter, was completed in 1891 and erected by public subscription at All Saints.*

Above right: *Ian Cann, the mainstay of church choir and music at the church organ console, All Saints.*

Left: *The brass lectern is in memory of John Downall (vicar 1850–72), All Saints.*

Below centre: *Stones from the old church inscribed with dates and initials, All Saints.*

Below right: *This photograph of houses beside St James' was dated 1860.*

Right: *The pulpit, showing St John the Baptist, in memory of John Downall, 1843–88, All Saints.*

Far left: *The south porch of All Saints where history lies beneath visitors' feet.*

Left: *Octagonal font of Bath stone, erected soon after the fire of 1842, All Saints.*

fashion of the times. They also objected to the old rood loft at the east end of the church, partly because it prevented them hearing the minister clearly and also because it was 'disfigurative to the church and chancel'. It was taken down and re-erected between four pillars at the west end, permitting the supervisor and officers of Excise with their families on the north side and Latin scholars from the little grammar school, packed four to a seat, on the south side to see the new altar-piece in wainscoting, with the Ten Commandments, Lord's Prayer and Creed on its panels.

Seats in the church were highly valued and the access to some could even be locked. 'Rights' to seats might be purchased or sold, given in gift, or even inherited by good fortune. Their size and shape bore witness to the relative importance in the parish of the occupant, and testified to their ownership of certain property. Mr William Weekes, with this in mind in 1704, considered that the £500 he had paid to purchase a particular estate entitled him to the seat of the deceased owners, but when his wife went to use 'their seat' she was shocked to find herself 'locked out' by the occupant, John Nosworthy, who let in only whom he pleased. While this was his 'right', probably by previous gift or purchase, the fact that Nosworthy and his wife were Dissenters, and his wife attended church but four times a year, served to further adversely affect the health of Mrs Weekes, a state of affairs which continued for some months.

Social distinctions were important, even in death. A mortuary fee of 10s.0d. (50p) was received by the vicar for those dying worth £40, but only 3s.4d. (18p) for any dying worth only £20. The sexton had to put up with a flat fee of less than £1 a year. Churchwardens were by this time responsible for the binding out of parish apprentices, supplying money and necessities to the poor and, assisted by the overseers, the administration of poor relief while, within the terms of the various charities' money, bread and wood were distributed, almshouses maintained and clothing provided for the poor. Expenditure during 1705 included:

Dorothy Rendell's house hire	2s.0d.
For bleeding of Mary Northcott and for	
* tape and salve*	2s.6d.
Paid by order to James Davy in need	1s.0d.

Among 30 or so different charities were those specifically for 'the relief of the poor', the care of 'decayed inhabitants', and another for those 'overburdened with children'; all were both well administered and used.

One notable vicar of the eighteenth century was Edward Cornish, a man of great learning, with a proper respect for the health of the parish. Prior to his appointment in 1711 he had been chaplain and schoolmaster for several years. He left elaborate instructions for his burial in case of his death from 'a contagious distemper'. Sometimes the parish had to bear the cost of burying a pauper; in 1720 John Denybold's 'burying suit' cost the Corporation 5s.3d., digging his grave 1s., and beer supplied at his funeral, by order of the Mayor apparently, accounted for another 2s.6d.

Accounts for 1728 showed that the bell ropes broke four times, but there were two bells used constantly; one for curfew, the other for services or to mark the death of any person within the borough.

Towards mid-century church attendance was dropping and communicants declining. In 1744 about 80 were reported but a steady decline continued and by 1779 the numbers had reduced by around 25 per cent. Visitations by bishops or deans also consumed cash. The rural dean's Visitation in 1750 revealed, among other things, that the clerk's Common Prayer book was too bad to be used and a church door was both in need of repair and a lock and key. In the same year six bells, replacing the old peal of five, were cast and hung and the rural dean found that 'ledges or other conveniences for kneeling are wanting in the seats and loft.' The parish band that accompanied the singing took over the loft in a church bereft of heat and lighting, evensong was held by mid-afternoon in the winter, and pest control was a matter for churchwardens who paid young lads, 'by the kill'. During the 1770s 'Paltridge's boy' earned good wages killing bullfinches and other birds at a halfpenny a time, hedgehogs at 2d., foxes at a fantastic 3s.4d., while the super-league vixens earned him a tremendous 6s.8d.

Towards the end of the century Napoleon's desire to see France dominating Europe dragged British troops into a war-torn period that lasted over 20 years until he met his Waterloo. Men and materials were consumed by the war effort, trade collapsed and agriculture was in difficulties; the churchwardens were distracted by the increasing difficulty in collecting church rates and the increasing numbers of the poor. The Chapel of St James fell on hard times and was in ruins; the school had already ceased by the end of the century.

Nelson's great victory at Trafalgar in October 1805 came only months before the last appointment of a chaplain was made, and the Quarter Sessions were all but abandoned. It was not until 16 years had passed that the vicar could report good attendance at his Catechism lectures, and that Sunday School might soon start. By 1833 this popular project had 178 pupils and a lending library, but the town's charity schools were becoming incapable of providing education so the Revd James Whyte put all his energy into the fight to establish a National School, which eventually opened in 1837.

Revd Robert Tanner (1834–40) built the new Vicarage, helped with the formation of a Bible society and the establishment of a benevolent society to help the poor while his successor, Revd Bourchier

The thirteenth-century interment stone found during the rebuilding of All Saints bears the remains of an inscribed cross and an inscription deciphered as 'Hic jacet Robertus de Moles'.

Wrey Savile (1841–47), 'an excellent young man, truly evangelical in his views and liberal and friendly in his spirit', promoted the cause of the Missionary Society.

During these years Okehampton was virtually controlled by a single patron – Albany Savile, who built Oaklands (originally named Sweetlands). While it is said, and is probably true, that his main interest was in controlling local parliamentary elections, he was certainly a benefactor to both church and town. For the latter he constructed Lodge Road and New Road, to the church he presented an organ, the player of which received a generous salary of £40; which was reduced to £30 for his successor. Savile's benefaction was to have awful repercussions after he provided the church with a stove 'to air and keep dry the instrument'. Tragedy struck on February 13th 1842. The sexton inspected the stove, before going about other business, at around 1.20p.m. By 2.00 the church was ablaze and, despite the vicar's fervent call, 'Oh save my poor church', and the valiant efforts of the town's fire brigade, it was reduced to ruins within an hour.

Rising, pheonix-like from the ashes, a new church much like the old one was opened on April 11th 1844 at a cost of £3,160.6s.2d., which was in the main provided by subscriptions large and small. Of its 600 sittings, 200 were free; for the rest pew rents were paid. Members of the Corporation paid £50 for their new seats, a collecting box at the White Hart brought in £1.12s.3d., the licensee being a churchwarden, and only £1,000 was borrowed from the Public Works Loan Office. The new church was insured for fire risk. The first heating in the church was provided in 1847 when two stoves were installed and a great deal of consideration was given to methods of arranging the flues; but a lightning conductor for the tower was not installed until 1882.

A census of church attendance was conducted in March 1851, and on the census Sunday 250 were in the congregation both morning and afternoon, with 200 present at the evening service. Some 80 Sunday school scholars attended both morning and afternoon.

During the 1800s the Revd John Downall, as curate or vicar, proved to be a man of great capability, serving on most local bodies from the Lighting and Watching Committee to the Board of Guardians and the Town Council. His main interest was in education, namely in the National School (founded 1837) and he vehemently opposed the proposal to establish a rival Nonconformist British school. He cared about the needs of children in the workhouse, visiting them regularly, and was pleased in 1861 to find their schoolmistress providing 'useful Religious, Moral and Practical education' to her charges. He also welcomed the formation of a school board, just before his death in 1872, at a time when a renewal of church life was dawning and church affairs moved forward.

A dispute that had endured for over 300 years over the lands held by the church and borough was ended and a dispute over the rights of the vicar in the Corporation chapel was amicably settled; this had reached its height in 1790, when a brawl at the chapel door led to a case before the Church Courts. The ancient but disputed right of the Mayor to nominate one of the churchwardens was abolished. Improvements were made to the church, the gallery was finally taken down, the organ moved and enlarged, and the churchyard was extended. Sit at the back of the church now, consider the past for a few moments, and it may just be possible to visualise the old, low gallery with the organ in the centre, and capture a fleeting glimpse of the inmates of the workhouse, in workhouse uniform, sitting on the south side, with the Sunday school children sitting on the north. Then, see among them the sexton, watchful and formidable, 'armed' with a long rod to rap the heads of the inattentive or refractory. In its time, the disappearance of that gallery was unmourned.

The parish worked hard to relieve the distress of the poor. Regular distributions of coal and other necessaries were made and a Church Benevolent Society did excellent work. The work of the church, too, extended into the furthest parts of the parish, for services were held at Brightley and a small chapel built at Meldon.

The *Parish Magazine* was started in 1887. In the last decades of the century the life of the parish was thriving. The church became the centre, not only of religious matters, but of social activity also. There were Bible societies and missionary societies, meetings for young men and girls, a continuing temperance campaign, bazaars, concerts, teas, lantern lectures, evening courses of lectures undertaken by vicar and curates, and summer parties on the Vicarage lawn. Annual outings of the Sunday school were begun in the 1890s, at first to Exmouth and later further afield. At the turn of the century, among those enjoying the outings, who had yet to reach their teens, were some whose names can be read today by any who walk the church paths and pause at the memorial to men, and women, of the First and Second World Wars. Many of those later named had once, like those who had gone before them, attended Sunday school, fidgeted during sermons and enjoyed the outings. They too knew the fine church tower, 80 feet in height, that survived the fire. Theirs was a church more filled than ours, but then churches on this site for over 1,000 years perhaps have witnessed the rise and fall in the numbers congregating there. While we witness a fall, a rise is sure to come.

The origin of the Chapel of St James is generally attributed to a papal bull, issued by Pope Alexander II in 1178, granting the right to Sir Reginald Courtenay and his wife and their heirs to have a free chapel at Okehampton exempt from the jurisdiction of any other person. Dame Joan Courtenay endowed it with land for two priests to say Masses for her brother's soul. In 1381, Bishop Brantingham granted a licence for the celebration of divine service in St James', which probably marks a rebuilding of the original chapel. Of this medieval structure only the tower remains.

The building was once hemmed in by Middle Row, that ran almost from its door down nearly the length of Fore Street. Four houses built against its walls were leased out by the wardens and the money used for the upkeep of the chapel. On the far side was the 'pigs' ground', where the 'scavenger' pigs, driven from the streets, were penned. The chaplain lived in Back Street, in a house called Luce Chyrche.

During the nineteenth century, the neglect of St James' was a long and continuing cause of concern to Revd John Downall, who wanted it put to proper use, and partial success came in 1848, when he persuaded the Corporation to repair it sufficiently to permit occasional services; but not enough to prevent the bell from falling in 1851. Revd Downall, who was also chairman of the Okehampton Agricultural Association, resumed his 'save St James' campaign', directing attention yet again upon the Corporation which eventually sanctioned the restoration of the chapel in 1862 at a cost of about £600. The nave was enlarged slightly and provision made for a north aisle, which wasn't introduced but was to be considered again later. Funding for this was partly borrowed from the annual allowances granted by the trustees and the remainder was raised by public subscription, and while it was agreed to hold regular services there, management changes were not far off; when town and parish charities were put under the control of charity trustees in 1873, despite the Corporation's protestations, responsibility for the chapel went with them.

It wasn't long before easy access to the new railway station, via St James' Street, was a topic of conversation that became a serious issue. Despite the £600 spent on it two decades earlier the chapel was still in poor shape; but it was attached to an ancient tower. A letter signed 'Nonconformist Committeeman', from Okehampton, appeared in the *Western Daily Mercury* on April 1st 1884, supporting earlier writers in 'deploring the present unsightly condition of the edifice', and suggesting that while the tower could remain (as a clock tower) there was a local builder willing to demolish the rest for £150. But, just as the majority of the town's leaders were

The committee of Okehampton C of E Bible Class, c.1925. Miss E. Janes seated with stick, Revd Welchman seated right.

St Boniface

Left: *The present church forms one part of a house that is thought to have formerly been one of Okehampton's private schools.*

Below: *The altar at St Boniface serves two areas of seating for the congregation, adding to evidence of there having been two schoolrooms here until the late 1920s. The picture also shows the unusual and possibly unique font, together with the splendid candle holder.*

Above: *The first Roman Catholic Church was established here c.1906.*

Below: *The church organ was provided in memory of Mabel A. Carey, who died on June 16th 1981.*

Bottom right: *The blocked fireplace in this part of St Boniface adds weight to the case for there having once been schoolrooms here.*

The origin of this exquisite and delicate wall plaque at St Boniface remains as much a mystery as most of the church's history.

ready to demand the removal of the chapel, the Revd C.W. Holley proposed, through the governing trust, that a second aisle should be built onto the chapel – thereby creating an even greater hazard.

An inquiry into the whole situation, conducted in the Town Hall by Mr S.H. Terry, an inspector of the Local Government Board, in February 1888, turned into a near riot during proceedings which a reporter described as being:

> ... of such a boisterous character and the applause was so frequent that the Inspector had several times to interpose to preserve order and the audience was also reminded by the hall keeper from below that, if persons stamped their feet so, they would all come through the floor, [the] building not being very firm.

Without space to include the full reports we can only recommend their reading elsewhere at your leisure; suffice to say that there was to be no winner – the chapel was not removed, nor enlarged. Services continued, with the vicar acting as chaplain at the invitation of the trustees, but at the turn of the century a new 'High Church' vicar caused eyebrows to be raised and muttering to be heard when the choir appeared in surplices; and other changes alarmed some of the trustees. The outspoken curate protested that services at St James' were rarely reverent, and that most of the congregation had not learned how to kneel, while he couldn't find words to describe the awful music.

Within the chapel The Tables of the Law were a Christmas gift from the Revd John Downall in 1863, and the south-east window was also given by him in 1862. The font was given in 1922 by Anne Dove Dumville-Lees, in memory of her grandparents Thomas Bridgeman and Patience Luxmoore. The finely carved and coloured Royal Arms on the front of the gallery are those of Victoria. The tower contains the clock and Westminster chimes given by the town in commemoration of the Silver Jubilee of George V in 1935. A large bell, considered to date from the middle of the fourteenth century, has the inscription 'Est michi collatum I.H.S. isted nomen amatum' (Jesus that beloved name is bestowed on me). An interesting feature of the interior is the Jacobean woodwork incorporated in places with that of 1862; it is what remains of the reseating ordered by the Corporation in 1625. The pulpit, dated 1626, shows figures of angels holding shields painted with devices now unclear but possibly attempting to depict the town and castle, together with either the town or the Courtenays' arms. The small curfew bell of St James' rang out at dusk until the mid 1950s to signal the way to safety for any late travellers. The town Receiver acted as chapelwarden and records of dealings, related to the chapel are scattered among the borough archives, especially the Receivers' accounts.

The Church of St Anne, Meldon

The increase in Meldon's population during the late-nineteenth century led first to the holding of services in Meldon, then to the building of the little chapel of St Luke in 1898, during the vicariate of the Revd F.W. Saulez. Said to have been a corrugated hut, this was not an impressive building, and there is the suggestion locally that a 'chapel' in several locations provided for the people of Meldon. For whatever was being used there did eventually come a replacement. The pleasant little Church of St Anne was built in 1957 in memory of Anne Dove Dumville-Lees and dedicated by the Lord Bishop of Exeter on June 19th 1958. The church is now a private house but, since its conversion into a beautiful home, a plate or panel that is said to have been placed in the church, 'In affectionate memory of Sidney Dove Dumville Luxmoore of the Manor House Okehampton who died December 21st 1944', is no longer to be seen. There are various opinions expressed about the actual wording, longer in some instances, so there is still much yet to learn about the church or churches and chapels of Meldon.

St Boniface

The heritage of the Roman Catholic Church in Okehampton is probably contained in the events of less than a century. There is no one to blame but ourselves for thinking that church details and information would be readily available. They were not, or perhaps we've been looking in the wrong places. Father Koppel, the priest at the time of writing, would welcome, like us, more information about the history of his church.

We understand that church members first celebrated Mass in the town in a small corrugated iron building that was erected in 1906 in Station Road and seated 160. That building has since been converted into a comfortable home but it was used until c.1922, if not later, until the present church was built as an addition to an existing property further up Station Road.

Local builders, possibly Maddafords, were engaged to build the addition to a house, or house and schoolroom, which became a fascinatingly different church and one to which Major Frank and Mrs Marguerite Murphy of Dunsland Court, Exbourne, became substantial benefactors.

Statues of Mary and Jesus in St Boniface.

Part of the old Star Inn. The upper floor was used for religious meetings during the nineteenth and twentieth centuries and the building was demolished in 1989.

The Star Chamber of the old inn was the room generally favoured by religious leaders of many denominations for use by their congregations.

The Church at West Turnpike Gate

In 1797, a shoemaker named Mr Wellington opened his house in North Lane to a Methodist preacher who came to Okehampton from Launceston. One who listened, a Mrs Mallett, was deeply moved by the preaching and became one of the leading spirits of early Methodism in the area. In 1800, Mr Trampleasure was sent from Launceston as a Home Missionary and did excellent work in Okehampton, Belstone and Sticklepath. Like many of the pioneers, he did not escape ill-treatment and on one occasion was only saved from being thrown into the river by some rowdy soldiers by the intervention of one of their officers. Mrs Mallett's home, in one of the buildings down the centre of Fore Street, became the meeting-place of the Okehampton Methodists; later Joseph Guest also opened his house in East Street for preaching services.

In 1811, Okehampton had been made a Home Mission Station with a preacher appointed by the Conference and meetings were transferred from the humble dwelling of Joseph Guest to the Star Chamber, a rented room over the Star Inn. A piece of ground was purchased for the erection of a chapel, but was never used and was eventually sold at a loss; becoming the subject of an appendix to the minutes of the 1818 Conference.

The congregation, dissatisfied with sharing their place of worship with imbibers below, removed from the Star Chamber back to Mrs Mallett's room in Fore Street, then again to a place 'fitted expressly for the purpose', according to Circuit records, in Red Lion Court, but it was not long before they again moved; back to Mrs Mallett's.

Mrs Mallett eventually moved to Sticklepath, where regular preaching continued in her home until her death. Betty Bennett's parlour, in Easterntown, became the Methodists' meeting-place for a time, before they returned again to the Star Inn and its upper chamber, and afterwards they found accommodation in Painter's Court. These latter moves had been occasioned by the revival of the work in 1826 by Mr Trampleasure, who had returned to Okehampton in his old age.

A legacy of £150, left by Mr P. Brook, c.1828, towards the erection of a chapel at Okehampton, was used partly to put in order the room used as a chapel at Painter's Court and the remainder to form the nucleus of funds which eventually secured a site near West Turnpike Gate. In 1833 a house was rented in East Town for the resident minister, and three years later, by which time membership had grown to over 100, a second minister had been appointed and Winkleigh had been added to the Circuit. By 1841, the building fund that had begun with part of Mr Brook's legacy in 1828 was allowing building to commence on a plot in West End, and in May 1842 a new 'Commodious Chapel' was opened at the corner of New Road and High Street. It was later to become 'Days' garage for many years, then to house a business selling clothing, before reverting to what it was originally intended to be, a place of worship, by providing a home to the New Life Church.

The Ebenezer Chapel

The ancestry of the Ebenezer Chapel, which later became the Congregational Church, takes us back to the late-eighteenth century, to a dingy room behind premises that we now know as the London Inn. At that time the room was being used by Nonconformists as their meeting-place, while the main building was a merchant's shop and dwelling. After gathering for many years in primitive surroundings, the members moved themselves to 'an upper room', believed to have been in a building close to their first meeting-place.

In 1781, a Nonconformist by the name of the Revd George Castle was preacher but there does not appear to be any connection between him and those who established themselves in 1800; the date of foundation given in the *Congregational Year Book*. Around the beginning of the 1800s, the little company in the 'upper room' received the accession of a young solicitor, a William Burd, who was a native of the town. Whilst serving his articles in Totnes, he had received religious impressions by reading *Pilgrim's Progress* and was influenced by a Mr Windeatt, who preached in Totnes whilst carrying on a secular business in the woollen trade. In 1818, the young solicitor established the first and, for many years, the only Sunday school in Okehampton, following the example of Mr Windeatt, preaching in cottages and in the surrounding villages.

The first baptisms recorded in registers kept by the minister, Mr Newcombe, are those of a Linda Weeks and Edmund Edye Lake, on June 20th 1802. The latter was the son of John and Emmet Lake; attesting witnesses were N. Newcombe, William Burd, Deacon, George Moase and William Moase.

With the need for a chapel pressing, as was the custom at the time, Mr Newcombe went to London with the 'Chapel Case', presumably to present to the relevant authorities the need for an Ebenezer chapel in Okehampton. His reasoning attracted the attention of William Wilberforce, leader of the movement that resulted in slavery being abolished in the British West Indies in 1807. Mr Wilberforce donated £5 to the proposed new chapel, then a substantial sum.

Designer of the first chapel was Mr Newcombe himself, who chose to make it egg-shaped, with a coved ceiling which provided excellent acoustic properties, not dissimilar to those boasted by the Whispering Gallery in London's St Paul's Cathedral. However, the chapel's heavy roof, without tie beams at the foot of the principals, made the walls bulge and it became obvious within a few years that this egg-shaped house would have to be rebuilt. The walls of the second building were both stronger and supported by buttresses, but nevertheless, one Sabbath part of the ceiling fell down and a person narrowly escaped injury. A new site was sought but most land in and around the town was owned by a churchman who refused to sell them a building plot, and they were compelled to build at the bottom of a meadow belonging to William Burd. The meadow stretched from the rear of Mr Burd's house in Eastern Town (East Street), down to the lower end of North Lane (North Street), and here, as they dug the foundations, they found fund-saving sand that they were able to use for building, which would otherwise have had to have been obtained at considerable cost.

The Ebenezer Chapel foundation-stone was laid on May 21st 1822, but the money to complete it still had to be found; £60 from the sale of the old chapel ruins and ground did help, and many gave their labour free. A friend, experienced in building, supervised construction, the building exterior remained unplastered and the little cemetery included in the conveyance unenclosed. From the old chapel to the new came doors, windows with large panes of glass, and pews with their high straight backs; in all, it was a very pleasant building. There was a gallery at the north end for the singers, but side galleries, half-way through the chapel, were not added until ten years later, for the Sunday school children.

The chapel was opened on Christmas Day, 1822, by neighbouring preachers. After a flourishing start and a period of stability, it began losing members to the Plymouth Brethren and the Anglicans, and 45 years after opening the church was in need of extensive renovation. The roof was repaired and to replace the (by then rotted) windows brought from the egg-shaped building, Mr Brock, a Bristol builder and former Sunday school scholar of the Ebenezer Chapel, presented a new set of windows. Pews which had come from the old chapel were replaced with new, making it practical to kneel for prayer, and the galleries were extended to the full length of the chapel. Three memorial tablets were introduced; on the right-hand side on entering there was a stone in memory of the former minister, Mr Nicholas Newcombe, who had died in 1832. He was also described as the first 'Calvanistic Minister'. A tablet to the memory of William Burd was placed on the east wall, near the pulpit, and also on the east wall, in a complementary position, was one in memory of Mr Underdown Burd.

Other than the walls, little remained of the 1822 building. Throughout its history, it appears that the chapel retained independence, neither applying for nor receiving aid from any society in London or elsewhere to support its ministry. Its first three pastors, ministering for over 50 years, were not 'regularly' trained, but followed secular callings; the first, Nicholas Newcombe (1800–20), was a shopkeeper; the second, George Moase (1820–25), a schoolmaster; the third, Mr (but later Revd) William Burd, 1825–49, a solicitor. The wages received by Mr Newcombe, who was inducted in 1825, were probably balanced by the expense of building the chapel; the linen draper was no architect. Christopher Moase, who was in the service of William Burd and his son, John Marsh Burd of Goldburn, for 42 years, left his entire life's savings of his wages for the building of an organ and to go towards a schoolroom. John Marsh Burd obtained liberal subscriptions from his Anglican friends.

By 1836 there were between 60 and 70 Okehampton members subscribing weekly payments towards the purchase of Bibles. The seat rents at this time were £2 a year and contributed to renovation costs and also helped to pay off a debt of £125, which was due when Mr Burd took the pastorate; a debt incurred when the aisles were floored, the chapel painted, the drainage installed, and the burial-ground enclosed. Further renovation was carried out in 1878, and Mr John Pearce of Hatherleigh reopened the chapel.

Heating was installed in 1882 at a cost of £90 and on March 30th 1890 electricity was installed. In 1900, the minister's house was sold, and there were also centenary celebrations; but nothing appears to relate the events to each other. The Sunday school was flourishing and increasing numbers meant that an extension to the original Sunday school (of 1836) in North Street became urgent. An extension was eventually completed and opened on December 17th 1924 and the chapel members had their own benevolent and missionary societies, a flourishing Boys' Brigade and a membership of around 120.

However, a further period of decline seems to have started in 1937, when for six years it appeared that they could not sustain a minister. Again, between 1945 and 1947, a similar situation arose, to be followed by another period of recovery, but from 1959 onwards there was a steady decline in the numbers in the congregation.

The last renovation of the Ebenezer Chapel was carried out in 1964/5 and it was reopened in 1965 by its oldest member, Mrs Elizabeth Drew. During the late 1960s and early '70s, Congregationalists and Presbyterians met to consider the way ahead, with a view to amalgamation with the Okehampton Methodist Church; a union that was favoured by members because of declining membership and falling finance. Further talks took place at a meeting held in January 1974. The secretary, Mrs Rosemary Humphreys, told a meeting of members that, because of the rapidly declining numbers, there were too few to carry on the work of the Church, emphatically stressing that the Church could no longer sustain a full-time minister. It was amicably agreed that the United Reformed Church would merge with the Okehampton Methodist Church.

The organ from the Ebenezer Chapel was installed in the Baptist church. The chapel's hanging light cluster, made by Avery's building company, went to the Fairplace Church, as did the organ from East Street Methodist Church, and the original Fairplace organ was taken to Folly Gate Methodist Church.

The East Street Churches

The Bible Christian movement was formed in the autumn of 1866, when a Mr and Mrs Rich came from Tavistock to live in Okehampton. They wrote to the Revd R. Kelley, who was travelling in the Chagford Circuit, saying they felt like fish out of water, because there was no Bible Christian Society in the neighbourhood and stated that they were willing to place their kitchen at the disposal of the denomination, if services could be arranged. The matter was discussed at the Chagford quarterly meeting – their offer was accepted and the Revd Kelley was appointed to preach on the first Sunday, but when he arrived to preach he was told by Mr Rich that the owner of the house had strictly forbidden the holding of religious services on his property. Kelley himself described what happened next:

We earnestly implored the greater proprietor of the universe to open the way and provide a place on which we could pitch our tent and as I perused the sacred scripture, my attention was drawn to the following passage, Mark, chapter 14, verse 15: 'and he will show you a large upper room, furnished and prepared, there made ready for us.'

About noon of that day, a person was sent from the Star Inn to offer the use of the two rooms in which we could conduct our services, one room in the parlour on the ground floor, the other room on the first storey. Having my mind still impressed about the upper room as described in the sacred scripture, I wasted no time inspecting the lower room, but repaired directly to the upper room and there as described, was a large upper room furnished with seats and a table on which to place the Bible and hymn-book. Here we offered our tributes

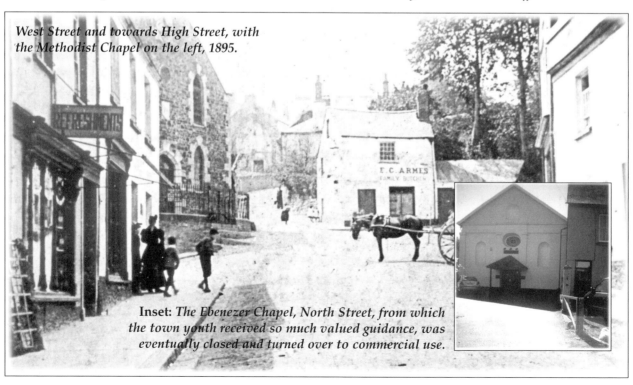

West Street and towards High Street, with the Methodist Chapel on the left, 1895.

Inset: *The Ebenezer Chapel, North Street, from which the town youth received so much valued guidance, was eventually closed and turned over to commercial use.*

of praise and thanksgiving to him who had made the rough places smooth and the crooked places straight. Thus we commenced our mission and continued to preach Christ, Sunday after Sunday, to a full and sometimes overflowing congregation.

While the congregation may have been overflowing, Mr Hocking, the landlord of the Star, discovering that the services seriously affected his business in the bars below, gave the Methodists notice to quit.

Confronting the problem through prayer, the congregation gained permission to hold their services at the Fountain Inn but, once there and with a continuing overflow, it was soon felt that a chapel was needed. One site only was available, for the large sum of £50, on the corner of Victoria Street and Exeter Road, opposite the hospital entrance. The cornerstone of what was to become Mount Calvary Chapel was laid on July 14th 1868, by Mr S.L. Thorne. The building was duly completed and the opening services were conducted by John Dymond on March 7th 1869; it was extensively altered in 1906.

From the outset, Mount Calvary Chapel was continually beset by debts; £180 was still outstanding from the building. In June 1883, a new trust was appointed but, despite all efforts the debt was not cleared until 1892, at the time when plans for the erection of a new schoolroom were being finalised. The room was completed the following year, at a cost of £163. Membership of the church had by then reached 80, 17 Sunday school scholars had been received, and 40 further persons had proffered conversion. The little chapel was fast becoming too small for the growing urban church.

In 1895, an American organ of some kind was purchased at a cost of no less than £45 but, even with the new schoolroom, the need to re-house both it and the congregation in new premises became ever more clear. From 1897 onwards, money-raising events for a new chapel became frequent and on Thursday March 1st 1898, a special fund-raising service was held. The Revd Bourne preached an impressive sermon in the morning. In the afternoon, the church was filled to hear Mr Bourne's well-known and ever-fresh lecture on 'Billy Bray'. The Chair was occupied by his Worship, the Mayor, Alderman J. Jessop, and the financial report for the year showed a balance in hand of £2.4s.7^1/₂d. A very successful bazaar for the new chapel was held on Wednesday and Thursday, July 26th and 27th 1899 in the Market Hall, at a cost of £4.18s.9d., with total receipts of £90.0s.9d. and showing a net profit of £85.2s.0d. To this could be added £8 in hand, £30 which the Christian Endeavour had in the bank, and £50 or £60 in reliable promises. Cash and pledges of around £183 were bringing new buildings ever closer.

The purchase of a site, on the corner of East Street and Mill Road, became possible in 1904; trustees appointed were: W. Linscott, J. Glass, R. Stoneman,

G. Nicholls, W. Pike, W. Avery, R. Doidge, E. Stoneman, T. Smale, J. Risby, F.C. Gay, Shipman, Ricit, P. Stone and W. Knapman. There were by then 110 church members, 55 Christian Endeavour members, 25 Junior Christian Endeavour members, 130 Sunday school scholars and 17 teachers.

The stone-laying took place in September 1904, followed by a public luncheon with 300 people at table after which the company adjourned to the site of the new building and 45 stones were laid. With further stones being donated by church members, at a cost of between 5 guineas to £100 each, it was anticipated that £1,000 would be realised by the chapel opening day.

The site of the church was formerly filled by 11 cottages, seven of which were demolished and rent of £24 per year was expected from the remaining four. Two of the cottages had been used as a mess room by Frenchmen, refugees from the Peninsula War; relics of an old winding staircase and an ancient granite staircase were found. The church, built in the Gothic style, seated 300 on the ground floor, provision being made for a future gallery. Building costs were estimated at £2,000, exclusive of the £1,500 for the purchase of the site, and eventually probably reached £4,500.

On Tuesday August 1st 1905 at 11.15a.m., with the Mayor (Alderman German) and Corporation attending, the new church was opened by Mrs W.R.K. Baulkwill, wife of the President of the Conference, before a crowd assembled in East Street. The key was turned, the doors opened, and the crowd, including people of all denominations, quickly filled the building – eager to participate in a service during which, departing from the customary observance, the doxology had preference over the National Anthem. The dedicatory sermon was preached by the Venerable Dr Townsend of the Methodist New Connection.

The turning of the key also unlocked two problems for the members. They had to deal with the burden of a £2,759 debt and solve a need for ministers. In the following year, Okehampton staff were increased to two ordained ministers and a hired local preacher, which led to a dispute and several rows erupting between the churches within the Circuit. Northlew wanted to continue as head of the Circuit, but Okehampton, now so much more developed, and with its magnificent new church, felt it should take this position. It took until March 1908 to arrive at a diplomatic solution with regard to ministers, accounts for Okehampton being kept separately and the town being responsible to the Conference only; Okehampton became a pastorate in its own right and not responsible to the Superintendent at Northlew after that date.

In that first decade of the twentieth century no one could have considered that passing wheels were already beginning to seal the fate of their new church in a town where the motor car was still a wonderful

Fairplace (lower centre) to Crediton Road and the outskirts of town.

new machine that children, and many adults, gazed on in awe.

Through two world wars the church in Okehampton continued to grow stronger and make a considerable contribution to the life of the town. It theoretically remained part of the Northlew Circuit until the realignment of 1947, when it was included in the new Okehampton Methodist Circuit. In 1963, its congregation were faced with the proposal to close their church to permit the formation of a single Okehampton Methodist Church at Fairplace, uniting two branches of Methodism, both of which had begun together during the last century in the upper room of the Star Inn. It was a proposal bitterly opposed. The last service in the East Street church was held on Sunday May 10th 1964.

The Union of Faith at Fairplace

The site of the Fairplace church was secured in 1895 by Revd John S. Jones, the Superintendent Minister, at a cost of £450; the erection of the boundary wall cost a further £30. In 1901 Revd James Finch from Sticklepath was appointed Superintendent and, under his able and enthusiastic leadership, proposals for a new chapel costing £2,420 (including site) were prepared by May 1902 and approved by the trustees who, in September, commissioned Mr I. Wills, of Derby, as architect. In January 1903 the old chapel in West End, near Turnpike Gate (now the New Life Church) was sold for £550, but building costs were rising. Later, when Mr Henry Geen was contracted

to build the new chapel, albeit with a schoolroom, the cost had risen to £3,159. The contract called for the foundation-stones to be laid on May 25th, and building was to be completed by October 17th; Mr F.J. Worden was appointed the Clerk of Works.

In May 1903, £1,100 was added to the building fund, due in part to a generous donation of £200 from Mr William Beer of South Molton, a former local preacher in the Circuit and, as construction continued in July, Mr and Mrs J. Bird German of Tavistock offered to present the window in the chancel as a memorial to the memory of their parents – in three panels depicting Christ, the Light of the World, Christ Blessing Little Children and Christ the Good Shepherd.

By September, Messrs Jones and Co. had been engaged to install the heating apparatus at a cost of £139.10s.0d. but the planned opening day passed with work still in progress. By November, it had been agreed that the organ could be moved from the old chapel by Messrs Hale & Co., of Plymouth, at a cost of £15; the choir accepted responsibility for raising this sum. Four and a half months overdue, but nevertheless with great rejoicing, the buildings were opened on March 1st 1904, by the President of the Wesleyan Conference, Revd Marshall Hartley. The Bible and hymn-book for the pulpit were presented by Mr and Mrs Wilson – and the trustees later presented to Mr and Mrs Tickle a Bible and hymn-book in commemoration of their being the first couple to be married in the new chapel. It was hoped that the new premises would tend, not only to the

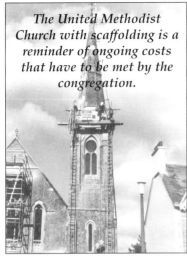

The United Methodist Church with scaffolding is a reminder of ongoing costs that have to be met by the congregation.

advancement of Wesleyan Methodism in Okehampton, but to the moral and material improvement of the town.

Troubled trustees met on March 28th 1904 to approve the final accounts, which had escalated to £4,300, leaving the members to find £1,141 more than had been anticipated. It was necessary to secure an overdraft of £880 to meet the debt, which was sanctioned by the Chapel Committee. Members rallied to support their leaders and reduce the debt and by 1907, with the help of a legacy of £100, a grant of £100 from the Chapel Committee and £200 from a bazaar that year, the debt was reduced to £400. The balance remaining in 1911 was incorporated with a Circuit debt, half to be found by Okehampton and half by the other chapels in the Circuit. Thus, within seven years of being erected, the fine block of buildings was paid for.

On September 25th 1932, the Wesleyan Chapel at Fairplace became the Methodist Church, when the Wesleyan Methodist Church, the Primitive Methodist Church and the United Methodist Church merged into one united group of worship. In the jubilee year of 1954, Alderman and Mrs G. Gratton made a gift to the trustees of the beautiful Gratton Hall. Splendidly appointed and capable of seating 150 people, the hall was officially opened on 13 January 1954 by Mrs G. Gratton and dedicated by the chairman of the District, J.K. Whitehead, BA.

It was the wish of Alderman and Mrs Gratton, and the hope of the trustees, that the hall would serve as a meeting-place for the aged folk of the borough and as a youth centre for the Methodist youth of Okehampton.

In 1963, the Methodist Conference decided that only one Methodist place of worship was needed in Okehampton and this resulted in an argument about which church should be closed. Both East Street and Fairplace were financially viable. East Street had by far the largest congregation and the biggest Sunday school, but was in a very unsuitable location on the main A30 trunk road. The merger should have taken place on September 1st 1963, but the two congregations were deeply divided. An independent commission, set up by the Plymouth and Exeter District of the Methodist Church, ruled that Fairplace was to be retained and known as the Okehampton Methodist Church and that East Street was to be closed. The advantageous position of Fairplace with its adjoining Sunday school, and the value of its

Gratton Hall as a place for public meetings swayed the decision and in November 1963 East Street Methodist Church was advertised for sale.

A new trust was formed and it studied an architect's report, in which recommendations for alterations and renovations to Fairplace were made at a cost of between £6,000 and £7,000; costs that would, of course, be more than covered from the proceeds of the sale of East Street. Included in that sale were the schoolroom, the kitchen, cloakroom and four cottages.

The last service in the East Street church was held on Sunday May 10th 1964 and the Service of Amalgamation was held on Wednesday May 13th. Fairplace then officially became the Okehampton Methodist Church.

On Tuesday December 10th 1974 a service of dedication was held and a covenant entered into between the United Reformed Church and the Okehampton Methodist Church, to be known, henceforth, as the Okehampton United Church.

Hence, Fairplace, which started life 90 years earlier as the Wesleyan Chapel, became in turn the Methodist Church, the Okehampton Methodist Church and then the Okehampton United Methodist Church of today.

The Gratton Hall was further enhanced between September 1981 and March 1982, when an additional storey extended the Sunday school accommodation at a cost of £22,000, with most of the labour being given free. It was officially opened by Mr Alec Rolls, the District Youth Training Officer of the Methodist

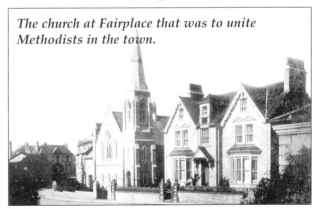

The church at Fairplace that was to unite Methodists in the town.

The foundation-stone of the church was laid on May 27th 1903.

Baptists

Above: *The Baptist Chapel appropriately has a Christian bookshop next to it now.*

Below: *Remembered as a lost architectural gem, the East Street Methodist Church stood on the corner of Mill Road.*

Above: *Mr and Mrs Trott at their shop beside the chapel.*

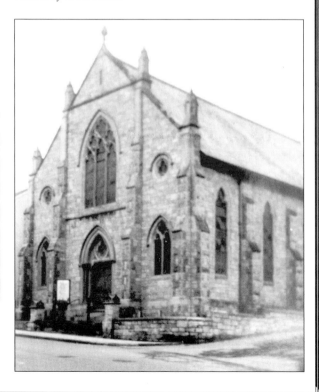

Church. One room of this extension is dedicated to the memory of Grace Gay, a primary and Sunday school teacher for many years who passed away, suddenly, on August 28th 1981, aged 62 years.

In 1985, the organ was rebuilt. Its 700 pipes were cleaned and tonally extended to match the acoustics of the building and, when completed, it was declared officially open by Mrs Kathleen Lee, who first played the organ in the old Methodist Chapel in East Street 54 years earlier.

A fully computerised central heating system was installed in the premises in 1991, which gave Fairplace as fine a block of premises as may be found in any town of a size comparable with Okehampton.

Girls' Life Brigade

Following their success in forming the 1st Company Boys' Brigade in 1916, the members of the Ebenezer Congregational Church in North Lane decided that a girls' organisation should also be started. In June 1912 the 1st Okehampton Company of the Girls' Life Brigade was formed under the leadership of Miss E. Oag, with Miss D. Stinchcombe as Lieutenant, attached to the Congregational Church but open to girls of all denominations.

Following Miss Oag's resignation in 1916, Miss Stinchcombe took over the company and led it for two years until she also resigned. Her younger sister, Miss M. Stinchcombe, then carried on with the help of Miss B.B. Hill and Miss Rose Williams as Lieutenants, the latter retiring in 1924.

In August 1924 a dozen girls, with the Captain, Mrs Brooking (née Stinchcombe), and Lieutenant B. Middleton went to Dawlish Warren to camp where they joined with girls of the 1st Exeter Company in having a very enjoyable time, the Okehampton girls winning the silver medal for tent inspection and doing very well on sports day.

Unfortunately the week ended in tragedy – Lieutenant B. Middleton was taken ill on the last day and her mother and sisters hurried to Dawlish and took her home to Okehampton, where she died the next day. This was a great shock and bitter blow to everyone, as 'Beattie' was loved by all.

Mrs A.E. Stinchcombe became Lieutenant in 1925 and she and Mrs Brooking took the girls to camp at Dawlish again but, on the second day in camp, Mrs Brooking became ill, leaving Mrs Stinchcombe in sole charge. The girls responded to the situation excellently, helping wherever possible, and also winning a medal for tent inspection and general efficiency, which pleased the adults.

In 1928, visiting officers from London granted commissions to Queenie Crocker, Winnie Lee, Florrie Knight and Beattie Sillifant, which strengthened the group, but later the same year, due to domestic reasons, Mrs Stinchcombe resigned.

In 1934 Mrs Brooking resigned for domestic reasons too, leaving Mrs Hoare in charge, helped by Queenie Crocker, and for a year the company continued until Mrs Hoare left the town and the company was disbanded. This was obviously a disappointment to all the girls and it was not until 1950 that the GLB was started again. The company this time had the benefit of leadership from Miss J. Pauley with Mrs Hoare and Miss Hill as Lieutenants and a committee comprised the following: Chaplain Revd Marsden, chairman Mrs Brooking, secretary Mrs Hoare, treasurer Mrs Stinchcombe, Mesdames Green, Brewer and Smale, and Miss Sillifant. It was decided to ask Mrs D.P.K. Ryan to be President. In the Congregational schoolroom on Tuesday May 16th, the first meeting was held, attended by 40 girls, at which Maribel Bond, Christine Bubear, Gillian Hosgood and Kathleen Medland were made leaders. The company met every Tuesday evening and on completion of required tests it was accepted as a recognised company on November 7th.

On Advent Sunday the company was dedicated and members enrolled by Revd J.P. Marsden at a special service to which parents, the Boys' Brigade and members of the public were invited. Little more than five weeks later the girls went carol singing for charity, which was enjoyed so much by singers and listeners alike that it became an annual event.

As the months passed so membership increased, and by the end of March 1951 membership stood at three officers, eight seniors and 29 juniors who were all invited to the Mayor's service on May 27th and proudly paraded with other organisations to the Congregational Chapel.

The girls' first camp was the next milepost, a weekend one at Throwleigh, not far away, and a great success. Growing more ambitious, the Company decided to hold a masked ball in aid of funds at the Drill Hall and made it a great success, even if the dancers did not actually conform to the rules of unmasking at midnight. Asked to help their brother organisation, the Boys' Brigade, the girls willingly volunteered for duty during the week of 8–15th October with their annual appeal and collection for the Cancer Campaign Fund. By December 3rd, Advent Sunday, a truly strong Company held its rededication service and was honoured to be presented with the Queen's Colours by Major and Mrs Ryan and the Company Colours by Mrs Brooking and Mrs Stinchcombe (former Captain and Lieutenant). These were accepted by the Captain, Miss J.E. Pauley, on behalf of the company, after they had been blessed and dedicated by the Chaplain, Revd J.P. Marsden.

Following the death of King George VI in 1952 the company solemnly attended a commemoration service on February 15th at the Parish Church. With lighter hearts on May 25th they joined with other youth organisations and, led by the Borough Band,

Boys & Girls' Brigades

Below: *The Life Boys aka the Junior Boys' Brigade. Left to right: W. Macbeth (Captain), B. Sillifant (leader), P. Henwood. R. Green, R. Horne, K. Chowings, A. Hatten, D. Chammings, B. Smale, A. Furse, A. Lowe, P. Lee, J. Westlake, M. King, P. King, J. Arthurs, W. Passmore (Lieutenant).*

Above: *An* Okehampton Times *newspaper cutting regarding the Boys' Brigade in Okehampton.*

Below: *An early photograph from the 1st Okehampton Girls' Life Brigade.*

Left: *Destined for the GLB, and to be Mayor, Joan Pauley with Clifford and Tiny the dog in 19.. no, we'll not give a lady's age away!*

Some of the girls were finding that fire-lighting could be fun, c.1956.

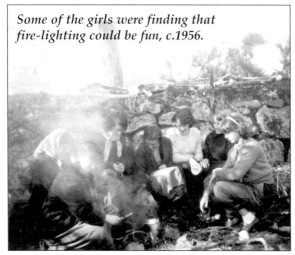

Mrs Ryan, Miss Pauley and GLB members 'officially' opening the GLB room in the Congregational Church schoolroom, October 31st 1956.

attended an Empire youth Sunday service which was conducted by the vicar. Saturday June 25th saw two buses speeding excited girls away to Looe on what was later to become an annual event. From August 27th to September 2nd they held their first long canvas camp at Throwleigh. Extracts from a diary kept of that camp survive:

Wednesday, August 27th, 1952
The Boys' Brigade tents had not arrived so five girls and Miss Pauley came out to the camping site in the afternoon to pitch some tents which had been borrowed from South Zeal Scouts. The girls, with the help of two men, put up a tent for all the girls to sleep in. The other eight girls came by taxi with the luggage. The cooks then made a hot drink to go with our sandwiches for our supper. We made our beds and went to bed. We spoke for a while. Then we went to sleep for a while then we woke up to find Judith snoring. Most could not sleep very well except Maria who had a lielow who slept soundly. We were all very excited.

Thursday August 28th
Today we were getting settled down, or trying to in the big tent. Everybody was trying to make gajets and leave room for their feet at the same time. The cooks were told they done very well but they thought that they could have done better if they had had more cooking utensils. Everybody said that the 'lat' was very bad, and were telling people to be careful not to fall head first into the 'lat'. But none of them did.

We were all at our wits end thinking the tents would not come. About two cars went by and everybody looked up, hoping, but no it was not. Then somebody shouted 'There here.' Every one of the girls suddenly felt like working. Down came the big tent, up went another, and in about ten minutes all the tents were up.

We all went in our tents and settled down for the night. Two people were ill, the bad people.

Monday September 1st
The cooks had to be woken up at 6.45 but by the time the cooks got out it was seven o'clock. For breakfast we had two pieces of fried bread and a good helping of scrambled egg. Just before breakfast Beryl went into Miss Pauleys tent and found Miss Hill asleep so they let down her li-lo and woke her up by tickleing her feet. Next we let down Miss Pauly's li-lo. After this we had breakfast. When we had cleared this away we peeled the potatoes and apples. While dinner was cooking we passed the time away by scragging Miss Pauly and Miss Hill. When we finished this we had our dinner. In the afternoon Miss Hill went to Gidleigh with Marcia and Jean while Miss Pauley went into Throwleigh with Beryl and Simone. The four small ones went on the common to play Cowboys and Indians and succeeded in getting themselves plastered in mud.

An inspection of the company by the Commandant

of the Battalion, Mrs Luckham, came in October, and she reported that the company was one to be proud of. The discipline was exceptionally good, and it was a pleasure to see so many girls in uniform. A pattern had by now been created that many girls would enjoy, recording their events in the diary.

With Christmas approaching the girls were shocked and saddened to hear on the evening of their carol singing for charity of the death of Chaplain Revd J.P. Marsden, who was 'an inspiration to the girls and... always ready to help – a sincere Christian whose gaiety and personality none could but notice and be affected by.'

There is mention in the diary of what was an annual and helpful event – collecting eggs for the local hospital, which some say had its origins way back when a similar thing, but not just egg collecting, was done for residents in the almshouses and the sick and needy. Others, separately, link the regular event with the world wars so there appears to be a history to the collection of eggs for the hospital that, when fully revealed, is likely to show Okehampton's attention given to those in need stretching back a long way.

As well as being guided and entertained through their membership of the GLB within the company, some entertainers were developing who, in April 1954, staged a concert in the Congregational schoolroom for company funds. The programme opened with a piano duet by Marcia Day and Valerie Rees and was followed by songs from the juniors and cadets before the Hosgood sisters, Gillian, Jennifer and Mavis, tapped their way around the stage performing a Dutch dance. Recitations by Judith Nash and Pauline Jewell, songs from soloist J. Marles, and three plays – *The Toy-Maker's Dream*, performed by juniors, *Our Betty*, staged by the seniors, and (after the interval) *My Kingdom for a* ..... The entire Company closed their show by singing the Girls' Life Brigade Hymn and were no doubt joined by the audience in singing 'God Save The Queen'.

By 1955 GLB membership was shown as comprising one officer, 24 cadets, 27 juniors, 18 seniors and half a dozen pioneers – a total of 75 girls. The cadet section had been increasing immensely due to the leadership of Mrs Taylor and they proudly paraded for the first time with the company on Anniversary Sunday. One event that was regularly awaited with excitement was the GLB Rally, which meant a trip to London. The diary records:

We left Okehampton just after 7.30a.m. and arrived in London about mid-day after a hectic journey with plenty of fun. We went straight to Hyde Park from Paddington, and everyone settled down to a greatly needed meal. Incidentally, the swans and ducks got lots of scraps. Eventually we arrived at the Albert Hall in one piece. We thoroughly enjoyed the display, and the performances were all of a high standard, particularly the girls from Ireland who appeared on television the following day. When we came out of the Albert Hall, we went to a tea-garden for tea. After tea we went sight-seeing for a while. Some of the places we managed to see were Trafalgar Square, Buckingham Palace (where we tried to make a guard laugh!!) and Piccadilly Circus. We then returned to the station. Of all the nights to come back on, it was the night of the rail strike, so we wound up the day by leaving a deserted railway station in the early hours of May 27th. We arrived back at Exeter St. David's at about 6.00a.m. on Sunday morning. Some very kind fathers came to fetch us and most of us slept through Sunday after a very nice outing.

This was by no means the only highlight the girls recalled in their diary and the company was of course occupied throughout the year and enjoyed participating in local events, honouring God and helping charities:

October 8th we got second prize for our tableau at Okehampton Carnival. The tableau was called 'The Plague.'

On October 15th we won third prize at South Zeal Carnival and on November 8th second prize at Exbourne carnival.

November 27th our Re-dedication Service was held at the Congregational Church. Mr Taylor conducted the service, the lessons were read by members of the Company. After the service we paraded through the town.

December 20th we went carol singing, which made a perfect ending to the year 1955.

The youth of the GLB in 1956 certainly appear not to have had time to be bored.

On 17 January the following year 'the seniors helped to organise the cadet party, which was a great success.' On February 15th, the GLB, the Boys' Brigade and the Junior Church combined to present a concert in aid of the heating of the room. Part of the programme included a play by members of the GLB. They included Dilys Jordan, Hilary Bird, Paddy Collacott, Eileen Kelly, Margaret Barkwill, Mavis Hosgood and Anita Luxton. On February 20th, eight members of the Company set out in macs, scarfs and boots to hike through Ball Hill out to Waters Glide and on to Belstone Cleave where, with the help of Graham Hosgood, they managed to light a fire although the snow was still on the ground. The diary continues:

About an hour later we had our dinner and continued to walk over the moors to the point. By the time we arrived home we were all very tired, particularly our feet!!

May 12th, seven of us caught the bus out to Sandy-Park and walked along the river. While we were having our dinner by the water-fall, we were infested by ants, they got into all our dinner and even in the Billie-Can!!

We walked along to Fingle Bridge along the road and over the fields down past Drogo Castle and back to the road and just caught the bus back home.

May 18th we held a Jumble Sale at which we made almost £20. With this money we bought an electric gramophone.

May 20th arrived, the day we had all been waiting for. We were going to London for the Annual Display in the Albert Hall. We set off at 7.30a.m. from Okehampton station. To begin with we were all very disappointed because our Captain, Miss Pauley, had German Measles and was unable to come with us. However, once the journey started we were very happy and high-spirited, but we remembered Miss Pauley all day. We had a very enjoyable journey and arrived in London at about mid-day. After this the fun started!! We began by going to the Houses of Parliament, then we went across the road to Westminster Abbey, this was under repair so we could only see part of it. Next we went to Madame Tussaud's which we all found very interesting. We had our tea on the steps of the Royal Albert Memorial. After we had finished our tea we went into the Albert Hall, where we saw a fine display of everything a Brigadier should be able to do!! When we left the Albert Hall it was about 10.30p.m. and we stopped on the way to the station for a hot drink. We then took the underground to Paddington where our train left at 12-0 midnight. We sat on the station for a while then when our train came in we walked up and down the outside of the train but couldn't find our reserved carriage. Eventually we found it at the very front of the train. At last we got settled and started to sing. After a while some went to sleep (well, a sort of sleep!!). We arrived at Exeter at 6a.m. and came home from Exeter in cars. When we arrived home we all slept until well after mid-day. It was a most enjoyable day and we are all grateful to those who helped raise the money which enabled us to go.

A great many activities also took place within the local community. On June 9th 1956 the GLB enjoyed a dance in the Market Hall and on June 27th members were manning stalls selling sweets and trinkets at the Congregational Church's garden party at the 'Mance' ,Exeter Road, Okehampton. Halloween, October 31st, that year was particularly exciting for the girls:

... as it was the day when our own room in the schoolroom was opened by Mrs D.P.K. Ryan. The church had kindly given us this room, and during September and October we spent most of our Tuesday nights distempering the walls very professionally. We had all embroidered our names on two pieces of black cloth and made it into curtains. We varnished the floor and were kindly given a couple of chairs and a table.

One annual event, regularly recorded, was held the same year on December 2nd:

... our Re-dedication Service was held in the Congregational Church. The service was conducted by Rev. Taylor, and members of the Company read the lessons.

The first event of 1957, when membership stood at 77 with one officer, was the parents' and former members' party on January 18th – followed the next day by a party for the seniors.

In spite of the snow some of the seniors went for a hike on February 25th and on March 7th he company entertained the fellowship with a skiffle group under the capable leadership of Margaret Barkwill as conductor; the class of performance was apparently improved by a violin solo by Trixie Spencer on her two-stringed instrument. There were performers aplenty in the GLB it seems:

After weeks of practice we performed the tableau 'The Light of the World' as our contribution to the Youth Display held in the Town Hall on 29th March. On 11th April we again performed our tableau at Exeter.

Almost a week in May was spent collecting eggs for the local hospitals, but no figure was shown. From July 27th to August 3rd, the seniors and Miss Pauley went to Treyarnon Bay and extracts from notes kept of that holiday include the following:

Monday 29th July
After we finished our dinner we packed a picnic tea and went down to the beach. We explored the rocks and watched the fish until the tide came in, and then five of us went swimming in the sea. Miss Pauley had her bathing costume on, but that was as far as she got.

After tea we had a game of rounders on the beach and then came up to change and get ready for the cinema. On arriving at St Merryn we found the parish hall, where the film was to be shown, closed. We then looked at the shops, and some of us had ice-creams and ice-lollies. Still eating we made our way to the parish hall, and found a long queue awaiting us. After a wait of about 15 mins we finally found ourselves inside the hall. Some people bought tickets while others hurriedly bought sweets. The films were the 'Ladykillers', and a cowboy film. Everyone who managed to squeeze into the hall was feeling in very high spirits, and before the show started there was much talking, laughing, whistling and clapping. After what seemed a long time the lights went out and the film started. All through the film the high spirits remained, and there was much laughing. At 10.45p.m. the show finished and feeling very tired we made our way back to the caravans. It was a beautiful evening; cool & clear. Arriving back rather foot weary but very thrilled with the beauty of the evening, the starry sky above and the dark sea on the horizon, three of us with Miss Pauley's assistance had the joy of emptying the 'Elsans'.

After a great deal of wandering about in the dark we finally found the disposal spot and after handing over to Miss Pauley, quickly returned to the caravans where supper awaited us. By this time we were all very tired and willing to crawl into our beds, in no time to drop off to sleep.

Later that year, on December 18th, the annual cadet party was held and the seniors attempted to keep them amused by presenting *Cinderella* in rhyme, with a cast consisting of Margaret Barkwill, Anita Luxton, Paddy Collacott, Elizabeth Brock, Mavis Hosgood, Cecily Medland, Janet Brewer, June Harris and Hilary Bird. A sad postscript was added to one diary that simply said:

We were very sorry to lose our four NCOs Kathleen Medland, Diana Worden, Gillian Hosgood and Pat Dawkins this year.

It was a year during which the company had collected £79.5s.10d. for charity and collected 53 dozen eggs for the hospital.

The activities and interests stimulated by the GLB leaders were extensive and if one thing went wrong they had contingency plans ready – 'the committee arranged a picnic for the cadets, and did it rain, however the bus took us to Winkleigh Aerodrome, where we were able to wander around.' On July 15th 1958, at the castle, 'a Barbecue was held... the Seniors did country dancing, & the Boys' Brigade & Scouts lit a bonfire at the top, the Cadets danced around the Maypole.' Later that year, on December 10th, the cadet party was held once more where 'the Seniors presented two pantomimes in rhyme, *Red Riding Hood* and *Goldilocks & The Three Bears*; the Cadets thought these pantos were lovely, thank you Seniors.' Five days later the girls were out carol singing: 'North St, Northfield Rd and Saville Mead were visited, then Wardhayes and Castle Hospital on Dec 16th. We collected £2.5s.0d. for the cancer.' Other monies raised by the company that year amounted to £96.16s.1d. On May 10th 1960 the egg collection amounted to 33 dozen eggs and £28 in cash.

Obviously, people were by now giving money instead of eggs but this was the last time that the egg collecting was mentioned in any of the diaries and scrapbooks we have so far been shown. Perhaps it was a sign of the changing times but, if egg collecting continued, it would be nice to know for how long.

On Friday June 15th 1962, two excited young ladies caught the 9.33a.m. train to London – Gillian Hosgood and Caroline Hellier were to represent the company at the Diamond Jubilee Parade in honour of Her Majesty the Queen and afterwards at a service in Westminster Abbey. Miss Pauley met them at Waterloo. In the afternoon they all went for a boat trip up the Thames to London Bridge and after an enjoyable trip they looked around Westminster

Girls' Life Brigade

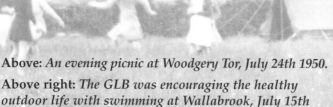

Above: *An evening picnic at Woodgery Tor, July 24th 1950.*

Above right: *The GLB was encouraging the healthy outdoor life with swimming at Wallabrook, July 15th 1955.*

Right: *Feeding the famished on the steps of the Albert Memorial in May 1955.*
Background: *The first long camp at Throwleigh in 1952.*

Abbey. The girls were staying at Wimbledon and so they caught a train from Waterloo to there. They were staying with Mr and Mrs L. West, she being an old member of the company. The couple took the girls on a sight-seeing tour of Wimbledon, during which they caught sight of the famous tennis courts and Atkinson Morely Hospital, where Stirling Moss was a patient. The diary records:

At 10a.m. in the morning went back to London and met Miss Pauley. They walked around London for a while, then had lunch and afterwards went on a 2 hour bus tour of London. They saw Trafalgar Square, Piccadilly, The Bank of England, The Mint, Hyde Park, Tower of London, Kensington, the West End, Houses of Parliament, and the Curiosity Shop of Charles Dickens' day.

At 2.10p.m. they all caught a taxi to Whitehall and then walked to the Mall to form in their Contingents. Gillian amongst the Pioneers and Caroline, the Seniors. At 2.30p.m. they got into ranks and at 3.00p.m. everyone marched down to Horse Guards Parade, headed by G.L.B. bands. After standing for ½ hour they were reviewed at 3.40p.m. by H.R.H. The Duchess of Gloucester, Brigade Patron. During the assembly incidental music was played by the 1st Broadstairs

Company. At 4.30p.m. the parade marched down to Westminster Abbey for the service, after which two proud but hungry young ladies met Miss Pauley on Westminster Bridge, chattered their way through tea and then all walked together up the Mall to Buckingham Palace. At 10.00p.m. the girls went back to Wimbledon and the following morning went to church. At 2.15p.m. next day they arrived at Waterloo, to catch the train back to Okehampton.

Miss Pauley resigned in 1970 and was presented with a Parker pen which she treasured thereafter. To simply record that she was much loved, and still is, is hardly sufficient. When one lady that had attended GLB and later went on to work with Miss Pauley said to us that she could never bring herself to address her in any other way than as 'Miss Pauley', it was but a casual comment. Hearing that same comment from so many others who knew her in different walks made it clear that this casual comment represented the deep respect which she earned from so many.

From 1972 the Brigade continued, first with Mrs Judith Harvey taking over to be followed by Judith Powell. But times were changing and numbers dropped until the 1st Okehampton Girls' Life Brigade faded into history when it was disbanded in 1972.

Jehovah's Witnesses

Okehampton's churches and chapels have provided a rich heritage, nurtured over centuries. Okehampton's Jehovah's Witnesses have become part of the fabric of the town in little more than four decades. Shortly after the Second World War, Jehovah's Witnesses Fred and Katherine Pitcher came to preach in the North Dartmoor area, but it was not until the 1960s that pioneers were assigned to Okehampton. Christine Branton had been in Cheshire, but after illness, she returned to her home area of Bude to recuperate. It was from there that she was asked in 1963 to move to Okehampton to continue her pioneering work. Her sister, Marjorie Fellows, moved from Putney to join her and expand the preaching work in the town and nearby villages. The sisters lived together in a flat in No. 2 Fairplace Terrace, in a house owned by Mr and Mrs Jordan who, although separating themselves from personal involvement, permitted the ladies to hold their first meetings in their sitting-room.

The Okehampton congregation expanded with the arrival of Roslyn Sillifant, and then two brothers from Holsworthy, and a lot of dedicated effort was made by these few souls to spread God's Word, often travelling for miles on foot and by bicycle.

In 1966, with more interested people coming to the meetings, it was necessary to find a larger room than the Jordans' sitting-room so, surprisingly to some perhaps, the lecture room at the Plume of Feathers public house was chosen. The congregation by this time had grown to nine and was then cared for by the first local congregation overseer, Mike Bidmead, who continues to serve the congregation as one of the body of Elders today.

In 1969 the meetings were moved to a room in North Street opposite the library and in the same year the small congregation managed to purchase the building opposite McCullocks Garage, East Street. The hall was furnished with pews, having previously been used by the Salvation Army, whose officers objected to the transfer of the building. In consequence, and after some difficulty, the hall was eventually purchased privately for £373.17s.0d. and later presented to the Jehovah's Witnesses for use as the first Kingdom Hall in Okehampton.

These premises served the steadily growing congregation well for 18 years, until it became too small and, with land available in the old Star Inn yard, East Street, the congregation proposed to purchase it and erect a purpose-built hall to seat 200. In June 1987 their application for planning permission was rejected, on grounds of access and amenity. A renewed application was made and in a letter to the committee the Jehovah's Witnesses pointed out that the use made of the proposed new building would reflect that of the building in use at the time. Since its opening in 1969, as far as they were aware, there had been

no complaints about noise. The congregation did not use tambourines, drums or any loud instruments during services, which revolve around Bible discussion, talks, and a song accompanied by piano at the opening and closing of meetings. The new hall, it was testified, would not be used for social activities of any kind and the building would not intrude in any way; in fact, it would make a marked improvement of current use of the site as a builder's yard and an area for dumping and at times burning rubbish.

A report in one local paper on Wednesday August 26th 1987 was headed, 'Plan for religious hall sparks row', and went on to say that the Jehovah's Witnesses in Okehampton had 'stirred up a hornets' nest'.

A petition against the project was raised by nearby residents. On September 24th, the *Okehampton Times* reported that the Jehovah's Witnesses:

... turned the other cheek to townsfolk who protested. Minutes after receiving planning permission for the controversial project at Okehampton they extended an open invitation to the objectors – including the 32 people who had signed the objection, to visit the building once it was built. Mr Raymond Cottrill, an elder of the congregation, added that the aim of the congregation was to make the hall a credit to the town.

By the end of January 1988 the purchase of the land, at £20,000, had been completed and a building schedule confirmed for the congregation to build their hall themselves.

Work for the volunteer army of builders began on April 2nd with rubbish removal and land clearing and, on a firm foundation, the building's walls were going up in August. By the end of September the gable ends were completed and, thanks to continuing good weather, trusses were soon being manhandled into position and secured. A special effort, made through 4–6th November, saw hundreds of tiles moved up to the roof one at a time and six days later the congregation could gather under their own roof, ready to start on the interior work.

Paul, a young blind but determined member of the congregation, slid around the floor clearing concrete spillage, ladies tackled the stripping and complete renovation of cinema theatre seats for future use, and plumbers and electricians took care of other necessities. Throughout the building programme members of other Jehovah's Witness congregations came to Okehampton whenever they could to lend a hand and the combined efforts of everyone ensured that the new Kingdom Hall was ready for its dedication on September 23rd 1989, when 191 gathered in attendance.

In 2002, the congregation in Okehampton consists of about 90 active members, plus children, who are proud of their town, at peace with their neighbours and, as a result of Jehovah God's blessing, they are sure, it is a congregation that will continue to grow.

Jehovah's Witnesses

Above: *Site clearance of the old Star Inn yard –*
preparing to build Kingdom Hall.

Above right: *July 1998 and no access for*
lorries meant that Kingdom Hall floor
concrete comes in a dumper truck.

Below: *Along a human chain hundreds*
of tiles were taken up to the roof.

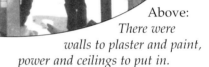

Above:
There were
walls to plaster and paint,
power and ceilings to put in.

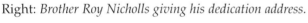

Right: *Brother Roy Nicholls giving his dedication address.*

Below: *Some of the 191 attending the dedication of the new Kingdom*
Hall, September 23rd 1989.

9

In Service & In Remembrance

Okehampton Camp

'Every penny spent at Okehampton camp is well laid out. As a practice-ground it is doubtful if it has its equal in the world.' Those words, written in 1902, have remained true ever since. Indeed, the site has enjoyed military importance for the past 2,000 years. Recent investigations have confirmed the very early use of the area and through every era of history there is sufficient indication to show that the strategic values of the moorland heights have been recognised; and once recognised, used. And yet few local people have ever set foot in the camp or know of the importance of the site to the Armed Services. We listen to Radio Devon to learn which 'firing ranges' to keep away from when planning a moorland walk and occasionally on those walks we encounter young soldiers, often tired and footsore, heading back to camp. But of their experiences we know nothing. A newspaper report may pop up that provides information regarding the Army on the moor, such as:

The Duke of Cambridge paid his first visit to the Camp on Saturday morning, when the Second Division were inspected and went through some manoeuvring. Later in the day the First Division was paraded, but no extended operations were attempted.

Monday was the first field-day. After an inspection and march-past of the whole Army Corps in the presence of the Field Marshal there was a sham fight, in which the enemy – represented in 'skeleton' by two companies of the Royal Engineers – and two field guns, each supposed to be a battery, were opposed by the combined forces of the First and Second Division, whose business it was to dislodge them from a position they had taken up. After a day of very exciting and rather rough work, the bugle sounded 'cease firing', and the decision of the umpires was that the enemy was defeated.

The people of Okehampton know their local weather well enough and are best placed to understand what troops are enduring when they read items like this:

THICK GRUEL
The weather at Dartmoor has not been altogether favourable for the manoeuvres of the Army Corps. Soaking rain such as is not seen in any other county of England, has made the ground of about the consistency of thick gruel, and when the rain has ceased it has often been succeeded by an impenetrable fog, making any attempt at the management of troops little better than guesswork. There have, however, been occasional spells of clear weather, during which the men have been by no means idle. There have been several engagements during the week in which both divisions have been employed, and the work done is generally spoken of as creditable to all concerned.

The Army's interests in and activities on the moor extend far beyond the northern region near

The camp of the 9th and 11th Gloucesters on the moor.

Okehampton Camp

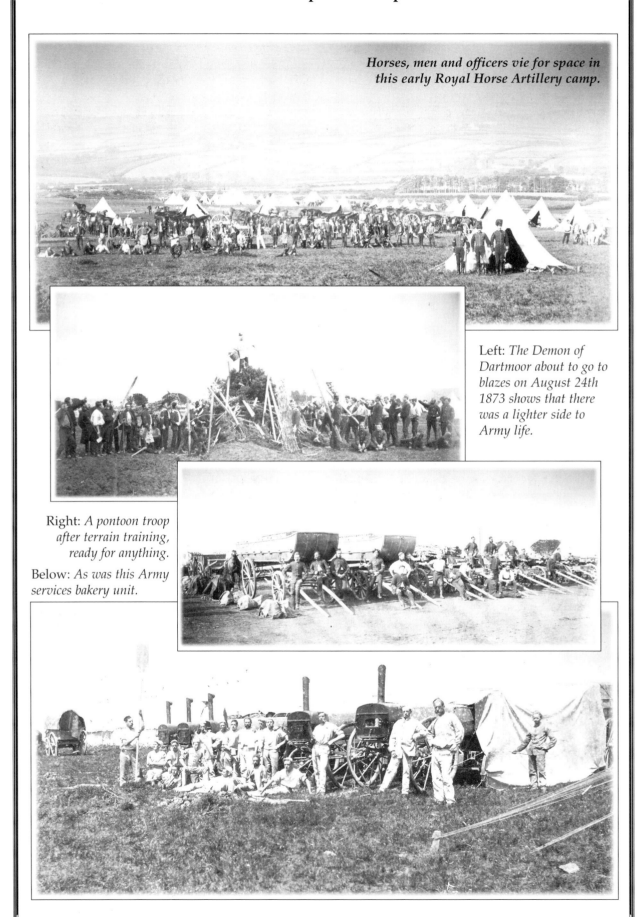

Horses, men and officers vie for space in this early Royal Horse Artillery camp.

Left: *The Demon of Dartmoor about to go to blazes on August 24th 1873 shows that there was a lighter side to Army life.*

Right: *A pontoon troop after terrain training, ready for anything.*

Below: *As was this Army services bakery unit.*

Okehampton:

LOST IN MIST
During manoeuvres, some of the ammunition waggons were lost in the mist, and one whole regiment was marching up Bellever Tor, right away from its destination, when it was fortunately met by a civilian who happened to carry a pocket compass.

On Wednesday, the weather became so bad in the neighbourhood of Princetown that Gen. Staveley abandoned the scheme of operations for the week, and sent the men back to Yannaton as fast as the defective means of transport would permit.

The camp is closed at a certain hour, after which every good soldier is either on guard or asleep within his tent. The patrol's stern demand, 'Any soldiers in here?' is, indeed, a terror to the truant soldier, who may have stayed too long over his pint and pipe in the tap room of the Red Lion, for he knows that absence without leave is one of the most heinous offences he can be guilty of.

It would not be fair to the present-day Commander at the camp if we did not admit that the reports quoted were drawn from the *Graphic* of August 1837. The Army of those days was here long before a National Park was thought of, or preservationists wanted them off the moor; but the weather was the same and the Army's needs for training today are no different.

During the past 145 years the Army has trained on Dartmoor at the Okehampton camp in readiness to defend this country and resist oppression in other parts of the world. Modern warfare needs modern methods of training but these methods inherited values from the past. When the war with the Afrikaners broke out in 1880 and the Transvaal under Kruger rebelled against the British Government, few would have considered that the Boer Wars would not end until the second year of the next century. Few would have thought that the men of the Royal Artillery arriving at Okehampton camp the following year were, in peacetime 1903, back in a country that just 11 years on would be embroiled in the absolute horror of a world war.

In 1903 the Royal Artillery was sending as many as 30 batteries for periods of two weeks to practise on the ranges installed just prior to the turn of the century on the moor above Okehampton. Each battery consisted of five officers and 166 men with six guns and nearly 100 horse. Over 5,100 officers and men and around 2,700 horses were in camp and being trained each year. The type of training that they came to receive had been, in 1902, the subject of the following article published in the *Windsor Magazine*. The reporter was a Mr Archibald Spicer and his words still provide, a century later, a detailed account of the manoeuvres being carried out. The original article was illustrated with photographs by E.J. Saunders of Winkleigh and E.J. Lugg of Okehampton:

WHEN the Duke of Connaught some time ago announced his intention to visit the Summer Practice Camp of the Royal Artillery, under the shadow of Yes Tor, Dartmoor's second highest peak, the officers busied themselves in making the best possible arrangements for His Royal Highness. Special furniture was brought up from the sleepy little town of Okehampton, 1500 feet below in the valley, over which a ruined Norman castle, arrayed in its mantle of ivy, stands as a spectral sentinel. It was conjectured that this officer of royal blood would be at least as particular about his temporary quarters as any other general. At last, when all the preparations were complete, the Duke arrived, and after a long and tiring day on the moorland, watching the guns belch forth destruction at imaginary foes, he was shown the arrangements that had been made for him, with apologies for their scanty character. The excuses were, however, cut short by the royal visitor: "Oh! I am not going to sleep in any building, thank you. I shall sleep under canvas as the men do, so that I may know what it is really like up here."

Accordingly, when the officers turned into their comfortable quarters, the Duke lay down in an ordinary bell-tent, just as the 500 or 600 gunners do every night. The next morning, when asked how he had fared, he replied cheerily: "Well, I turned in with a racking toothache, and woke this morning to find it had quite gone, thanks to the splendid air up here." And the Duke added that in future he should recommend all his friends who were out of sorts to try the effect of tent life in the invigorating air of the western highlands.

This camp has now superseded Shoeburyness as the new practice-ground of the artillery, owing to the long and irregular ranges obtainable. It is delightfully situated on the northern margin of Dartmoor. To the south, rising high above the undulating river-riven moorland, are the tors strewn with clatters, looking like extinct volcanoes – as some geologists, in fact, believe – and from their heights the eye travels to the rugged coastline of North Cornwall, to Bude, and to Boscastle and Tintagel, of Arthurian story; while to the south, west, and east lie heather, bracken, and gorse which lends a wealth of colour to these great uplands of Devon. Because at Princetown, in one corner of these highlands of the West, the old buildings that sheltered many of the French prisoners taken in the wars of the early years of the last century still stand and with new erections serve as penal establishment, the whole of Dartmoor has come to be regarded as a bleak, barren waste, fit only as a place of enforced residence for the criminal outcasts of society. In truth, the whole centre of Devonshire is wild, picturesque, high moorland, some 130,000 acres in extent, which forms part of the Duchy of Cornwall. It is the source of most of the rivers of the county, to which the valleys owe their world-famous charms. Swept by the breezes of the Atlantic on the one side, and by those of the English Channel on the other, Dartmoor is the greatest and most invigorating "lung" of the West Country, and is increasing in favour every year as

Okehampton Camp

Above: *Piper Cubs using the camp airstrip provided Gunnery officers with overhead eyes.*

Above right: *USA Captain Arthur L. Flinner, Battery C. Commander at Okehampton camp.*

Above left: *Three former (USA) COs of the 110th Maryland meet up on the moor.*

Left: *Okehampton's military sidings as a Battle of Britain class – Bulleid 4-6-2 steams past. The class was introduced in 1945 and rebuilt after 1957.*

Above left: *Sappers installing a bailey bridge before the old West Bridge was demolished in 1956.*

Above right: *The moment of destruction.*

Right: *Royal Marine Commandos at the town's 2002 Jubilee celebrations gave young visitors a taste for the life.*

a holiday centre for those who, satiated with town life and civilisation, are content with a tract of country that remains to-day very much as it was in the times of the Druids, its fabled inhabitants of pre-historic times. It appeals to the angler, the fox and otter hunter, to the pedestrian, and to all, in fact, who love to live under the canopy of heaven, away from encircling bricks and mortar, and to drink in health and cheerful spirits from lusty ozone-laden air.

For twenty-five years camps for artillery-men have been held every summer on a comparatively small scale on one portion of these uplands, but now Okehampton has become one of the great permanent military establishments of the country. Old wooden structures have given place to well-built substantial day-rooms for the men; an excellent recreation-room, with reading-room, library, and refreshment bar, has just been completed; a large church finds a place, and even the guardroom is being enlarged – almost doubled. Many thousand pounds are now being spent by the War Office in order to render the camp a more pleasant place of temporary residence for the hundreds of officers and men who in future will be sent either into Devonshire or to Salisbury Plain to practise with their guns. While the men continue to sleep in tents, they have comfortable rooms in which they have meals, and increased provision has recently been made to enable them to spend their hours of leisure pleasurably, without over-running the little town in the valley below, which has few amusements to offer to a soldier.

The batteries, from all parts of England, visit Okehampton in turn, and the arrival and departure of the units lend to the railway station quite a warlike appearance. Formerly the batteries travelled by road, being billeted at night at public-houses, but this mode of removal was so slow and expensive that it has been abandoned. Now each battery, however far it may have to travel, bring with it by rail its own horses and guns and complete equipment of every kind, so that not only are the men tested as gunners at the admirable irregular ranges, but the horses are trained to cover the difficult country swiftly and with unfaltering step, and the harness and weapons, as they are rattled over great boulders and through ravines and streams hidden away in the folds of the moorland, are put to a trial that could not be provided anywhere else. In the course of a season from 20 to 30, and some-times even more batteries pay flying visits of a fortnight each. Three batteries at a time are thus always using the ranges. There is also one unfortunate unit which is selected at the beginning of the summer to remain as permanent fatigue party to keep the camp in good condition, speed the parting guests and welcome those arriving, and to carry out all the weary, heavy work in connection with the care of the targets.

When it is stated that each battery consists of five officers and 166 men, with six guns and at least 89 horses, it will be understood that these fortnightly removals entail a great deal of exertion, but with

practice the men are becoming adept at entraining and detraining their weapons and horses. It is astonishing how soon after the arrival of the special trains they manage to get the horses harnessed and the weapons limbered up, and are ready to drag them up to their temporary home on the moor. The carriage of the guns is a matter of great responsibility, for they are somewhat delicate and very costly. Each 12-pounder of the Royal Horse Artillery, though it looks so small beside such monsters as carried on board our war-ships, costs the War Office £242, and its carriage another £262; while each time it is fired, cordite and metal of the value of 28s. is sent into space. The 15-pounder of the Field Artillery is more expensive, while the 5-inch breech-loading howitzer is still more costly. As each battery is allowed 600 shells for the fortnight's practice, and 90 of this number are for the special training of recruits, it can be readily understood that the annual expense of maintaining this camp is not a bagatelle, though tile rent which the authorities pay to the Prince of Wales as holder of the Duchy of Cornwall is inconsiderable.

As one stands on high ground with the staff officers, in a place of safety, as I was privileged to do, and watches the hail of shells at 28s. each being hurled through the air, it is impossible to stifle thoughts of the amount of good that might be done in the world with all this money and the many millions besides which are devoted by the Powers of Europe to the training of their great and continually increasing standing armies. There is only one satisfaction. Every penny spent at Okehampton camp is well laid out. As a practice-ground it is doubtful if it has its equal in the world. It is as though the northern portion of Natal of glorious and yet sad memories, had been set down in the middle of Devonshire. The system of practice is most ingenious and practical, and in striking contrast to the old and stereotyped methods. Until they are actually on the moor, neither officers nor men know the details of the day's work that is before them. When the guns have been swung up to a part of the moorland, as directed by the senior officer, then the general plan of operations is communicated, but the details as to the movements of the enemy – represented by target – are often not revealed until the moment arrives for altering the disposition of the guns. The following is a sample of the 'general idea' for one day's operations, which resulted in most interesting developments:

Exeter is held by a hostile force which has landed at Exmouth, and is being invested by a northern force. A portion of this northern force is detached to Okehampton, and the enemy are endeavouring to pass a convoy into Exeter via Chagford. The brigade division will rendezvous north of the East Okement Farm enclosure, and the enemy are reported to be moving – by the track passing by Oke Tor to Belstone.

Such schemes as this are set to the batteries when they

practise in divisions, after they have spent several days under their individual officers, so as to become expert in the use of their weapons. To encourage healthy emulation, badges ranged in four classes are awarded, besides a cup which is held for a year by the men who most distinguish themselves. These awards are, of course, in addition to the monetary prizes that are won before the batteries come to Okehampton, and which are given, not for actual firing, but for smartness in drill and gunnery knowledge.

The official staff of officers in charge of the camp have evolved a most elaborate system of targets, which at a distance of a mile or two, the usual range of the guns, bear a very close resemblance to the cavalry, infantry, and artillery which they are supposed to represent. Some of these dummies are stationary, and consist merely of boarding cut in the shape of soldiers, sometimes hung with old uniforms, and with a spike at the foot to enable them to be fixed into the ground at any distance apart, to resemble men in close formation or skirmishing order. Some of these figures are made short, to represent men kneeling in the act of firing, and others are longer, to show that the enemy are standing. A new feature is the crouching bodies of the wooden army to be found at every spot where the slightest advantage can be taken of cover, in faithful imitation of modern sharpshooters. These targets are very simple, and such fallen heroes of the mimic battles that are waged almost every day through the summer months are to be seen all over this portion of the moor, more or less damaged, and evidently supply the residents in surrounding districts with an unfailing stock of fire wood. Thirty mile of rope, which lies over the surface of the moorland, laced and inter-laced in the most surprising way, are the chief indications of the many moving targets that it is the business of the fatigue battery to place in the positions desired by the Camp Commandant, and to manipulate as though they were active foe. By means of the various types of targets, every phase of an engagement is reproduced – charging cavalry advancing behind the shelter of moorland tors into the open, infantry creeping up the dry bed of some erstwhile turgid stream, dummy guns of wood manœuvred by unseen foes, and skirmishers afoot and on horses, which appear and as quickly disappear among the hills and ravines as though controlled by some magical force. In fact, when the guns are belching forth flashes of fire and raining metal on the enemy, the face of the moor looks not unlike the stage of a marionette show of exonerated proportions. But the secret of these mysterious movements is easily solved, for beyond the zone of fire can be descried, possibly a mile away, the horses and drivers of the fatigue battery dragging at the ropes, which by means of pulleys and other ropes give activity to the figures. No one who has not witnessed these lifeless warriors and their guns suddenly creep forward from behind some hillock can appreciate the realism which is imported to the scene.

One exercise in fire discipline of which the staff are not a little proud is the direct outcome of the 'white flag' incidents which disgraced the warfare of the Boers. This drill is most ingeniously arranged.

While the batteries are peppering away their hardest at the distant foe, suddenly an umpire, who is concealed in a 'splinter proof', by pulling a string causes a white flag to rise above the enemy as a token of submission. But as soon as the British gunners have ceased to fire, by pulling another string, the officer explodes a small charge of black powder as an indication that the enemy, having succeeded in their ruse and obtained a momentary lull in the deadly hail, have opened fire again. Immediately the puff of powder is seen by the British artillery men, they 'switch' on their fire once more with surprising rapidity.

The feature of the drill for artillery as seen at Okehampton is the entire absence of shouting and confusion. Almost every command is communicated either silently or in conversational tones. A whistle's shrill alarm denotes that attention is required for some order, and for the rest semaphore motions of the hands and arms suffice to direct the operations. The clenched hand moved up and down between the thigh and shoulder shows that the battery is to trot, while a circular motion of the hand in a vertical plane, as though whipping up a horse, is a signal that the trot is to become a gallop, and so on.

In this wise, by whistle and the twist of his hand, a commanding officer can control his guns far more efficiently than was the case in the old days of violent yelling, some swearing and not a little confusion.

In every respect the drill of artillery has become more intelligent and better ordered. In their practice the officers are not left to blunder along, in their ignorance. Every shot that is fired is noted by the umpires, and word is passed to the batteries of their success or failure, and there are frequent 'pow-wows'.

Most mornings, before the work on the moor begins, the officers gather in the little lecture-room, where the colonel commanding the camp explains the faults in the previous day's firing, and the subordinate officers have every opportunity of discussing questions and even defending their action. It is apparent that by these means the artillery is being converted into a far more intelligent arm of His Majesty's service than hitherto, since the officers are encouraged to take a deeper and more thoughtful interest in their work, and to study the problems that present themselves from time to time, instead of proceeding by rote.

Another excellent practice is to anticipate the thinning of the ranks from wounds, and to make provision for the gaps thus caused being filled efficiently and without any confusion. Frequently word is passed to an officer or man that he is as good as dead, or at least so wounded that he cannot any longer perform his duty, and he has immediately to fall on his knee and then, standing up, remove his haversack, retire to the rear, and, in the words of Bret Harte, 'the subsequent proceedings interest him no more.'

The advantage of 'making casualties' in a battery is that the junior officers and the men obtain practice *which familiarises them with the duties of those immediately senior to them, so that if an officer or man is incapacitated in real warfare, there is no uncertainty or disorder, but his junior at once takes his place with all the calmness acquired by frequent practice. Sometimes the umpires will go to the length of telling the major commanding a unit, that he has been killed, or even the divisional commander himself, a Lieutenant-Colonel of the Royal Regiment, will be put hors de Combat.*

THE NATION'S GAIN IS DEVONSHIRE'S LOSS.

One result of pitching this military camp at Okehampton is that a large portion of the moor is practically closed to those who are wont to roam over Dartmoor in the summer months. The military authorities have, however, conceded one important boon. As a rule they avoid, as far as possible, all firing on Saturdays, thus enabling holidaymakers to wander about in perfect safety. So complete is the system by which the public are warned when firing is in progress that, although tourists have had narrow escapes, no serious damage has been done except to some moorland cattle. On the days that the batteries are going to practice, men are despatched early in the morning and laboriously climb to the top of Yes Tor, which rises 2,027 ft. above sea level, and there and on other distant elevation they hoist red flags of warning. These signals are supplemented by many permanent notice-boards, and from sunrise on firing days a number of shepherds in picturesque red coats are busy driving all cattle into valleys where they will be out of danger.

It is hardly necessary to add that though the area reserved for the practice of the artillery is large, the greater portion of Dartmoor is open to the public at all times. One may still take a day's tramp without running any danger from the firing of the guns. Practically all the central part of Devonshire is moorland, and it is impossible that the War Office will ever require the use of much more than they have secured at present; and, as a matter of fact, the presence of the camp above Okehampton and the daily practices are considered by most visitors an additional attraction to this side of the moor. As there is no county in England more beautiful than Devonshire, so there is no part of this country more wild and invigorating than the 130,000 acres of Dartmoor, the rugged highlands of the west.

While much has changed during the past 100 years one may still take a day's tramp without running into any danger from the firing of the guns. And there is a strong feeling in the town that those who demand the 'right to roam' at all times are unlikely to be among those first to take up arms when called on in war. Their more likely cry, it is suggested, would be, 'Why aren't our Armed Forces prepared?'

Forces from overseas have been grateful for the opportunity to train on Dartmoor, including the 110th Field Artillery, Maryland, USA. In his book on the history of the 110th, John P. Cooper junr, Colonel,

Maryland National Guard, writes of the men leaving the relative comfort of Tidworth Barracks, near the Wiltshire-Hampshire border and the eastern edge of Salisbury Plain:

From its new station the battalion frequently made motor marches to the Okehampton Artillery Practice Camp on Dartmoor, beginning its first week-long stay at the range on November 27th, 1942.

The artillerymen found that winter on the moors was dismal, damp, foggy, windy and cold, but agreed that the experience was novel and toughening. At Okehampton the cannoneers progressed importantly in efficiency, for as ammunition became more plentiful, they fired thousands of rounds in practice exercises. For the first time, most of the officers conducted fire with the 105-mm. howitzers. Here, too, the unit received shipments of a new, high-explosive, time-fuzed shell designed permanently to replace shrapnel. Quickly officers and men mastered the new weapon, including the rapid techniques necessary to mass the battalion's fire following adjustment by a single battery or gun.

At Okehampton, moreover, the 110th developed a standing operating procedure to speed up the handling of observed fire missions through the fire direction center. In this method of action number two gun replaced number one as the base piece in each battery, thus eliminating the computation to center the sheaf – or pattern of shellbursts – when bringing batteries into fire for effect. Then a practice of closing the sheaf on number two gun and opening on number three practically cancelled the slight theoretical off-center result. When seconds counted in battle, this procedure saved valuable time in firing for effect, and the cannoneers used it successfully throughout the European campaign.

During one of the 110th's stays at Okehampton, the division ordered cannon companies organized for each of its three infantry regiments. Captain Arthur L. Flinner of the 110th conducted the initial training of the units, including their operation as batteries under fire direction control. In addition, to provide an experienced cadre for the 115th Infantry Cannon Company, the 110th promoted and transferred several capable cannoneers to the new unit. Since the function of the 110th was to support the 115th in battle, the teamwork developed with this company at Okehampton and later in Cornwall was invaluable.

Okehampton's Army camp has served both town and country well for several centuries and in the twentieth century helped train those who served King and country in both world wars. Now many local people express concern about Europe for a third time. In some future time if Devon and other South-West counties are forgotten, absorbed into 'Region 28', or some other such numbered outpost in the new country called 'Europe', there may be no need for an army to be training on the moor. On the other hand, there may be one of occupation there.

Above: *USA 29th Division infantrymen leaving the moor after wartime training.*

Right: *For over a century, through two world wars and countless conflicts, Royal Artillery training has been conducted at Okehampton.*

Below: *HM Royal Marines who have an illustrious history at the camp.*

The Royal Horse Artillery at a ford on the moor.

The 19th Hussars took full advantage of the moorland terrain.

Field cookery was always needed.

We Will Remember Them

Down through the centuries men and women of Okehampton have taken up arms in defence of their country and beliefs, fought on this island and overseas, and many have never returned home. During the Second World War the moor claimed the lives of a number of airmen, all of whom are still remembered on or near November 11th each year. Thanks are due to Mr Frank Harper, 76, from Cornwall, who flew more than 30 raids over Germany. Since retiring, he and his wife, Joyce, 75, have helped families of missing airmen learn the fate of their loved ones; the truth of which was kept from families at the time for reasons of national security. The couple were recently recognised by the *Daily Express* Jubilee campaign to honour unsung heroes of Britain, and they were also introduced to the Queen and Prince Philip at Truro Cathedral on the first day of the Golden Jubilee Tour. The records which Mr and Mrs Harper gathered during extensive research include the names of those who fortunately survived their moorland crash. As veterans we salute them too.

An aerodrome at Folly Gate came into use soon after the First World War and Mr Harper confirms that by 1928 it was being used by Army Co-operation aircraft during artillery practice on the Dartmoor ranges from May until September each year up until the outbreak of war in 1939. The squadrons involved were Nos 13 and 16 using Bristol F2B, Atlas and Audax aircraft. The personnel lived in tents on the airfield.

In 1932, there was local opposition to use of the aerodrome on a Sunday for an appearance of 'Cobham's Flying Circus' which was touring the country, led by aviation hero Sir Alan Cobham. In 1926 he had flown from Rochester to London, by the way of Australia, landing on the River Thames in front of the Houses of Parliament before an estimated million people thronging the bridges and embankments; he was knighted soon afterwards.

By 1932, Cobham's enthusiasm had turned towards providing touring air shows with a fleet of aircraft and airborne performers including skilled aerobatic pilots, wing-walkers, parachutists and novelty turns that would thrill crowds the length and breadth of the country. Sundays at that time were far more strictly and religiously observed than today with most shops closed, opening hours for pubs limited and little or no entertainment permitted. The Lord's Day Observance Society naturally therefore objected to any of Cobham's shows being presented on a Sunday. It was eventually agreed that since local authority approval and licensing was required for shows any that were approved should not take place during church service times. Cobham's squadron of entertainers came to Folly Gate where other squadrons had been using the aerodrome for four years.

Above: *One of the airliners offering flights to Okehampton people in August 1932 when Sir Alan Cobham's 'flying circus' came to town.*

Left: *Sir Alan Cobham.*

Below: *Flying Officer Turner Hughes, almost seen here, held the record for flying-upside down when he appeared at Okehampton with the flying circus.*

Following the outbreak of war the airfield remained unused until August 1940, when 16 Squadron using Lysanders returned and became involved in coastal patrols covering Lyme Bay, and a stretch from Portishead to Barnstaple. Bad weather restricted flying, and in May 1941 it became a satellite for Western Zoyland and 16 and 225 Squadrons used it as a base while cooperating with Army units practising on Dartmoor. A decision was made in March 1942 to use the site as a Forward Holding Unit for aircraft spares and 73 MU was formed. WAAFs started to replace airmen in February 1943 and it became a major unit supplying aircraft spares and equipment to most of the airfields in south-west England.

A little flying took place during this period using light aircraft, including units of the American Army. It was closed as an operational unit in 1945, its responsibilities transferred to other MUs and the airfield was used occasionally by Auster spotting aircraft up until the 1950s when it was sold.

While RAF aircraft crashes on Dartmoor took many lives there were survivors. Mr Harper's records, for quiet contemplation, include:

16th May 1940
Blenheim L 9031 of 2 School of
Army Co-operation based at
Andover, Hampshire, crashed
5 miles south of
Moretonhampstead on high
ground in fog. The aircraft
was on a training flight. The
crew were killed.
P/O M.L. Patton-Bethune
RAF (VR)
Sgt. K.A. Stokes RAF (VR)

21st November 1940
A Gladiator N5644 of 247
Squadron based at Roborough
on a routine flight, but in dete-
riorating weather flew into
high ground at HIGH WILL-
HAYS. The pilot, Sgt. R.T.
Thomas RAF (VR) was killed.

23rd February 1941
Blenheim T 2040 of 59
Squadron based at Manston in
Kent crashed near Lamerton
following compass failure
returning from operations
against Brest.
The three man crew survived.

21st March 1941
Hamden X 3054 of 49
Squadron based at Scampton,
Lincolnshire, was returning
from a raid on Lorient, and
crashed on Hameldown Tor in
bad visibility.
The crew were killed.
P/O R.D. Wilson RAF (VR);
Sgt. R.L. Ashburton Ellis RAF
(VR);
Sgt. C.J. Lyon RAF (VR);
Sgt. R. Branes RAF (VR).
There is a memorial to this
crew at the site of the crash.

28th March 1941
Anson L9150 of 3 OTU based
at Stranraer crashed on
Halfinger Down following a
structural wing failure.
The crew were killed.
Sgt. K. Klyszce (Polish);
Sgt. A. Cheetman RAF (VR);
Sgt. R.J.R. May RAF (VR);
Sgt. E.R. Devereux RAF (VR).

4th April 1941
Hampden AD748 of 83
Squadron based at Scampton,
Lincolnshire crashed on
Hangingstone Hill at 0200
hours in bad weather conditions returning from
mine-laying operations in
the Brest area.
The crew were killed.
F/Lt. R.P.C. Thompson RAF
(VR);
P/O L.R. Evans RAF;
Sgt. A.M. Murray RAF (VR);
Sgt. L.R. Eden RAF (VR).
A farmer high on the moor
heard the crash but thought it
was thunder. He found the
wreckage two days later, and a
naval party from Plymouth
were called out to recover the
bodies and carry them to the
nearest road.

20th April 1941
Hallow K7015 of 271 Squadron
based at Doncaster, Yorkshire,
crashed at Inwardleigh when
the port engine caught fire in
heavy rain. The aircraft was
on a routine training flight.
One man, F/Sgt. M.E. Price
RAF, survived but the other
four crew members were
killed.
Sgt. E. Procyk (Polish);
AC1 K. Robins RAF;
AC1 K. Beevers RAF (VR);
AC2 K.R. Moore RAF (VR).

21st August 1941
Lysander V9551 of A.S.R.
Flight based at Roborough suf-
fered an engine failure in bad
weather and crashed between
Okehampton and Tavistock.
The pilot P/O L.B. Wilton RAF
survived.

4th September 1941
Wellington W 5684 of 115
Squadron based at Marham,
Norfolk, crashed at
Horrabridge after flak damage
after returning from operations
against Brest.
The six man crew survived.

27th September 1941
Beaufighter R 2442 of 307
(Polish) Squadron based at
Exeter, Devon, crashed near
Widecombe in bad weather on
routine patrol. The Polish
crew were killed.
P/O W. Peleger
P/O W.J. Gaysler.

29th November 1941
Spitfire W3968 of 317 (Polish)
Squadron based at Exeter
crashed near Princetown in
bad weather. The pilot, F/O
K. Wojcik, was killed.

28th December 1941
Beaufort N 1086 of 5 O.T.U.
based at Chivenor, Devon,
crashed at Coombes Head six
miles west of Tavistock after
engine failure on a training
flight. The crew were killed.
P/O H. Isted RAF (VR);
Sgt. F.C. Baker RAF (VR);
Sgt. G.G. Sinclair RAF (VR);
Sgt. E. Robinson RAF (VR).

28th December 1941
Wellington Z 8971 of 75 (New
Zealand) Squadron based at
Mildenhall, Suffolk, crashed on
Dartmoor returning from
operations against Brest.
The six man crew survived
Sgt. Machin, Sgt. Thompson,
Sgt Buckby, Sgt. Balshaw, Sgt.
Clements, Sgt. Bourne.

10th January 1942
Wellington W 5682 of 311
(Czech) Squadron based at
East Wretham, Norfolk,
crashed 2$\frac{1}{2}$ miles from
Tavistock after engine failure
returning from Brest.
The Czech crew were killed.
Sgt. J. Fina RAF (VR);
Sgt. K. Mazurek RAF (VR);
F/O K. Slama RAF (VR);
Sgt. J. Svoboda RAF (VR);
Sgt. F. Sipula RAF (VR);
Sgt. F. Raiskup RAF (VR).

7th January 1942
Hudson AM 741 of 224
Squadron based at St. Eval,

First World War

Right: *Christmas gifts on their way to men at the Front, 1914.*

Below: *For over a century Dartmoor has provided a training ground for the Military. Through the Boer War, and especially the First World War, a special kind of bravery was needed by those trained on the moor in the use of the tethered balloon, which was an easy target.*

Below: *The 2-6th Devonshire Regiment serving in India, 1914–18, included George Hawking, reclining 3rd from left front row.*

Cornwall, crashed near Princetown after flak damage while on patrol along the French coast. The four man crew survived.

24th May 1942
Lancaster R 5617 of 207 Squadron based at Bottesford, Leicestershire, crashed on Standon Hill near Peter Tavy in poor weather on a training flight. Four of the crew were killed.
F/Sgt. R.L. Mellish R.C.A.F.; Sgt. C.A. Pankhurst RAF (VR); Sgt. A.P. Paterson RAF (VR); Sgt. L. Smith RAF (VR). The remaining two crew members survived; Sgt. T.K. Paul and Sgt. T.A.M. Whiteman.

6th October 1942
Wellington BK 281 of 142 Squadron based at Grimsby crashed on moorland above Tavistock in poor visibility returning from Aachen. Four of the crew were killed.
F/O G.H. Edgett R.C.A.F.; Sgt. R.H. Baston RAF (VR);

Sgt. J. Bennie RAF (VR); Sgt. R.L. Partington RAF (VR). The other crew member, F/Sgt. K.S. Nicholls, was seriously injured but survived.

2nd December 1942
Spitfire EP 749 of 19 Squadron based at Predannach, Cornwall crashed into a hill in bad weather between Okehampton and Mary Tavy while on routine patrol. The pilot, P/O W.M.M. Ciechanowski (Polish) RAF (VR) was killed.

1st June 1943
Wellington MP 597 of 3 OADU on flight from Hurn in Hampshire to the Middle East crashed into Kitty Tor.
An injured member of the crew found his way to Meldon Quarry and workers from the quarry spent most of the day in driving rain and thick mist searching for the aircraft. Late in the afternoon the aircraft was found and the injured crew were carried to waiting ambulances and taken to

hospital. Sadly, one man was found dead in the wrecked cockpit. The crew were:
Killed – Sgt. J. Dixon RAF (VR); Survived F/O G.S. Watterson; Sgt. G.V. Collins; Sgt. W.U. Simpson; Sgt A. Mooney.
A scroll presented by the Directors of the Southern Railway was presented to the Quarry as a tribute to the men who took part in the rescue, with miniature scrolls presented to each of those who took part.

5th December 1944
Wellington NC 967 of 22 OUT based at Wellesbourn, Mountford, crashed on Westacott Farm near Okehampton in poor visibility. The crew, all Canadians, on a training flight, were killed.
Sgt. G.A. Chevrier RCAF; F/Sgt. P.A.N. Jobin RCAF; F/O J.L.G.G. Dumas RCAF; Sgt. J.J.P.O. Berlingue RCAF; Sgt. J.L.N. Savard RCAF; F/Sgt. J.L.M. Dube RCAF.

A true appreciation for what people have done for us in the past is, for us and many others, felt most acutely each year as Remembrance Sunday draws near. For an individual family that appreciation comes twice or more times each year as its members recall a particular date, perhaps associated with battles of the Somme or Passchendaele when a loved one was lost. Or it may be that battles at Caen or Falaise in 1944 are remembered, or any of the days or nights when death dealt a wartime blow.

Some say that the past must be put behind us, old wounds allowed to heal, distant days allowed to be forgotten, and local or national remembrance services ended. It is not a view we share so we have no hesitation in adding to our picture of Okehampton the details of the annual Service of Remembrance that can be turned to at any time. Fortunately, in recent years, the country has been turning its collective conscience to silent moments of remembrance at precisely 11a.m. on November 11th, whatever the day.

Each year also, in a public demonstration of appreciation and remembrance, our civic leaders, representatives of organisations, and many people of the town and hamlets continue to gather to walk up the hill to the Parish Church, in procession, to be

ready at the eleventh hour, on the Sunday closest to the eleventh day in the eleventh month, to participate in the Royal British Legion Service of Remembrance for the fallen. The Service begins in silence. A poem or other suitable epitaph is then read before the act of remembrance at the War Memorial:

Vicar: Let us remember before God, and commend to his sure keeping: those who have died for their country in war; those whom we knew, and whose memory we treasure; and all who have lived and died in the service of mankind.

The names of those to be remembered are then read out by the Mayor:

1914–1918
Montague Anning, George Baker, William Bickle, Thomas Bowden, Arthur Bowdidge, Sydenham Carpenter, William F. Chapman, Reginald Clinnick, R. John Clinnick, George Cole, Francis William Cornish, Harold G. Crews, Charles Dart, Bertie R. Day, H.E. Dewdney, Percy Drew, Albert Fairchild, Alfred Ford, Thomas H. Fox, John Friend, W. Harry German, Samuel Glover, Maurice Gregory, Wilfred S. Hamlyn,

Second World War

Local men served on HMS Andromeda, here seen in commission.

H-XE 12 coming alongside to be replenished by local men in the 1940s.

Top: *Okehampton Civil Defence Rescue Group 1939–44. Left to right, back: ?, Mr Dunstan, Eddie Vanstone, 'Tapper' Johns, ?, ?, ?, Fred Bullen, ?; middle row includes: Mr Wayborn, Mr Dyment (?), Tom Spear, Reg Ball, Joe Bond, Les Jeffery, Mr Guscott, Mr Orville, Mr Maddaford, Mr Horne, ?; front: Arthur Seymour, Bert Richmond, Mr Brunskill, Mr S. Sims, Bert Hawkins.*

Right: *Local doctors served the town during times of war and peace, seen here on 9 December 1966 at a tree-planting ceremony in memory of Dr Allen-Price and his wife.*

Remembrance Day

Right: *Remembrance Sunday, 1944 – 1212 Squadron ATC on parade.*

Below right: *The War Memorial at All Saints Church to some of those lost on HMS* Verulam, *September 3rd 1919.*

Below: *Members of St Johns Ambulance attending the Remembrance Day service.*

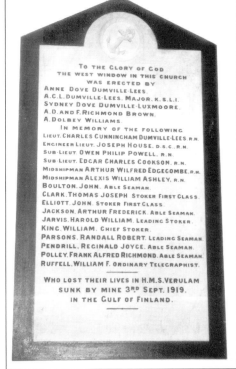

Right: *Okehampton's ATC Squadron no longer bears arms or wears poppies, as here, at the Remembrance Day parade.*

Below: *Remembrance Day parade, 1995. Leader Helen Cooke, also including Grace Thorpe, Tessa Cooke, Martha Unwin, Rachel Murray and Rebecca Coe.*

TO THE GLORY OF GOD
THE WEST WINDOW IN THIS CHURCH
WAS ERECTED BY
ANNE DOVE DUMVILLE-LEES.
A.C.L. DUMVILLE-LEES. MAJOR. K.S.L.I.
SYDNEY DOVE DUMVILLE-LUXMOORE.
A.D. AND F. RICHMOND BROWN.
A. DOLBEY WILLIAMS.
IN MEMORY OF THE FOLLOWING
LIEUT. CHARLES CUNNINGHAM DUMVILLE-LEES. R.N.
ENGINEER LIEUT. JOSEPH HOUSE. D.S.C. R.N.
SUB-LIEUT. OWEN PHILIP POWELL. R.N.
SUB-LIEUT. EDGAR CHARLES COOKSON. R.N.
MIDSHIPMAN ARTHUR WILFRED EDGECOMBE. R.N.
MIDSHIPMAN ALEXIS WILLIAM ASHLEY. R.N.
BOULTON. JOHN. ABLE SEAMAN.
CLARK. THOMAS JOSEPH STOKER FIRST CLASS.
ELLIOTT. JOHN. STOKER FIRST CLASS.
JACKSON. ARTHUR FREDERICK. ABLE SEAMAN.
JARVIS. HAROLD WILLIAM. LEADING STOKER.
KING. WILLIAM. CHIEF STOKER.
PARSONS. RANDALL ROBERT. LEADING SEAMAN.
PENDRILL. REGINALD JOYCE. ABLE SEAMAN.
POLLEY. FRANK ALFRED RICHMOND. ABLE SEAMAN.
RUFFELL. WILLIAM F. ORDINARY TELEGRAPHIST.

WHO LOST THEIR LIVES IN H.M.S. VERULAM
SUNK BY MINE 3RD SEPT. 1919.
IN THE GULF OF FINLAND.

Right: *The Royal British Legion leading the Remembrance Day parade on November 9th 1958.*

113

William Heysett, Percy Hockin, Percy Webber Hockings, James Hodge, John Horn, Richard Horn, William H. Hucker, James Hutchings, John Kennard, John Kingdon, William Lang, Mortimore Lee, Charles C. Dumville-Lees, Tom Lias, L. Herbert Lobb, P.A. Maddaford, Ernest Mansley, Charles McKenzie, C. O'C McSwiny, Frederick Metters, John Milford, Frederick Mogridge, Joseph Mott, Arthur Northam, John Oag, James Opie, Charles Pearce, John Pearse, Harry Pedrick, Robert Pudner, Frederick Pyke, Reginald Sherriff, John Slee, William Slee, George Smale, John B. Smale, Ernest Southcott, Leonard G. Stoneman, Alfred Triggs, William H. Weekes, John Westcott, Fred Wilde, William Woolridge, William Yelland.

1939–1945
Seth Allen, Stanley Beer, Cyril J. Bevan, Norman Blight, Bobbie Bolt, Samuel Chowings, George Eric Coldwell, William F.L. Cole, William J. Connor, Wilfred A. Dymond, Charles Foster, Geoffrey U. Fulford, John W. Harder, Frederick Heywood, Reginald Hooper, R. John Hutchings, Francis S. Lake, James Mallett, Sidney J. Martin, Leslie P. Nash, Derek Newcombe, Bert K. Payne, Albert Pedrick, Sydney J. Rice, Naomi E. Salmon, Edward G. Shaddick, Tom D.F. Slaughter, Reginald S. Soby, Walter H. Sowle, Donald Spry, Frederick Steer, Reginald Strong, Robert C. Symons, William T. Vanstone, Albert Wright, Paul C. Wyatt, Norman G. Yeo, William J. Yeo.

They, shall grow not old as we that are left grow old. Age shall not weary them, nor the years condemn. At the going down of the sun and in the morning we will remember them.
[And all shall repeat]
We will remember them.

[Here follows the silence]

Vicar: Almighty and eternal God, from whose love in Christ we cannot be parted, either by death or life: Hear our prayers and thanksgivings for all whom we remember this day; fulfil in them the purpose of thy love; and bring us all, with them, to thine eternal joy; through Jesus Christ our Lord. Amen.

The Royal British Legion Branch President then lays a wreath on the War Memorial and the service continues with hymns and prayers. The War Memorial in All Saints Parish Church bears these words: 'In grateful memory of those from this parish who gave their lives for God, their country, and us... their name liveth for evermore.'

The 50th anniversary of the ending of the Second World War was marked in Okehampton with celebrations in two stages. Victory in Europe, May 8th 1945, was remembered with events on May 5th, 6th and 7th 1995 with bingo in the Drill Hall and a

'Bombed out' auction in the Royal British Legion Club on the Friday. A victory dance in Charter Hall and a teenage disco in the Okement Centre were the Saturday events and, not forgetting the young ones, there was a tea party and entertainment for them in Charter Hall on the Sunday. Victory in Japan, August 14th 1945, was remembered with a full programme of events on Saturday and Sunday 19th and 20th August 1995, starting on the first day at 9.45a.m. with a victory peal of Parish Church bells at St James' Church, in which a flower display had been arranged for everyone to enjoy. The Mayor and Councillors visited the Royal British Legion coffee morning in Church Hall and by 1.30p.m. they were all on parade, quite literally, together with other organisations, led by Okehampton Excelsior Band, from St James' Church to Simmons Park where there was a tree-planting ceremony by the Mayor and dedication by the vicar. The townspeople turned out for two days of fun. On behalf of the VE/VJ event organisers, their secretary, Marilyn Poat, made the following address to the veterans:

Ladies and Gentlemen my name is Marilyn Poat, I came to live in Okehampton in 1979 – irrelevant information – what is relevant is that I was born in 1946 and that tells you that I experienced nothing of the events of 1939–45 that we are here today to commemorate. So what do I know? The only knowledge I have has been from my family and the media, as at school I was taught how the Romans invaded Britain not how Hitler invaded Poland which led to the war in Europe or how Pearl Harbour was attacked which led to the war in the Far East.

Like most families I was raised to show respect on Armistice Day, now Remembrance Sunday, and have watched on television, many times, the Royal British Legions Parade of Veterans at the Cenotaph in London and heard the commentators speak of 'The Ultimate Sacrifice', those who returned as 'The Lucky Ones' and 'The Forgotten Army'. I knew what they were talking about but did I really understand – maybe not. Then in 1991 my parents invited me and my husband to join them on holiday in Crete, my father was in the Royal Marines and a Crete Veteran. Most of you here will know that Crete was not a successful campaign but the people of Crete hold the British and Allied Forces in such high esteem that they have a national holiday to commemorate their efforts.

During that fortnight we visited many villages where due respect was paid to the veterans followed by much celebrating. However, on the last Saturday a coach trip had been arranged to a place called Souda Bay and as I walked through a pair of wrought-iron gates I could see the sea shimmering in the distance, but most of all I could see row upon row of beautifully tendered graves. Walking through those graves and seeing aged 19, 22, 24 – the eldest I saw was aged 34 – and some 'Known unto God', I learnt the full meaning of the words 'Ultimate Sacrifice' and the reason why those who returned consider themselves 'The Lucky Ones'. At dusk a Commemorative Service was held and at the end an elderly Maori Gentleman stood and addressed those gathered there and told them that he was here today to say farewell to his friends. He had visited them for 50 years but now he felt his own journey was coming to an end so he would be unable to visit again – but 'in saying farewell I can say YOU WILL NOT BE FORGOTTEN – YOU WILL BE REMEMBERED.' Listening to his words and watching the Veterans I became aware that although acknowledging their 'Luck,' they too had made a sacrifice.

I know of one, whose 18th birthday was on September 3rd 1939. Today, it would be a much celebrated occasion – then, I am sure, it was a happy family occasion but with, I suspect, his parents feeling a tinge of sadness because that youth had become a young man – old enough to fight for his country – but not to vote. The young man did enlist and thankfully was a 'lucky one' and when he speaks of those years he speaks of the comradeship and how when he received his letters from home he would share what he could with those comrades who had none – the darker side of those years remain personal to him and his privacy is respected.

'The Forgotten Army' – The only knowledge I had of these is from my family when I have heard them say how glad – if it is possible to be glad in such dark times – that they did not get posted to the Far Fast. However, all that changed in April, when I was asked if I would be willing to help with the Commemoration/Celebration arrangements of VE Day – there I learnt about VJ Day and that Victory in Europe was in May 1945 but Victory in Japan was still another three months away – and it is that we are commemorating this weekend and in doing so telling 'The Forgotten Army' you are not 'forgotten' – you will be remembered. It is now that we celebrate – peace. 'The Lucky Ones' – referring to the Veteran I spoke of earlier, he was a 'Lucky One' and, thankfully, like most, rebuilt his life having children and now grandchildren, all of whom he is extremely proud and throughout the year he receives postcards of all sorts of places – Portugal, Italy, Greece – from them on their travels. He, like all of you with your families, is extremely proud of their achievements but you should also be proud of yours because the sacrifice of your youth gave them, next to love, the greatest gift of all – freedom.

Ladies and Gentlemen, I am honoured to be here today to say, on behalf of all post-war babies and the generations that follow – to those who gave 'The Ultimate Sacrifice', 'The Forgotten Army' and 'The Lucky Ones' for your sacrifice: YOU WILL BE REMEMBERED. With DEEPEST GRATITUDE and a SINCERE THANK YOU.

Mr Jeffe Cunliffe then spoke – a man who came to Okehampton during the war and here found both a future home and a wife. Indeed, he subsequently served as a councillor and as Okehampton's Mayor. He replied on behalf of the Veterans:

Ladies and Gentlemen I am here today as a veteran and on your behalf I thank Marilyn and all her ladies for their hard work in preparing the excellent 'reception' we have had today. As a veteran I have often wondered whether the young really understood about 'The Forgotten Army', but today you have made it clear that they are NOT 'Forgotten' and there is no doubt your remarks will be of great comfort to all here today especially because as a post-war baby, while still quite young, you took it upon yourself to find out what 'The Ultimate Sacrifice' and 'The Lucky Ones' you heard about on Armistice Day was really about. Never have I felt that the words 'deepest gratitude' and 'sincere thank you' would mean so much – To you Marilyn, on behalf of all of us here today I say thank you – and I am now sure that as you said – 'We Will Be Remembered.'

Miss Joan E. Pauley, Mayor of Okehampton at the time, later recalled those festive days:

The weather was perfect and Okehampton rose to the occasion. The organising of events by the Royal British Legion was much appreciated by all. We remembered those who gave their lives to win a peace. The simplicity of the service conducted by Reverend Russell Chamberlain, Father Hay and Reverend Graham Stone, was a reminder of those battlefield churches, 'Where two or three were gathered together – there I am too.' This was a thanksgiving service for the veterans, before we sat down to eat a meal together. There was the symbolic planting of a walnut tree, which will grow and remind the younger generation of this special celebration and their future. The young people will be the future of our town. They will come to realise that without firm foundations, you cannot build. The foundations are in place. Those who witnessed and took part in the Community Celebrations August 1995, know the development and future of the town will depend on those young people, to whom we hand on our heritage for which lives had been given. It is to them we say God Bless, the future is yours the past is ours. Treasure them both and make Okehampton a place for all to live in peace and beauty.

Mayor, Cllr L.J. Hayward MBE, VRD at the service of remembrance 1998.

The War Memorial at All Saints Church.

Post-Haste!

Russell & Co., the biggest hauliers of their day operating from Falmouth to London via Okehampton.

The Quicksilver coach, the fastest mail delivery to the South West, provided hair-raising travel, often at more than 10mph.

Above left: *The popular Comet offered cheaper travel to London, via Salisbury, if an extra day or so journey time was of no consequence.*

Left: *Moorland mail delivery, with Moor View Villa in the distance.*

Right: *During the late 1800s this Chagford-bound coach picked up rail passengers at Yeoford, but why was it in Okehampton in the early 1900s? The White Hart and the Fountain each had their own, similar 'courtesy' coaches while a general coach service also operated between Fore Street and the station.*

10

Business, Travel & Communication

We open this brief view of trade and commerce in the town with a snapshot of Okehampton during the period 1823–30, when Mrs Lethbridge was postmistress of the Chapel Street Post Office, and received mail from Exeter every night at midnight and mail from Falmouth every morning at 1.00a.m. The town housed five attorneys: Wm Burd in East Town; Henry Robson Colling (who was also a fire office agent) and Henry Hawkes, both in Back Street; and Solon Luxmore and Thomas Bridgeman Luxmore, both at Fair Place.

For those needing medical attention at the west end of town there was surgeon Wm Legge at West Bridge, whilst those in town could use the partnership of Lethbridge and Thorne in Chapel Street – or any of them could choose, if they preferred, Thomas Parsons on Church Hill. William Bassett was running his boys' day-school and John Goss had another boys' school, boarding and day. Miss Arabella Wheeler, later Mrs Arabella Ponsonby, a 'professional' person, ran a ladies' boarding-school at West Bridge and nearby were the shops and premises of Wm Aggett, linen draper, Wm Heanes the builder, Jn Newcombe, tanner, and the cooper, Daniel Ward.

The area was well served for liquid refreshment by The George, run by Mr Thomas Morcombe, Mr Bond's, New Post Boy and, of course, the Old Post Boy, in the capable hands of publican, John Frost. Taking a stroll across the West Bridge into town, on the Parade one would have found Aaron Bazley's shop, selling drugs or groceries, Thomas Cartwright the mail-coach proprietor, and then the shop belonging to William Taylor, the linen draper. Before setting off around town one could rest awhile at the White Hart Hotel, where the staff of landlord John Crotch would be pleased to attend to one's needs; and also deal with stagecoach bookings.

There was also a great deal on offer in Fore Street. Edmund Brooks, the druggist, had his grocery shop here, as did the alternative druggist and grocer, George Lacey (with larger premises, as he was a wines, spirits and seed merchant also, as well as being the agent to the West of England Fire Office). When Emanuel Newcombe took over as druggist, grocer and spirit merchant, he left it to William

Ponsford to offer his services as a fire office agent. Cath. Tapson, along Fore Street, was one of the other linen drapers in the town. Philip Brook, Henry Newton and William Treliving also had shops, while Henry Pitts divided his time between being foremost a linen draper and then a saddler.

Trading competition for his secondary occupation came from three other saddlers. Anthony Bulleid, his son John, and Thomas Joyce. William Cann was the town's builder and ironmonger, but as far as the latter goes there was also John Elford the ironmonger nearby. John Carpenter the timber merchant could supply any timber needed by Mr Cann's company and John James the carpenter, Edward Lillicrap, Joseph Moore and Charles Palmer, the joiners, were available for work. Thomas Painter, the only plasterer, and George Lewis, the sole painter and glazier in town, were probably heavily occupied. Blacksmiths included Thomas Mallins, William Partridge and Joseph Rowe, and William Moore, the mason, had set up a smithy too. Wheelwrights included Henry Holloway, Richard Holloway and Thomas Tutcher. William Dunstan's rope-making works was the only one operating and Samuel Harris the only wool-stapler in town.

When it came to good boots and fashionable or sensible shoes there were six makers: William Corom, Thomas Brown, Henry Palmer, John Partridge, and Samuel and William Heanes, all in their respective shops and works, providing strong or fancy footwear for the gentry, merchants, traders and everyone else in town. There was also Richard Heanes, but he dealt in household china too. William Ashley the currier provided them all with fine coloured leather, which he obtained from John Newcombe, the cooper, who owned the tannery. For the gentlemen the town sported three fine tailoring establishments run personally by George James, Thomas Fried and John Moore but, for the ladies, dressmaking was something, of course, that was done in the home – there were many fine seamstresses and needlewomen available for this work. For good quality china or glass, Joseph Ceeley's was the shop to try, and Maria Pedler was the only earthenware dealer in town.

Mary Palmer and Christian Pitts each had their straw-hat-making businesses while Mary Brandon

Public Houses

Left: *Guy's Posting Stables, providing wedding carriages among other services from the Kings Arms.*

Below: *The Exeter Inn was offering good stabling in the 1920s and '30s.*

Below right: *The Fountain Inn in 1920 provided a service to the station for its guests.*

Below: *The Plume of Feathers in the 1870s, with access to its yard and stables.*

Bottom: *The Red Lion in c.1911 by Davidson's Cash Stores, and could that be a young Mr Lugg interested in the camera?*

Morcombe and Maria Pitts were milliners capable of making all manner of hats to suit any occasion. For those special, entertaining occasions Elizabeth Pitts the baker and confectioner in Back Street or George Partridge, the other baker in town, could be relied upon. As for butchers, there were John and William Perry and John and William Palmer ready to provide the finest cuts.

The town was pretty self sufficient, and it even had two watchmakers, Richard Philp and William Bassett vying for trade, but James Rendle the auctioneer and land surveyor had the area's business to himself. There were even two booksellers, Ann Smale and Thomas Simmons; separately of course. They each provided stationery and pens for those who could write. Of course, none of this includes the many people who came into town each week to set up a stall in the market.

Besides the White Hart the town was well supplied with taverns, inns and public houses. There was the Butcher & Ox in Fore Street run by John Palmer, the Golden Lion kept by Richard Heanes, and John Ponsford's hotel of course, the Red Lion, run by Richard Rich, Joseph Drew's Plume of Feathers, the Town Arms owned by Richard Lillicrap, Will Soper's Barnstaple Inn down North Lane, the Kings Arms, run by Geake Digory in Back Street and John Palmer's New Inn. On past Josh Richardson's, the printer by East Bridge, one arrived at the Fountain occupied by John Stanley in East Town, the Exeter Inn, held by William Morcombe, and the Star belonging to Joseph Seymour. This is a healthy number for a parish with not very many more than 2,100 inhabitants but Okehampton was a very convenient crossroads for stagecoaches and carriers; a major contributory factor to the growth and expansion of the town.

Stagecoaches operating at the time included the following:

To LONDON, the Royal Mail (from Falmouth) every morning at four; goes through Honiton, Axminster, Bridport, Dorchester, Blandford and Salisbury.
To BARNSTAPLE, the North Devon (from Plymouth) every Tuesday, Thursday and Saturday afternoon at one; goes through Hatherleigh, Great Torrington and Bideford.
To EXETER, the Regulator (from Falmouth) every evening (Sunday excepted) at six.
To FALMOUTH, the Royal Mail (from London) every night at half-past nine – and the Regulator (from Exeter) every morning (Sunday excepted) at ten.
To PLYMOUTH, the North Devon (from Barnstaple) every Monday, Wednesday and Friday afternoon at two; goes through Tavistock and Devonport.

The local carriers were also providing services:

To EXETER, William Davis, from the Exeter Inn, every Monday and Wednesday.

Russell & Co. from their warehouse – William Alway and Alexander Northan, from their respective houses, every Monday and Thursday.
To FALMOUTH, Russell & Co. every Wednesday and Saturday.
To LAUNCESTON, Wm Davis, every Thursday and Saturday, and Russell & Co. every Wednesday and Saturday.
To PLYMOUTH, John Baker's Van, from the Golden Lion, every other Tuesday.
To SOUTH MOLTON, John Baker's Van, every other Friday.
To TAVISTOCK, William Alway, every Wednesday.

Added to these were the local coaches and carriers' wagons plying to and from Chagford, Hatherleigh, Moretonhampstead, Drewsteignton, Bow, and the villages all around the area.

While the stagecoaches rumbled into town, and along every road between the towns, the coaching inns thrived and prospered providing employment for local people which ranged from ostlers to handle the horses, to cooks and kitchen staff to cater for the travellers, and many more. Horse dealers, farmers, butchers, bakers, candlestick makers, chambermaids, carriage cleaners, and washerwomen were a few among the many who found their services regularly required. The golden days of the coaches and carriers have passed into history, but their achievements, for towns across the South West, such as Okehampton, speak clearly from the records.

The Victorian Arcade in Edwardian days on July 8th 1907.

Shops & Businesses

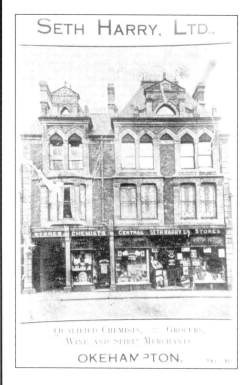

Above: *Devon Motor Transport buses covered a great deal of the region and the company employed these engineers in Okehampton in 1928.*

Left: *Seth Harry's promotion postcard, 1906; the jewel in the crown, and most remembered. All said that it was, 'a crime to pull such a beautiful shop down'.*

Above: *Formerly Ruby's Garage, then a petrol company's, I.G. MacCullock & Sons opened here in East Street, complete with roadside pumps, in June 1966. Nearby, they still serve the town.*

Above: *Mr Lugg at his Arcade studio in the 1920s; an exceptional photographer of his time who took family and amateur theatrical portraits that show period style and grace.*

Left: *The Mart; among the most remembered shops. Mr Westcott, Mayor (1889), built the shop up to sell almost everything while generating its own power until 1956; it closed in '58.*

Shops & Amenities

Fore Street in 1908, before Lloyd's Bank.

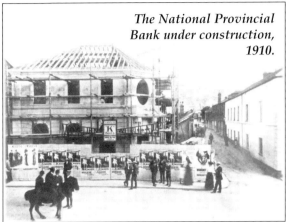

The National Provincial Bank under construction, 1910.

Above: *Okehampton Telephone Exchange in operation during the 1960s.*

Below: *Work in hand, but soon to close, one of the town's cobblers.*

Above: *John Palmer's Arcade Hotel in 1906 was newly built and boasted electricity.*

Below: *This is thought to have been one of the town's post-war chemists. Weighing the baby in the shop continued until the 1960s.*

Left: *Mr Jim Balkwill, outside his shop in February 1980, was 33 years a butcher in town and served in the Special Constabulary from April 1958 to December 1978, achieving the rank of Sergeant.*

While researching this book we were privileged to meet people who had known Okehampton for all, or much of, their lives. Over 30 hours of taped conversations with many now form the basis of a valued recorded history. In April 2002, Mr Charles Westlake, a local businessman and historian, reminisced about the Okehampton he knew half a century ago. The following are extracts from his memories of the town in the 1950s:

Next to the Town Hall was International Stores, with original Victorian shop front; it had been a grocery shop for generations before it was 'International'. The left-hand side was tall wooden shelves from the floor to the ceiling and a wooden counter in front with a row of glass-topped biscuit tins selling loose biscuits, mainly semi-sweet but also some cream ones and plain ones as well; weighed on brass scales. The other side was provisions. They had a marble display in the window, and marble-topped counters and shelves behind the counter with fresh provisions on. People shopped every day virtually for fresh goods and almost nobody had domestic refrigerators, and freezers were unheard of. The only shop that I can remember selling frozen foods in that era was the Shobrooks' at 1a Crediton Road and they had a fruit and vegetable shop and they used to sell frozen peas, which was quite handy when there was a scarcity of peas.

Red Lion Yard really was Red Lion Yard, the yard of the former Red Lion Hotel which became a temperance Hotel run by the Ball family. Red Lion Chambers, 3a Fore Street, housed the National Farmers Union offices and Mr Symons, optician; he attended on market day from Tavistock, on Saturday mornings. He was the only optician until Mr Rae came and bought Harris' chemist business. He was a pharmacist as well as an optician and ran both businesses for some years.

Mr Brock's shoe shop was at No. 3, Fore Street, which had been the Red Lion Hotel, then No. 4 was Mrs Stroud, fruit and vegetable shop, flowers, seeds, plants, groceries, provisions – a tiny shop crammed from floor to ceiling; well, it had a very low ceiling. Mrs Tolley took over the business afterwards and rather emphasised on groceries and provisions. Then, 4a and 5a, above 4 and 5 was Mr Clifford Hancock, accountant from Lydford; the only accountant in the town. There weren't near as many professions in the town then. Of course, No. 5, Donalds, was then Hepworths, men's outfitters, run by Mr Lobb as manager. Midland Bank chambers at No. 7 was Gordon Vick and Partners, estate agents and auctioneers. Nos 8 and 9 Fore Street was the central supply stores, Seth Harry, a high Victorian building dominating Fore Street – a remarkable building with wonderful architectural features, built in the late 19th century, and retaining its original shop fittings until it was demolished in the 1960s. The Harrys, in the 50s, were a dispensing chemist and a wine merchant, one of only two off-licences in the town, and they supplied most of the well-off people in the district. It was also very economical to shop there because

long after anybody else they sold a large number of items, loose. You could buy cereals for milk puddings, dried fruit, lentils, pearl barley, butterbeans, brown sugar of all types, all there by weight, in blue paper bags. They used to sell 28lb blocks of salt. My father had an allotment and had a surplus of runner beans. We used to buy these 28lb blocks of salt for cooking, and store them in the airing cupboard in brown paper, and use them salting runner beans in stone jars. Of course, like many women at the time my mother was a full-time housewife so she bought all these ingredients for all her cooking at Seth Harry's, because it was cheaper than buying the ones the other shops sold in packets. They also sold Bibby's green household soap in large bars. We used to buy large bars of it and cut it up with a carving knife. It was a wonderful shop, Seth Harry's, with a very high standard of service.

Next door was Glass's garage, and they'd had the shop-front taken away from No. 10 Fore Street and a petrol pump put in the front with an arm going over the pavement so the cars could park in the street and fill up with petrol. The recessed ground floor was their office, and shop selling paraffin and motor accessories. No. 11, the Okement Café, had been run by Mr And Mrs Spear and then it was run by Mr and Mrs Newcombe; he was an Oketonian and she came from Postbridge. They ran the café for several years there and also did catering for events, like dinners and wedding receptions. No. 12, where Cornish's jewellers is now, was Lennards shoe shop with Mr Vincent as manager; after that closed, Cornish's moved in there. No. 13 was Mr Webb, the barber's shop, and they had a little shop at the front run by Mrs Jeffrey from Northfield Road, in connection with the barber's shop, and Miss Gertie Williams ran a hairdressing salon for ladies upstairs on the first floor.

No. 14 is one of the few shops that, today, retains the same sort of business on the same site. It was Hutchings' dairy shop, George and Daisy; she was Daisy Yeo from Lower Upcott and they ran a dairy shop there and sold confectionery and ice-creams and did a milk round. We used to take a glass down to buy cream and they put it on the scales to see how much it weighed, then filled the glass up with cream for whatever amount you wanted. We never bought cream very much because we always scalded the milk and used the cream off the top of the milk. You had to do that to keep the milk from one day to the next in warm and hot weather.

Then, 15 and 16 was Westcott, the Mart, and they had a drapery shop one side and grocery and provisions the other – a huge business with a very large staff and, like Seth Harry's shop, they had a very narrow driveway into the street where they came out with a little van that delivered the groceries, going miles.

The next shop on was Mr Bate's boot stores, No. 17. Then 18 was Cornish's ironmongery and Cornish's jewellers, two shop units in the same property with two frontages. After their jewellers moved, after Lennards closed down, they extended the ironmongery shop. No. 19, was Miss Quance's confectionery with jars of sweets,

20 was Hawkings' butchers and 22 was Finucane's, and they had a very large shop and they never seemed to have very much in it, selling flowers and fruit and veg., and a few bits of groceries and confectionery. Endacott's bakery shop was next, No. 23, on the corner then, and behind that, in No. 1 North Street, was the Labour Exchange and National Assistance Office.

North Street was a very busy street. Believe it or not, it had two-way traffic in the narrow part in those days, and the primary school was down there with hundreds of children. Next door to it, the old mill was converted into Mr Maddaford's fish and chip shop, one of two in the town. Further down there was the forge, George Vanstone was the blacksmith down there, that was Lovell's forge originally. Brightley Mill, where they make the kites now, was a working farm.

In North Street was the Congregational Chapel. It had a beautiful gateway with an iron archway with a lamp on it, and the pathway going through the graveyard, and a big board said 'Ebenezer Chapel'. It was very well attended, a lot of business people went there, and a lot of families that weren't particularly Congregational but they lived in that part of the town so they attended it, and they had a big Sunday School, and uniformed organisations.

The Aggets lived in No. 50 North Street, they owned the old quarry and they took in washing. There's a car-parking space now where they had a three-cornered building where they used to do washing. No. 10 was a barber's shop at one time for a while. The library was the Congregational schoolroom and No. 2 was Mr and Mrs Gale's. Mr Gale was barber and Mrs Gale ran a tiny shop selling toys and tobacco, and stationery and confectionery and fancy goods. After he retired full time from barbering she extended the shop and ran it until she was in her eighties. They were an institution. Wonderful couple, much loved by the community, he was bandmaster for the Excelsior Silver Band; they were the only people who sold Sunday papers in the town.

No. 1 East Street was East Parade Store, run by Fretwell, and they sold groceries and provisions and sorts of china and glassware and kitchen utensils. No. 3 East Street was Mr Horne, the town's only saddler. Then behind No. 9, Gunn's, the coal merchants, ran a mineral water works behind there; the Misses Would ran a ladies hairdressing salon upstairs. No. 11 was the doctor's surgery, for doctors Routh and Jowett and Twining. Dr Jowett and his mother lived there and it had been a doctor's house for generations because it was the house where Dr Burd lived and they ran this three-doctor surgery with Mrs Ivy Carew from Sticklepath as receptionist.

Then there was a derelict site where the Star Inn had been, derelict until the 60s. No. 15 was where Mrs Medland and her daughter Alice lived. Alice worked at the Premier Cinema in Market Street. No. 19 was Yeo's, grocers and provisions shop, run by Mr and Mrs Cloke. No. 21 was Maddaford's bakery shop, as it is now, but they sold quite a few groceries there, though they had a grocery shop next door. In 23 Mr and Mrs

Taylor lived; he worked on Post Office telephones, and became Mayor, and Mrs Connie Taylor was agent for parcels for Devon General Buses. She had a big conservatory and they used to put the things in [there]. At No. 31 East Street, on the corner of Northfield Road, where the Chinese fish and chip shop is, Allins had a big shop selling wallpaper and paint and, down Northfield Road, they had a workshop and premises where they kept all their equipment.

There was a thatched house where the garage forecourt is of MacCullock's garage in East Street. The original garage was only where the showroom is and it was Rees and Lee's garage, run by Mrs Rees and Mrs Lee and the Reeses lived in the double-fronted thatched house where the middle of the garage forecourt is. Mr and Mrs Saville ran a ladies fashion shop at 10 East Street, and in 6 and 8 Hain's the decorators had a shop selling furniture and paint and wallpaper. They were one of the oldest established businesses in the town.

Then there was March Court, Mr Johns had a cobbler's workshop and Mr and Mrs Wonnacott ran a milk round from premises there. No. 2 East Street was the Trustees Savings Bank, the manager was Mr Discombe, who was a Church of England Lay-reader. Bridge House was Blatchford Ash and Company, which had previously been the Geens' business but the business had been taken over by one of the Geens' sons-in-law, Mr Blatchford. Now, Blatchford Ash and Company was a most amazing business. They had a furniture shop there and they also made furniture for people; they sold furnishings, and made furnishings, like curtains and chair covers and cushions; Mrs May Moulding, an aunt to John Hodge at Lower Halstock, worked there doing that. They were timber merchants, and builders, decorators, undertakers, upholsterers, and then sold decorating materials as well... for people to do their own decorating and had a huge premises up alongside the East Okement river, it really was a wonderful business.

No. 1 St James's Street was the Mill Bay Dyers and Cleaners, they used to take in dry cleaning and laundry there, and take it to Plymouth to be done. No. 3 was Bassetts newsagents and stationers, and tobacconists... and barbers in those days as well. They only had the top part of the shop and they later extended it the full length of the premises, No. 3... after the father retired from the barber's business.

The Carlton Cinema had a sort of tower on the front which disappeared at some stage afterwards. There were two cinemas in the town in those days, quite well patronised before television. They used to run buses in from North Lew on a Saturday evening for people to come to the pictures. Wright's ironmongery fronted both St James' Street and Fore Street. St James' Church was in use three times a Sunday then. They had eight o'clock Communion every Sunday, ten o'clock children's service... for children as well as having a church Sunday School in the afternoon, and 6.30 Evensong... and it was quite full on a Sunday night, mainly attended by people who didn't have cars to get to Evensong in

Getting Around

Devon Motor Transport, Okehampton Depot, c.1923.

Nicknamed 'the greyhound' and used on the Padstow line, the 30313 was withdrawn in July 1961 and scrapped at Eastleigh in September.

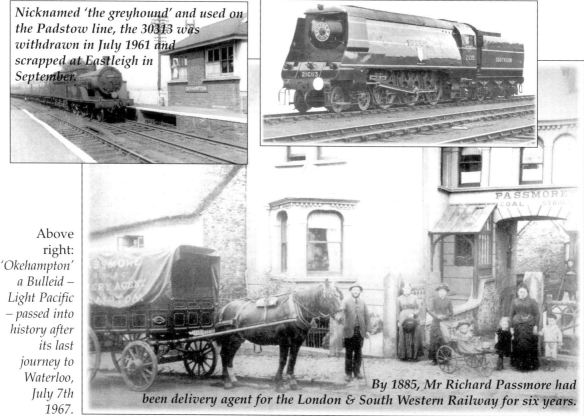

Above right: 'Okehampton' a Bulleid – Light Pacific – passed into history after its last journey to Waterloo, July 7th 1967.

By 1885, Mr Richard Passmore had been delivery agent for the London & South Western Railway for six years.

the Parish Church, although Okeridge Bus did run a bus service from the east end of the town to the Parish Church to the services. My mother used to play an American organ at St James' for the children's service in the morning, for some years, and my Grandmother played in the evening; and she had a choir of teenage girls there. They took on playing after Miss Bradley, who had been organist there, moved to Northamptonshire. Next door to Wright's, where Boots is now, was the Post Office, and behind that they had the Royal Mail deliveries... because all those properties had entrances into St James' Street in those days. There was quite a lot of people lived in the town centre in those days. Where Telecare is, was the Central Hotel and Green Lantern café; the last of Okehampton's temperance hotels.

Slees were greengrocers, fruiterers and flowers and plants, and they used to sell some confectionery as well. Then, No. 34 was Harris' chemist and stationers... and until well after the '50s they had all the original shop fittings there; it was like the preserved pharmacy in Plymouth that's in a museum now. It was a completely intact Victorian shop. The Arcade has had so many changes with the shops, people that have come and gone, but... in the '50s first on the left was Carr's motorcycle... sales and repairs, then the Arcade snack bar, run by the Carthews, then there was the Arcade Fernery, run by Mrs Boucher, then Worden's shoeshop, Nash's drapery [which] had three units selling linen and haberdashery and childrenswear. Then there was three units belonging to the Arcade Pram and Toy shops.

Coming down the right, the **Western Times** had an office there... for taking adverts and selling papers, and Nash's took over the unit vacated by the Stinchcombe's for a childrenswear shop, which left them more space in the other three units. There was the Bon-Bon Sweetshop, that was run by Mr and Mrs Percy, then it was bought by Mrs Holt, who was a Kelly from Okehampton; [she] still lives here, and after she sold it it was bought by Mr and Mrs Lee... then Weaver's tobacconists was there [and] Mr Eveleigh, barber, upstairs. He was the father of Mrs Boucher who ran the Arcade Fernery. There was Nuttall's menswear. [The] manager [was] Mr Dennis Wills, then somebody had a fancy goods shop there.

Nash's had a menswear shop... and then there was Mary Ashley's ladies' outfitters, and Molly's hairdressing salon, and on the corner the Dartmoor Boot Store, with Gerald Newcombe, before he had the newsagents. Then after that closed down, the son and daughter-in-law of Mr and Mrs Slee from the greengrocery took over the premises and created a cafeteria.

Back in Fore Street there was Dewhurst's butchers... they used to sell a lot of tinned items as well. The Plume of Feathers had a different frontage on the ground floor to now and it had a way through for a horse and cart into the yard from Fore Street, and next to the National Westminster Bank Knapman's had a butcher's shop; now part of the Plume's bar.

West Street and New Road were very busy, the White Hart very well patronised. Apart from the Okement Café it was the only place that did catering for meals and the only licensed premises that provided accommodation very much – for tourists and commercial travellers. They had a lot more trade from people stopping.

No. 1 West Street was still solicitors, J.J. Newcombe and Company. He was Town Clerk as well, and Churchwarden and I can remember their reception office being heated by a coal fire, with an iron surrounded grate with tile splays. Where the Tourist Information Centre is now was Mr Jordan's printing works, with his antique printing press still in regular use. He and his wife were both Okehampton people, they were lovely couple, and he did very high quality printing. No. 3 West Street was Hedley Stanbury, estate agent and auctioneer, [who] had a one room office in the front, the rest of the property was occupied by Mr and Mrs Lobb and their sons as residential. Plymouth Brewery's off-licence at 5 West Street had previously belonged to Newcombes who were also wine and spirit merchants. Next was the West End Café – a sort of snack bar and then Hutchings' bakers and grocers, and then, where Jacobs Pool House is, the site of the George Inn was occupied by agricultural engineers selling tractors and agricultural machinery. Previously it had been a bus depot for the Devon Motor Transport but, remember, the alignment of the road and pavements all round that area was completely different then.

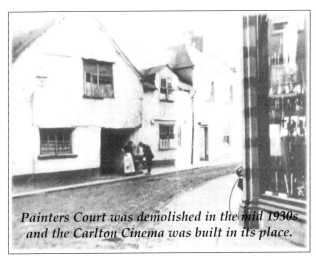

Painters Court was demolished in the mid 1930s and the Carlton Cinema was built in its place.

The showrooms of T. Day & Sons decorated for King George V's Jubilee, 1935.

Okehampton & District Chamber of Trade

The Chamber of Trade in Okehampton was started before the Second World War but there seem to be no records left from that time. The Chamber has always been an important organisation in town and in the 1960s and '70s its 'Annual Banquet' was a major social event, rivalled only by the Mayor's Civic Ball. Okehampton's *Town Guide* is a publication that has always been produced by the Chamber. Early editions from the 1950s still exist, providing a glimpse of a bygone age when the town attracted firms' representatives or 'travellers' to stay in the hotels and the town was a good place to spend a short-break holiday.

In the early '70s it was the Chamber of Trade members that brought Christmas lights to the town, lights that have become an asset to Okehampton and which are admired throughout the county. Local people and visitors alike welcome their annual return and appreciate the warm, traditional Christmas atmosphere they bring. In the early days Mr Howard Downing of Downings Motor Works was responsible for constructing the strings of lights and getting other traders to help. More recently, but for many years, Mr Don Rooke of Donald's Menswear has been responsible for organising, repairing and replacing these lights.

Throughout the summer months since 1992 the hanging baskets that adorn the town have been provided by the Chamber. Each year more baskets are provided, all helping to keep the town colourful and bright. The display is kept watered and maintained by Don Rooke and his team who spend hours during the summer looking after the baskets. Over the past five years the Chamber has produced town maps and 'Where to Stay', 'Where to Eat' and 'What to Do' in Okehampton... all provided free for visitors.

Secretaries to the Chamber of Trade have included Mrs Joy Vaughan JP, who served for many years in that role, and Mr Mike Wreford, secretary for 14 years from the mid 1970s. During the late 1980s the Chamber suffered declining membership and this was not reversed until the early 1990s when the then secretary, Mrs Jane Seigal, worked tirelessly to promote the Chamber of Trade and Okehampton.

Mr Peter Sworn, who was the landlord of the Plume of Feathers, served for many years as chairman, and was honoured by being made a Life Member of the Chamber. Another long-serving chairman is Mr Ian Bailey, of Ink Print, Okehampton, who has been in the chair since 1994. The Chamber recently added to its structure the position of President; at the time of writing this is held by Mr William Cornish of W.J. Cornish & Son, Jewellers. William's father was a past chairman of the Chamber and was an active committee member for many years. Following in his footsteps, William is also a committee member and is active within the organisation that now has over 80 members and looks forward to maintaining the position it holds in representing trades and business people in the town. The Chamber now meets once a month and has a varied diary that includes speakers on issues that affect local businesses, visits to other companies, discussion of local issues and social events.

Main: *John Cornish's 'Competitive Stores' in the 1930s.*
Left: *William Cornish at work, 2002.*

11

Stage & Screen

The Okehampton Amateur Operatic and Dramatic Society was founded in 1928 by Mrs R. Gorle who gathered around her a capable company that immediately set to and started entertaining Okehampton the following year. In a market filled with butchers' tackle and heated by open braziers and paraffin-oil lamps, a small audience saw *HMS Pinafore*, the Society's first show. Scenery and costumes had been fashioned by members of the cast themselves. A solitary pianist strummed out the musical score. Against all odds it would seem those plucky performers breathed life into a company that was to establish itself firmly, often with two operatic or dramatic productions each year, and achieve 17 successfully before the outbreak of war in 1939.

Mrs Gorle was a lady of considerable talent, a more than capable musician and, while being a competent conductor, was one who sometimes put singers and their songs before the musicians and their music. As a producer she was able to impart her knowledge of stagecraft to a cast of 45 or more sufficiently well to set them on the road to becoming one of the foremost amateur societies in the county. By the time the company was presenting *Iolanthe* and *The Mikado* as their Gilbert and Sullivan selections in 1930, the local reporters were noting that the town's Market Hall lacked facilities:

Mad Margaret, Ruddigore, 1931, magnificently played by Mrs P. Brooking and stylishly photographed by Mr Lugg.

... despite the unsuitable accommodation offered by the building it was made into a creditable substitute for a theatre. It makes one wonder, incidentally, whether there is not room in Okehampton for a better building for social functions and amateur shows.

Like all good amateurs the society members enjoyed their stage work and paid for it by giving the pro-

ceeds raised from performances to local charities and organisations; the Cottage Hospital having been an early beneficiary.

In the 1930 *Mikado* the title role was entrusted to the capable hands of Mr Eric McKean, who, for the company, also performed the less ostentatious role of business manager. Mr Frank Horn played Nanki-Poo, his son, while the object of his romantic attention, the attractive Yum-Yum, was played by Miss Joan Wright. The Lord High Executioner of Titipu and The Lord High Everything Else were played by Mr Reg Spear and Mr Norman Bickle, while Mr Charles Buxton found himself comfortably in the role of the noble lord Pish-Tush. Mrs Breakell and Mrs Wood took delightfully to the stage as Yum-Yum's two sisters, Pitti-Sing and Peep-Bo, the wards of the Executioner, and the main cast was completed by Mrs H. Brooking whose characterisation of Katisha, an elderly lady in love with Nanki-Poo, was considered to be magnificent; apart from her rather poor voice. The remainder of the cast were reported as being: chorus of schoolgirls, nobles, guards and coolies: Mesdames McKean, Reid, Cornish, Angell, Stinchcombe, Horne, Seldon, Glass, Brunskill, Palmer, Wilde and Day, the Misses Quance, Tippet, Wotton, Lawson, Pickering, Down, Edgecumbe, Reddicliffe, Loram and Messrs Hutchings, Day, Lawson, Breakell, Brunskill, W. Day, Howe, Eveleigh, Smale, Parker, Cornish and Gorle. Guards: Messrs E. Maries and B. Maries. Coolies: Messrs Tremain and Casley. Swordbearer: Master Eddie Lee. In this production Mrs Gorle as the hon. producer also received assistance from Mr Bickle but retained her independence as conductor of an orchestra.

Quite early in the society's history major changes took place. The founder-producer-conductor, Mrs R.

Early Productions

Left: *The new company's first production,* HMS Pinafore, *in 1929.*

Below: *Some of the ladies of the chorus for the 1935 production,* The Pirates of Penzance. *The full chorus was composed of Mesdames M. Archard, F. Beaven, M, Brunskill, M. Cornish, C. Kew, B. Lias, E. Angel, M. Palmer, V. Parsons, and R. Stinchcombe, and the Misses M. Bulley, B. Creek, J. Lawson, W. Nash, B. Newcombe, D. Squire, and I. Quance.*

Left: *Mrs Bickle made a somewhat uncompromising Queen of the Fairies in the 1930 production of* Iolanthe.

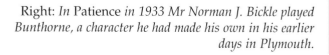

Above: *In the 1950s production local postmaster Mr Carter played his part.*

Right: *In* Patience *in 1933 Mr Norman J. Bickle played Bunthorne, a character he had made his own in his earlier days in Plymouth.*

Gorle, seemingly retired c.1931, having provided the company with a very firm foundation. Mr Norman J. Bickle, with his wife's support, was to become hon. producer for the company which, by then, had a core of some 60 or more performers, musicians and staff he could call upon. The choice for his first production was an interesting and spectacular opera, first presented 54 years earlier at the Savoy, although it was one that, at that time, was hardly as widely known as many others by Gilbert and Sullivan. Nevertheless, 'Okehampton Amateurs Shine in Comic Opera,' was the plaudit handed the company by the reporter of the *Western Times*.

On Tuesday November 17th 1931, the Society presented Okehampton with its version of *Ruddigore*, with the first performance under the distinguished patronage of the Mayor of Okehampton, Mr G.U. Fulford, and the Corporation. The reporter noted that the presentation had, 'something of a West Country flavour of the early-nineteenth century to it,' which was hardly surprising really since the scene in Act I depicts a fishing village in Cornwall. The scene opened with the village's professional bridesmaids, 'daintily represented by Miss Down and Mrs Horne,' singing before Rose's cottage, from which Mrs Bickle appears, as Hannah, to act as 'chorus' and sing the story of the legend of Sir Rupert Murgatroyd. Mrs Bickle obviously earned her part with her 'pleasing contralto voice', and she was 'well received by an appreciative audience.' The character, Mad Margaret, is for many one of the most highly regarded of Gilbert and Sullivan's creations, calling for the grotesque representation of the person to be contained in caricature and not slipping beyond it into the ludicrous. Styles of performance, and photography for that matter, have changed over the 70 or so years since Mrs P. Brooking played Mad Margaret and period pictures of players can be deceiving to the modern eye. It was therefore interesting to read that the reporter considered that she brought personality to her difficult part with marked success and that her facial expression deserved special mention.

The entry of Sir Despard, played by Mr Norman J. Bickle, was the signal for sustained applause, marking the early appreciation and regard that the man was to command as performer, producer and mentor to many for a great many years, and long after he made his final exit. One lady, who could just remember the 1930s operas, recalled Mr Bickle on stage, as a fascinating performer and as a strict disciplinarian during rehearsals. In 1931 those values were even then noticeable to the reporter who commented that his acting was 'in striking sympathy with the character', and that the 'finale to Act I was noticeable for the stateliness of the gavotte and the accurate dancing of the jig.' Yet the added comment that, 'The chorus work throughout was good, though the positioning on the stage left something to be desired,' certainly indicates that stagecraft, presence and positioning were still developing.

Local companies were not only taking an interest in the company's productions, they were actively engaged in them. Full recognition and credit was given by the reporter to Messrs T. Day and Sons Ltd, who were responsible for the lighting effects in the second act scene which is set in a picture gallery. They were responsible for lighting throughout of course and their work gained further mention when, 'Introduced and ended by 'Painted emblems of a race', the ghost scene was developed in a striking manner.' During the presentation of the ghost scene it was necessary to use a dimming apparatus but electricity was then still in its infancy – at least as far as Okehampton was concerned. The difficulty was met by manufacturing a resistance from a piece of slate off a billiard table by winding it with copper wire. It was probably the first 'dimming' contrivance ever used in the town.

The finale of *Ruddigore* brought a ground-breaking production to a climax, and there was long, sustained applause as a well-deserved tribute to one of the best performances the company had achieved, thus far.

The orchestra, which had been considerably strengthened, performed very capably according to reports, 'under the conductor, Mr H. Phillips', who, in turn, brought together even more musicians. The 'hon. producer' received special 'artistic' mention in one newspaper report that agreed:

... he merited the congratulations showered on him for a fine performance of one of the most difficult operas of Gilbert and Sullivan for an amateur society to undertake.

First night was under the patronage of the trustees of the Okehampton and District War Memorial Hospital; also in the audience were probably Mr Bickle's sternest critics, the officers and members of the Gilbert and Sullivan Fellowship, Plymouth.

The Okehampton company was now attracting civic recognition. Its headed notelets used in 1932 confirmed that it had a president, and holding that honorary but privileged office was His Worship the Mayor of Okehampton. It also advised note readers that Mr W.Q. Yeo was the hon. treasurer, and Mr E.G. Hawkins was hon. secretary, but omitted to give any hon. address to which a reply could be addressed. Nevertheless, the increasing size of the company confirms that budding thespians knew where to find it and reports of capacity audiences indicate that Okehampton's opera lovers were being satisfied.

The town was, at one time, considered as one to be added to the country's canal systems, but the plans never reached fruition and the opportunity of open-air opera in Okehampton was denied the hon. producer. This was perhaps most regretted when he launched the company into his production of *The Gondoliers* in 1932, and we shall never know just how far his undoubted talents as producer may have taken him. However, despite being hampered by the very small Market Hall stage the company sailed its way through another successful show. Once again, Messrs T. Day and Sons received special mention in the papers for their lighting effects, especially those first seen by the audience at the rise of the curtain on 'the Piazzetta, Venice'.

In the first-night audience was Mr W.B. Chamings, in a dual role as president of the company and Mayor of Okehampton. *The Gondoliers* added another success to the society's list, and the players were now well on the way through the Gilbert and Sullivan Savoy operas, although for their production in 1933 the hon. producer was forced to live up to a reputation he had gained in Plymouth some years earlier. As a leading member of the city's Gilbert and Sullivan Fellowship, Mr Bickle had gained a high reputation for his performances there in the role of Bunthorne, the somewhat fleshy poet in *Patience*.

In Okehampton by then it almost went without saying that an Operatic and Dramatic Society production would be a success, for on all previous occasions distinguished ability and histrionic talents had been shown by its members. This production was to continue to entertain as an amusing satire with dialogue and lyrics full of the richest farce. Mr Bickle lived up to his aforementioned reputation to score a big personal success in a wonderful production showing himself in a difficult part as an actor of great ability. 'Mr. Eric McKean,' said the papers:

... proved equally capable in the more robust part of Archibald Grosvenor (an Idyllic) Poet; Mr. Charles W. Buxton, as Colonel Calverley made a decided hit; and in Act II a trio by the Duke (Mr. Frank Horn), Major Murgatroyd (Mr Reginald Spear) and Colonel Calverley received an enthusiastic encore. The quintet, which followed and in which the Lady Angela (Mrs. D.C. Glass) and the Lady Saphir (Mrs. M.M. Reid) joined, was also a great successor and Mrs. Bickle's portrayal of the Lady Jane was a very finished performance.

The orchestra which played a most effective part in tunefully accompanying throughout consisted of: First violins, Mr. Mitchell (leader), Miss Pearse, Miss German; second violins, Miss Tippet, Miss Hamlyn, Miss White; violincello, Mr. Moir; flutes, Mr. F. Turner, Mr. W. Brown; cornets, Mr. H. Lee, Mr. W. Stoneman; contra bass Mr. Pranglin; clarinet, Mr. C. Purslow; drums, Mr. R. Lee; piano, Mrs. Tavener; conductor, Mr. H. Phillips.

With new hon. producers being encouraged to come forward and Mr Eric McKean taking on a revival of *The Mikado* as the next presentation the strong society was on such a successful course. We might have been tempted to leave a few years for a future fuller history of the society, but a 1934 cutting demanded further attention:

'Amateur success in spite of deranged cast'

It was all down to illness apparently, throwing the company into confusion, not a cast suffering mental affliction in memory of Mad Margaret.

During the weekend prior to first night two of the principals, Mr Frank Horn, a favourite with an Okehampton audience, who was cast as 'Nanki Poo', and Mr C.W. Buxton, who was taking the part of 'Pooh Bah', became indisposed. Saving the day at very short notice, Mr Bryn John (Exmouth Amateur Operatic Society), agreed to take Mr Horn's place, despite not having played 'Nanki Poo' for two years and only being able to attend one rehearsal. His performance, the reporters said 'was wonderfully good and of a high standard which won frequent appreciation from the audience.' Into the role of 'Pooh Bah' came Norman J. Bickle who enhanced his reputation with an outstanding performance. 'His acting and facial expressions gave an interpretation of this character, and he must be accorded the honours of the evening,' was the opinion in one newspaper. It was a baptism of fire for Mr Eric McKean the hon. producer but the papers lavishly congratulated him on the success of his first venture in that capacity in the local society and heaped glowing tributes on the whole company; almost.

The orchestra, conducted by Mr. H. Phillips, they conceded, added to the success of the opera, but then added that; 'there seemed times when their work lacked sympathy with the principals, and at least in one duet could have been more subdued with advantage.'

The company put up with the restrictions of the Market Hall stage in 1935 to present *The Pirates of Penzance* with Mr Norman J. Bickle returning as hon. producer, and with his resounding bass and convincing swagger making a great success of his role as the Pirate King. It was a production with impromptu variety, on the first night at least. The stage manager had previously drawn the attention of one of the piratical crew – an over-nervous curate – to a support holding up the scenery and warned him when making his entry to take care, but the reverend gentleman was so flustered that he fell awkwardly against the support and brought down the whole of the back scenery. Unaware of what had happened the principals continued with their performances. Needless to say, the audience was too polite to laugh.

Opportunities offered in *Cox and Box*, played as a curtain-raiser, were eagerly taken by players with little or no previous experience as principals. The newspapers noted that:

Mr. Jack Day was an able Box, and Mr. Douglas M. Archard, as Cox, was an outstanding success. The part of Bouncer was well played by Mr. Wallace Day.

By 1937 it becomes clear that the 'administrators' of

the society had achieved a great deal off-stage during the decade and in this instance 'administrators' probably includes a great many people. The society that had been founded by Mrs Gorle was now affiliated to the National Operatic & Dramatic Association and, not unusually, had a formal structure of officers and committee. The chairman was Mr T. Day, and vice-chairman W.Q. Yeo. Secretary was Mr P.J. Beavan, and the treasurer Mr R.W. Kew. The members of the general committee (with officers *ex officio*) were Mrs J.G. Tavener, Mrs W. Day, Messrs R. Day, H. Pyle, A. Stinchcombe and D.U. Archard, and there were sub-committees for opera and drama.

There was also an underlying strength that the society benefited from regularly which came from businesses and residents in the town and surrounding districts and the 'patronage rights' were conveyed upon specific groups for specific performances during the run of an opera or play – the first-night patrons being the Mayor, Aldermen, Councillors and officials of the borough, and thereafter on successive nights: pupils of Okehampton Grammar School; the Okehampton Simmons Bowling Club; Okehampton Rugby Football Club; and Okehampton Argyle Football Club.

A turn of events in 1937 has left something of a mystery that, 65 years later, still remains unsolved. The Society was staging *HMS* Pinafore that year with principal players Reginald Spear, Douglas U. Archard, Walter Mortimer, William H. Shellard, William Perryman, Richard Mills, Richard E. Yeo, Gladys M. Yeo, Hazel Wilson and Margaret A. Brooking; and supporting players Mesdames E. Angell, M. Lias, V. Parsons, M. Brunskill, C. Kew, M. Palmer, E. Routh, F. Beavan, H. Kitley and Misses M. Bulley, D. Squire, G. Squires, J. Lawson, B. Newcombe, H. Tapper, and Messrs W. Macbeth, C. Sillifant, S. Nash, S. Pook, P. Hayman, W. Seckington, S. Hales, W. Jenkins, W. Madders, J. Day, G.H. Dyer, R. Bissett and W. Jeffery. The orchestra under their conductor included Mr C. Faulkner Mutten; violins – Miss Pearse, Miss German, Miss Coldrey, Mr J. Bickle, Mr A. Millgate; violoncello – Mr F. Auty; contra bass – Mr W. Pranglen; clarinet – Mr C.S. Ireland; flute – Mr F. Turner; cornet – Mr W. Matthews; drums – Mr W. Crocker; and piano – Mrs M. Tavener. Mrs V. Parsons and Mrs W. Day assisted make-up supervisor Mrs M.A. Bickle, and Messrs A. Stinchcombe and H. Pyle were stage managers. Mr R. Spear was the carpenter. All of this represented a company of 57; with helpers, probably in excess of 60.

For their 1937 production the company staged their performances in Okehampton's new, and second, cinema; open for less than a year. It was built, the story goes, when the owners of the existing cinema in town, The Premier in Market Street, formerly the Okehampton Picture Palace, did not believe that anyone would be foolish enough to open a second one in competition. Mr W. Pope, an owner of

Above: *Okehampton's Carlton Cinema, being prepared for an evening, has served the town for over 60 years but shows no sign now of how major shows were produced in it.*

Left: *Cinema owner John Pope has spent much of his life behind the projector.*

'Cinedromes' in Liskeard, Wadebridge and Padstow, considered that there was business enough for two in town and was intent on adding another Cinedrome to his circuit. The site selected was a redevelopment area, formerly Painters Court, and Mr Pope submitted plans for a purpose-built cinema and two shops, one either side of the main entrance. The plan was rejected when it was realised that a right of way to Park Row had existed through the old passages of Painters Court. Alterations to the original plan and the deletion of one shop saved the day and provided for even better access, but Okehampton didn't get a cinedrome. The cinema's name was changed to the Carlton and, as such, has served the town for 70 years; continuing long after the Premier Cinema closed its doors. Today the Carlton, as an independent cinema, still serves the town well, screening new films soon after their general release and charging a very reasonable £2.50 admission charge; and long may it provide big-screen entertainment. That's enough of the commercials, what of the mystery?

The Carlton has remained unaltered since it was built and is now owned and run by Mr John Pope, son of the original owner. His original plans of the building, confirmed by the Town Council's copy, show seating for about 600, a shallow stage and limited wing-space leading to emergency exit doors. There was no provision made for a full, curtained stage, dressing-rooms, props, lighting controls or any other facilities to accommodate stage plays; or Gilbert and Sullivan operas. It was done, but no plans or records have been found showing how.

People, now in their mid-eighties, recall 'wonderful shows... on a fair size stage.' 'They had a good lot

1950s–'70s

Left: *The chorus for the 1952 production of* The Pirates of Penzance *included,* seated: *Mrs J. Hawking, and Mrs/Miss Bicknell, J. Slee, ? Cann.*

Below: *A scene from the WI production of* Snow White and The Seven Dwarfs *in January 1959.*

Below left: *The ladies of the WI ready for the 1973 Pageant at Okehampton Castle, in which the release of slaves in 1050 was depicted and they also resurrected the ghost of Lady Howard.*

Below: *A scene from* Boeing Boeing *produced in 1978; Donald Baker* (standing), *Maud Hall – maid, Roger Partridge* (seated) *with two of three air hostesses who were played by Grace Baker, Jenny Pedrick and Jackie Dagwell.*

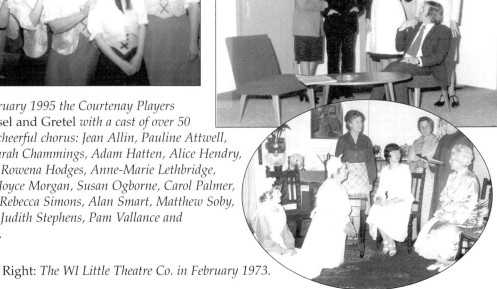

Above: *In February 1995 the Courtenay Players presented* Hansel and Gretel *with a cast of over 50 including this cheerful chorus: Jean Allin, Pauline Attwell, Val Bennett, Sarah Chammings, Adam Hatten, Alice Hendry, Susan Hubber, Rowena Hodges, Anne-Marie Lethbridge, Lita Meardon, Joyce Morgan, Susan Ogborne, Carol Palmer, Jenny Pedrick, Rebecca Simons, Alan Smart, Matthew Soby, Beth Stephens, Judith Stephens, Pam Vallance and Geoff Wheatley.*

Right: *The WI Little Theatre Co. in February 1973.*

In 1983 Okehampton Young Farmers' Club members took to the competitive stage, nationally, in Okehampton Goes To War, and came third.

of light. It was electric, you know, marvellous. We didn't have electric at home.' 'Oh yes, us went home through the big doors by the stage. There was a lady opened them… and let us out.' Mr Pope was unaware that the Carlton had been used as a theatre but, with emergency exits obviously available for use, had no idea how a large cast, crew, costumes and props could have been easily accommodated. Someone out there will have the answer, and possibly a stage-area layout, but until they are found or come forward the mystery remains.

The *Post and Weekly News* reporter was impressed enough with the show on November 16th to write enthusiastically that:

Okehampton possesses amateur actors of ability far beyond the average [as] realised by the audience present at the Carlton Cinema, Okehampton, on Tuesday night when the first performance of "H.M.S. Pinafore" was given by members of the Okehampton Amateur Operatic Society. The Mayor and Mayoress (Mr. and Mrs. S. J. Rich) and many members of the council with their wives were present and with the rest of the audience were enthusiastic in their appreciation of the talented acting.

The performance went through without a hitch, the nervousness which generally attends a first perform-ance being replaced by a joyous confidence... each member of it seemed peculiarly fitted to the part taken. It was a brilliant performance and enhanced a reputa-tion already high.

Advertisements in programmes sold for productions such as this are a rich source of information and can provide illuminating insights into services provided in the past:

EVENING SHOES Make your choice from the very Latest Styles in Dress Wear Coloured Crepe to match every shade... Bar or Court in Silver Kid and Gold Kid. ANY SHADE MATCHED IN 48 HOURS... 1937 Styles for the Christmas Festivities Worden's, Arcade, Okehampton

The Quality Shop 'Two Steeples', 'Sportsman' and 'Chilprufe' Knitwear for Ladies 'Celanese' and 'Chilprufe' Undies F.B. YEO 17, The Arcade

'Veritas' Perfection Oil Cooking Stoves. 2-Burner Stove 3-Burner Stove 4-Burner Stove £4.10s.0d. £5.12s.0d. £6.16s.0d. Single Oven 27/- Double Oven 33/- Single Burner Stove with Oven 48/- James Wright & Sons, Okehampton 'Phone 41.

NOW OPEN. NEW CARLTON SHOP – Adjoining the Carlton Cinema. For High-Class Confectionery, Stationery, Tobaccos, and Fancy Goods. Chocolates and Lyons Ices on sale at this Performance. Obtainable from the attendants.

BRITISH CARS ARE BETTER BUILT Study this – significant fact More than two thirds of total increase in New Car Sales for Twelve Months were Austins. The increase in new-car registrations in Great Britain and Northern Ireland for the 12 months ending July 31st, 1937, over the preceding 12 months was 23,414. OF THIS INCREASE 68.5% INCREASE WERE AUSTIN CARS !

No further proof is necessary that the public appreciates Austin quality. You buy a car – but you invest in an AUSTIN See a representative range of Austin cars at T DAY & SONS, LTD., OKEHAMPTON. 'Phone 7.

The Society's second version of *Pinafore* was given in a packed and comfortable cinema, and to the accompaniment of an orchestra augmented by late members of the old Theatre Royal, Plymouth. Contributing to the presentation in this largely agricultural district were chemists, watchmakers, butchers, drapers, bank clerks, railwaymen, commercial travellers, mechanics, postmen and, of course, farmers.

'Delightful from beginning to end' was the universal opinion of the audiences who, in March the following year, assembled at the Carlton Cinema again, to witness side-splitting performances of the farce *Tons of Money*. The play evolves around Aubrey Henry Maitland Allington being left half-a-million dollars which might otherwise have gone to his long-lost, presumed dead, cousin George. With creditors closing in Aubrey's wife has the bright idea that Aubrey should disappear, and that his death be presumed. Then, he would make a reappearance as long-lost cousin George, claim the fortune, cheat his creditors and later 'marry' the grieving widow. On Mr A.E. Stinchcombe and Mrs N. Day, as Mr and Mrs Allington, depended the success of the play, for on them devolved most of the work; and they responded admirably: 'Mrs. M.L. Tavener as Miss Benita Mullett, a deaf spinster aunt, proved a delightful comic', 'Mr. W.M. Day, as Sprules, the butler, was an undoubted success, as also was Miss Winifred Betts as Simpson the parlour maid.' Mr Reginald Spear as Giles, the gardener, had a smaller part to play than usual, but he acted in 'his own inimitable humorous style and his every appearance was greeted with applause and laughter.' Supported by Mr S. Nash as a prim and precise solicitor, Miss M. Tavener, a sentimental deserted wife, and Mr W.E. Seckington and Mr Harry Pyle, the company brought home another success.

Audiences left the Carlton looking forward eagerly to the next production. None could have foreseen that the following year's *The Rebel Maid* would be overshadowed by a Second World War, throughout much of which the society suspended its activities. In 1944 some from the society, but then as 'Okehampton Amateur Dramatic Club', staged *The Man in Dark Glasses*, following it up in 1945 with *Charity Begins...* and in 1946 with two productions, *Living Room* and *The Blue Goose*, and raising over £400 for charity by doing so.

The move away from Gilbert and Sullivan was not new. The society had produced *The Dover Road* in 1931 and, among others, *To Have the Honour* was staged in 1935 and the ever popular *The Ghost Train* the following year. The society members' revival of *The Dover Road* in 1947 preceded its new version of *The Mikado* in 1948.

Post-war England was far from finally emerging from the rigours of war, but while rationing was still restrictive and many foods scarce, society members decided that there was going to be no further rationing on the entertainment and they launched into a schedule that gave the town two productions in 1949, a fresh version of *Ruddigore* and a production of *Death takes a Holiday*. By now there were differences of opinion on future productions. Some members wished the society to continue with its mixed programme of Gilbert and Sullivan and straight plays, while others wanted to tackle other theatrical forms. What theatre-goers were to see was the decline of the Okehampton Amateur Operatic and Dramatic Society and the emergence of a new company, the Courtenay Arts Club; which was later to become The Courtenay Players.

On February 14th 1950 a 'membership' meeting was held at which 138 people paid 2s.6d. (12^{1}/$_{2}$p) to launch the club. It then included sections for film and photography but its first production was to be a panto, *Aladdin*. During the 1951/52 season, the old society produced *The Yeomen of the Guard*, followed by *Pink String and Sealing Wax*, and notes in the programme, priced 4d., sold at the 7–9th February performances informed patrons that the next production was to be *The Pirates of Penzance*, with *Box and Cox*.

With the enthusiasm for theatre generated by members of the new club, through the 1950s and '60s the town was treated to a veritable feast of theatre that satisfied all tastes. Among many others *Murder at the Vicarage*, *Charlie's Aunt*, *A Murder has been Arranged* and *Dry Rot* were produced and enjoyed and were followed by *The White Sheep of the Family* and *Night Must Fall*, to name just a few from two decades. The Courtenay Arts Club, however, was not the only performing force in town. In November 1971 Mrs Vera Hodgkinson turned back the clock and relived the past in what has been a familiar role for her. Mrs Hodgkinson was the wife of the licensee of the Plume of Feathers and she stepped in when Okehampton WI were looking for someone to produce their plays. She knows possibly as much as anyone what the stage was about. After studying at the Ben Greet Academy she was playing at the Garrick Theatre in London when she met her husband, Harold, who was rehearsing a part in *Dracula*. Together they ran their own repertory theatre in various centres in the North. In Exeter, during the war, they ran semi-professional shows for the troops and one of their achievements, after taking over the Three Crowns at Chagford, was to put in a theatre, the scene of many successful plays and pantomimes. Mrs Hodgkinson not only produced the WI performances, but provided the Bijou Theatre, converted from a small room in the yard of the hotel; which many may recall as the skittle alley. She furnished the stage and in setting it out was helped by Mrs Marion Dawkins. The Bijou Theatre certainly lived up to its name and in it, for quite some time, the WI were to perform wonders of movement in one-act plays.

The first play at the Bijou, *Untimely Ripp'd* by Maurice McLoughlin, was a thought-provoking drama on the rights and wrongs of abortion played in the atmosphere of an approved school for girls run by nuns. The subject was treated with delicacy and refinement and made an impact. Performances of real stature came from Joyce Morgan (Sister Pauline), Finola Rudd (Dr Ellis), Ernestine Morgan (Revd Mother), Jennifer Pedrick (Janet Logan) and Marjorie Whittaker (Mrs Owen, JP). The second, *Repent at Leisure* by Cherry Vooght, was a more light-hearted offering, showing the explosive qualities underlying pre-nuptial family tension when people of the argumentative calibre of Grandma (well played by Dorothy Matthews) are around. That all ended happily was due to Marjorie Elliott (Mrs Baxter). The cast included Susan Hearn, delightful as the bride-to-be, Rhoda Jordan (Aunt Margaret), Grace Brewer (Rose), Evelyn Spear (Lady Munday), and Adelaide Ward (Alice).

The WI has a high reputation nationally for one-act plays of high standard and the Okehampton branch maintained that standard. Not to be outdone, the Courtenay Arts Group treated the town to 'five' scenes in a single play the following year with Noel Coward's *Still Life*. The strong cast included Erica Tey, Patricia Crosbie, Pauline Wakeham, Christopher Bosher, John Crosbie, Margaret Boshor, Douglas Whittaker, Ivor Greenslade, Janet Dei'ert, Lily Allin and Roger Partridge. Roger, a relative newcomer, was to play a major role in the future of entertainment in Okehampton, writing and producing pantos, directing plays and revues, and nurturing new talent. In 2002 it is clear that his ability and drive have inspired others and ensured the continuing success of the club he first joined and the Courtenay Players, of which he is now President.

Back in the 1970s, though, even the strong arts club could not resist a good one-act play and slipped in, for pre-Coward hors d'oeuvre, *When the Cock Crows*, a rural comedy by Joe Corrie. And what an appetiser this turned out to be with Raymond Vallance sparking gales of laughter as George Hazelwood, a farm labourer with a honeyed tongue who sets out to win the heart of the dragon of a housekeeper for a bet. The papers said of Mr Vallance, who was later to take on the role of Mayor of Okehampton, that he 'proved himself a resourceful and ingratiating Petruchio and had an admirable foil in Joyce Pengelly as Eliza Bridwell, the modern Katherine.' Pauline Wakeham and Hilary Wreford acted as the maids, and Roger Partridge was the lovelorn nephew – who 'all hovered effectively in the background,' the report added.

The main course, from Noel Coward, was on the theme of *Brief Encounter* set in a station refreshment room in 1936 where, amid the life of the station, two strangers meet and fall in love and play out their affair. As the two lovers, John Crosbie and Erica Teys 'displayed all the frustration and heartache of romance and were splendidly supported by the rest of the players'; Chris Bother was an ebullient ticket collector and Patricia Crosbie a hard-bitten manageress. Other station staff included Roger Partridge, Pauline Wakeham and Janet Dei'ert, while, as travellers, Douglas Whittaker, Ivor Greenslade, Margaret Bosher and Lily Allin 'more than authenticated the buffet atmosphere.'

The plays were directed by Finola Rudd and C.D. Gerrard Mills and backstage or front of house were Cyril Dutton, William Strong, Victor Graham Deakin, Tony Short, William Savage, David Easterbrook, Margaret Vallance, Florence Freeman, Margaret Brooking, Marjorie Whittaker and Maud Hall.

During the 1970s the Courtenay Arts Club took the initiative in developing new productions and through them encouraged talent for variety to come to the fore. *Courtenay Capers* in 1972 provided an evening of music, sketches and comedy from a cast including Lily Allin, John Crosbie, Patricia Crosbie, Josephine Hooper, Michael Hooper, Norman Judge, Audrey Knight, Roger Partridge, Joyce Pengelly, William Strong, Raymond Vallance, Marjorie Whittaker and Deborah Young. Two years later the *Courtenay Revue* and a Festival Concert Party secured the future for some of the talents that had taken tremendous steps forward in a short period of time. For *The Camel's Back* in 1974 the club fielded a strong team in the form of Norman Judge, Hilary Wreford, Maud Hall, Deborah Young, Rosina Young, Roger Partridge, Erica Teys, Pat Crosbie and John Crosbie. Comedy came to the fore again in 1975 when the competent company switched from *Old Tyme Music Hall* to *The Chiltern Hundreds* and onwards into *Pools Paradise* – satisfying their audiences every time.

All tastes were being catered for, as confirmed with productions of *Tell Tale Murder* and *Lloyd George Knew My Father* the following year. The talents that had been developing were, by now, looking towards new challenges and, as with its Gilbert and Sullivan based predecessor, the Courtenay Arts Club appears to have been heading towards two paths diverging in a yellow wood, and some wanted to take the one less trodden. One thing was obviously not being forgotten – the charitable side of enjoying amateur dramatics. The 1978 'Music Hall' production produced a club donation to the town of £137.74, to go towards its St James' Church tower fund. The year also produced what now stands out as a turning point for amateur entertainment in Okehampton. The Stan Forrester production of *Boeing, Boeing* hilariously revealed to the audience that what goes on in a flat near the Orly Airport in Paris is nobody's business, unless they were fortunate enough to have a ticket for this show. With the help of what turned out to be an ideal cast the comedy written by Marc Camoletti

1950s–'70s

The cast of **Summer Showtime** *presented by the Courtenay Players on 20th July–24th August and September 21st 1994 included Hayley Allin, Jean Allin, Pauline Attwell, Christopher Bennett, Valerie Bennett, Graham Cross, John Hammond, Alice Hendry, John Hubber, Christopher Kite, Joe Lindsay, Lita Meardon, Carol Palmer, Roger Partridge, Jenny Pedrick, Carol Pellow, Karen Pellow, Alison Rounsley, Horace Rutley, Rebecca Simmons, Alan Smart, Ron Tudge, Maureen Venton, Pam Vallance and Perry Vallance. MD was Terry Bennet.*

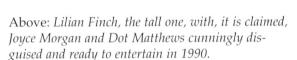

Above: *Lilian Finch, the tall one, with, it is claimed, Joyce Morgan and Dot Matthews cunningly disguised and ready to entertain in 1990.*

Above left: *The WI Little Theatre Co. produced* Untimely Ripp'd *in 1971 with Finola Rudd as Dr Ellis, Jennifer Pedrick as Janet, Ernistine Morgan as Revd Mother, Joyce Morgan as Sister Pauline and Marjorie Whittaker as Mrs Own JP.*

Below: *On or off stage the Handbell Ringers are always appreciated as here at Christmas 2001.*

Above: *Enjoying theatre at an early age are these woodland animals appearing in the 1995 Courtenay Arts production of* Hansel and Gretel: *Rebecca Butland, Samantha Durston, Katy Copeman, Alice Griffith, Lauren Hutt, Karen Jameson, Stacey Kettlewhite, Sophie King, Annette Mortlock, Jen Mortlock, Laura Mortlock, Martyn Partridge, Kathryn Penna, Amy Stephens, Sebastian Stevens and Lucy Williams.*

certainly took off as Bernard, a Gallic Casanova of the modern school, was seen to be making a habit of wooing airline stewardesses. A meticulous timetable ensures girls arrive and depart oblivious not only to being double-timed, but treble-timed. But, when turning up simultaneously, the timetable is well and truly upset. The result is a hilarious romp – of the 'Whitehall Theatre' genre that calls upon the players to 'live' the ensuing situations with a tremendous sense of fun and panache. Much of the action depends upon split-second timing and this, the newspapers reported:

... was achieved to a remarkable degree. In the Cary Grant-like role of Robert, the old school chum pitchforked into the heart of the polygamous happenings, Roger Partridge navigated a path through the complications delightfully. It was a performance to savour. As Bernard, Donald Baker made up a formidable team, extricating himself astutely from the rigmarole of embarrassments and showing a rich flair of humour. The performances of the three airhostesses were beyond praise. No American, German, or French airline could have had a more attractive or zany lot than Grace Baker, Jenny Pedrick and Jackie Dagwell, the last named making her stage debut, and what a good one it was.

Another notable contribution came from Maud Hall, as the unromantic, long-suffering maid doomed to turning out the appropriate Continental or New World dish at a moment's notice.

Rightly buoyant with success, the club launched into yet another theatrical art form – the musical – but problems began for the cast of *Salad Days* only hours before curtain-up on the first night. Peter Allcock and Jackie Downing had to pull out at the last moment – and other actors stood in or doubled up in roles. The cast, however, seems to have coped well with the situation. Director Mair Naris was congratulated for introducing a highly imaginative opening to the show. The audience was greeted by a Tramp, happily playing his piano, and then saw him walking away from it... with the piano still apparently playing. The stage was set, therefore, for the action with the audience already aware that this was no ordinary piano. After the opening chorus the two leading characters, Timothy and Jane, two university graduates (played by solicitor Roger Partridge and music teacher Carlyn Patterson) are alone, deciding their future. In the duets and solos that follow, Carlyn 'excelled herself by capturing the hearts of the audience with her sensitive acting and powerful voice.' Timothy, likewise, 'sang with feeling though he apparently found the extensive number of lines a little too demanding.' The newspaper report, perhaps a little unfairly, points to what was considered a fault in the production, when, to the reporter's knowledge at least, the parts of Rowena and PC Boot, two lovers in the show, were played by real-life mother and son,

Grace and Kevin Baker; who weren't criticised for poor performances. The second 'annoyance' the reporter suffered may have been much more justified: 'there was a lack of dance routines in a play whose central theme concerns a piano that makes people dance.' This was only aggravated during the number 'Out of Breath' where members of the chorus:

... walked backwards and forwards singing 'I'm spinning like a top,' and similarly, during Jane's solo 'I sit in the sun,' she didn't at all and went twirling around the stage instead.

However, the critic was impressed with a breakfast-room scene during which Timothy's mother (Aline Forrester), father (Stan Forrester), and the nagging Aunt Prue (Patricia Crosbie) combined their talents in a musical number that calls for split-second timing, and it was noted that 'the amusing over-exaggeration of Aunt Prue's character by Patricia Crosbie was especially well done. Not so appreciated were the Inspector, played by John Crosbie, and Timothy's mother (Aline Forrester) who 'threw away some of their best lines, though it probably didn't help having a rather slow audience.'

Norman Judge, juggling two roles, apparently, 'grew in confidence as the play progressed' and Donald Baker was 'excellent as Nigel' but was expected to 'probably wish to forget his performance in doubling up as the gay Ambrose, owner of a dress shop.' Good performances, however, were reported from Rosina Young (Lady Raeburn) and John Young (Uncle Zed), another mother-and-son duo, Beryl Bowles (Fiona) and Jackie Dagwell as the stunning nightclub dancer Asphyxia; and 'the scenery was scant though the piano well done.'

For the record the musical director was Maud Hall; stage presentation: Stan Forrester; choreographer: Grace Baker; house manager: Barry Matthews; wardrobe: Joan Barnes, Margaret Vallance; backstage crew: John Brockman, Janet Brockman, Dick Ames, Stephen Brockman, Kay Judge, Richard Johns and Richard Rose.

For many of the artistes the 'local crit' may well have been one that was upsetting. Under the circumstances in which they found themselves performing, they may have considered it unfair. One of the critic's final comments, 'the Courtenay Arts Club's ambitious production of *Salad Days* gave Okehampton its first real taste of a grand-scale, musical,' may have been appreciated while the comment, 'In essence *Salad Days* lacked salt and pepper', was probably upsetting.

If that were so it was unfortunate since the critic was probably the best friend that the Courtenay Arts Club could have come across at that time. Ignoring the strange remarks about mother and son, every production or performance criticism made provided actors and their producer with guidance to build on.

Regularly taking to the stage for many years has been the Okehampton Excelsior Silver Band, here seen in 1980 in competition at Paignton. Left to right, back row: A. Martin, R. Beardon, R. Mooney, J. Hawking, M. Vallance, K. Milton, J. Braizier, L. Hawking, N. Warren; middle row: A. Gilbert, A. Packer, M. Fallon, P. Martin, G. Stevens, R. Baker, A. Braizier, B. Vallance, E. Stapelton, N. Braizier, V. Packer; front: K. Bond, A. Vallance, K. Vallance, Reg Beardon, D. Allin, H. Woodley, D. Vallance.

The experience gained by the entire *Salad Days* company has undoubtedly filtered down to the performers and producers of today and it is highly likely that every single production down the years has benefited on the way. Since that time dozens of plays, pantomimes and musicals, including *Babes in the Wood*, *The Sound of Music*, *Arsenic and Old Lace*, and *South Pacific* have been enjoyed by thousands. And, soon after the *Salad Days* lessons were learned, as they surely were, the Courtenay Arts Club received this crit:

Boos, hisses, applause, and some lusty singing were provided by a willing audience at the opening night of Aladdin, *the Okehampton Courtenay Arts Club pantomime production – all in just the right places. These traditional panto ingredients were all that was required after the club members had written their own script, rehearsed, and prepared stage, scenery, costumes and lighting. The bouncy tale of the poor laundry boy who triumphs over Abanazar, the evil magician, and finally wins the hand of Princess Precious Moon, is peppered with plenty of lively singing and dancing – enhanced by the splendid scenery and beautiful costumes. Particular favourites with the many children in the big audience were Ping Pong, the colourful dog (Perry Vallance), the huge teapot, and the way the characters came off the stage and into the main hall. The hard work the cast had put into the preparations soon rubbed off – that's a pun – on the audience, but special mention should be made of Widow Twankey, a really professional*

performance from Roger Partridge. The wicked Abanazar was well played by John Brockman, a late replacement for Norman Judge, who was unwell; and Aladdin (Jenny Pedrick) and the Princess (Tracy Podd) tackled their major parts with imagination and spirit. The Genie of the Ring (Lindsay Jenkins) and the Genie of the Lamp (Lilian Finch) were also worthy of extra praise. Other characters: Wing Wong – Beryl Ames; Wing Wang – Maureen Venton; Grand Vizier Chop Suey – John Crosbie; Mandarin Ebenezer Chow Mein – Neil Allden; Lily Flower – Jackie Dagwell; Lotus Blossom – Mandy Jennison; Confusious Chang – Ray Valiance; Windywoo – Mark Drew. Hong Kong citizens – Doris Layton, Nibs Morgan, Joyce Morgan, Alice Hendry, Lilian Finch; principal dancers – Alison Bayfield, Helen Congdon, Sarah Moss, Rachel Moss, Julia Boreham; chorus – members of Langton School of Dancing. Stage manager – Gordon Naris; lighting – Richard Johns; musical director – Neil Allden; props – Margaret Vallance; wardrobe – Alice Hendry; pianist – Joan Barnes; front of house – Dick Ames; production secretary – Joyce Morgan; producer – Mair Naris. A donation was made to the Okehampton and district branch of the Muscular Dystrophy Group from profits.

The Okehampton Courtenay Players inherited a firm foundation when the group took over the role as amateur entertainment providers to the town and with each production they continue the tradition of providing the best their talents can achieve; just as Mrs Gorle's company of performers set out to do in 1928.

12

Heritage Comes in Many Valued Guises

Okehampton Fire Brigade

After entering Parliament in 1735 to represent Old Sarum, William Pitt (the elder) was returned to Parliament on December 11th 1756 as member for Okehampton, and in that year became Secretary of State and leader of the House of Commons. He also had strong family connections with one Thomas Pitt, his grandfather, but whether or not that gentleman, who died in 1726, was the Thomas Pitt who presented the town with a fire engine is not clear.

The honour of being the earliest club organisation or society still active in Okehampton goes to the Okehampton Fire Service; a worthy group of fully trained volunteers. It was Simon Newcombe who accepted the honorary post of Captain of the Brigade in 1900 and the fire appliance then being used was a horse-drawn pump. In 1941 the National Fire Service was formed as a temporary expedient in that time of crisis but following the war years the Auxiliary Fire Service was formed; later to be changed to the Devon County Fire Brigade. The original Okehampton Fire Station in Market Street housed one engine in a building that was part of the 'weighbridge' premises. In 1960 the present station was built at North Road, to house two fire appliances; the number required to be stationed in the larger towns only.

In 1973 the city brigades and Devon County Fire Brigade were amalgamated, resulting in the formation of the Devon Fire Brigade but this became The Devon Fire and Rescue Service in 1987 to better reflect the role of the modern fire service. Today, the North Road station crews attends over 200 calls per year, ranging from fires, flooding, emergency special service calls and road traffic accidents. The station has a complement of 18 men, retained and fully trained fire officers who, while having other jobs, provide Okehampton and the surrounding area with 24-hour, 365-day cover. The station not only responds to calls within its own station area but can attend any large fire in Devon; one appliance attended a fire which caused enormous damage to Dingles department store in Plymouth and helped stop it spreading further. In 1991 the Graham Reeves company in Okehampton suffered the most recent major fire. In a none-too-cautious age the retained firemen are often found at local fairs and village events where they can draw attention to safety awareness issues and meet the public in better circumstances than might occur if their safety messages are ignored.

Above: *Devon Fire & Rescue Service, Station 13, Okehampton 2001.*

Right: *Okehampton Fire Brigade of 1911 with Mayor John Cornish at German's boot factory.*

Freemasons

At a preliminary meeting held at the White Hart Hotel in January 1878, it was decided to endeavour to establish a Masonic Lodge in Okehampton and Bro. Brodie and others volunteered to investigate the possibility. The following month they reported that the Provincial Grand Master Bro., the Revd John Huyshe, had, after careful consideration, concluded the town could support a Lodge, there being a considerable population in it and a railway station about to be established. However, his support was conditional upon Bro. Brodie consenting to and being recommended as the first Worshipful Master of the Lodge. A petition containing the following signatories was drawn up and submitted to the Provincial Grand Master who attached his certificate recommending the granting of the prayer of the petitioners:

William Brodie	Semper Fidelis Lodge	No. 1254
William Pidsley	Semper Fidelis Lodge	No. 1254
Benjn Barber	Semper Fidelis Lodge	No. 1254
James W. Boon	The Lodge of Sincerity	No. 189
J.J. Ball	Semper Fidelis Lodge	No. 1254
Robt. T. Relf	Lodge of Concord	No. 463
G.W. Gould	Bedford Lodge	No. 282
A. J. G. Waters	Semper Fidelis Lodge	No. 1254
A. Paddon	Semper Fidelis Lodge	No. 1254

A Warrant of Constitution dated April 24th 1878 was granted by the Grand Master, His Royal Highness Albert Edward, Prince of Wales. The Lodge of Obedience No. 1753 was duly founded, constituted and consecrated on August 26th 1878, at a Provincial Grand Lodge held in the schoolroom in North Lane by the Right Worshipful Provincial Grand Master, Bro. the Revd John Huyshe, PGC. Over 400 attended the ceremony and Bro. Samuel Jones, PPGSD, was deputed to install Bro. William Brodie in the Chair as Worshipful Master for the ensuing year. Once installed, Bro. Brodie then appointed and invested his Officers; Brothers B. Barber, W. Pidsley, J.W. Boon, Revd C.W.H. Holley, R.T. Relf, G.W. Gould, A.J.G. Waters, J.J. Ball, A. Paddon and J. Coombe. The Lodge, ready to become part of the community, was far from secretive about this. The Brethren formed a procession and, headed by the First Devon Militia Band, marched to the White Hart Hotel for a banquet.

Freemasonry is not a religion, nor an alternative to religion. It demands of its members a belief in a 'Supreme Being' but provides no system of faith on its own. The Lodge was soon operational, meeting at the White Hart Hotel on the last Monday of each month, with a joining fee of 30s.0d., initiation fees at 5 guineas and annual subscription of 1 guinea. By March 1879 there were 20 members, an increase of 10 in under nine months, and soon after the turn of the century membership stood at 57. Members resided in the Exeter, Holsworthy, Tavistock and Plymouth area,

but the majority were in the Okehampton area. Distant members could travel by train and excursion tickets to Okehampton, which in 1897 were: from Exmouth and Lympstone 3s.0d.; from Topsham 2s.6d. by all trains up to 1.30p.m., returning 8.33p.m. or 9.45p.m.; from Exeter, Queen Street or St David's 2s.0d. by all trains up to 3.10p.m., returning 8.33p.m. or 9.45p.m.; from St Cyres or Crediton 2s.0d. by all trains up to 2.05p.m., returning 8.33p.m. or 9.45p.m.; from Holsworthy 1s.6d. by 10.50a.m., 12 noon and 2.22p.m. trains, returning 8.37p.m.; from Plymouth (Friary or North Road) and Devonport 2s.6d., Tavistock 1s.6d. by all trains up to 2.15p.m., trains for Friary returning 8.18p.m. or 10.55p.m. A special train left Okehampton for all stations to Exeter at 9.45p.m., connecting with last trains from Exeter to Exmouth, Dawlish, Teignmouth, etc.

In 1888 the Lodge purchased a Bell American Organ for £12.17s.3d., carriage paid from London, and with a six-year warranty. A regular topic of conversation was the need for permanent premises and a decision was made in 1899 to purchase land known as Nathan's Plot on which to build a Freemasons' Hall. Tenders were invited. Of six received, the lowest, at £415, from John Sleeman, was accepted, trustees were empowered to borrow from the bankers and to later mortgage the completed building. On August 27th 1900, the Brethren congregated at the Church Room, formed a procession and proceeded to the Town Hall where the Mayor and Corporation awaited them and who then headed the procession to St James' Church for a service. At its close the procession reformed and proceeded to the site of Freemasons' Hall. The ceremony there was opened with prayer by the Provincial Grand Chaplain. A silver trowel was presented to the Acting Provincial Grand Master, W. Bro. G.C. Davie, PGD, who, after addressing the assembly, placed a record of proceedings of the ceremony in position and lowered a Corner Stone onto it. On August 26th 1901, Freemasons' Hall was dedicated in due and ancient form to Freemasonry, virtue, universal benevolence and friendship by W. Bro. G.C. Davie, PGD, Deputy and Acting Provincial Grand Master. The cost of providing and furnishing the hall was as follows:

Item	£	s.	d.
Purchase of lease of site	165	0	0
Legal costs and expenses	15	6	0
	180	**6**	**0**
Amount of building contract	415	0	0
Extras on contract	79	2	0
	494	**2**	**0**
Furnishings	31	11	7
Mortgage and bank charges	15	12	0
Architect's claim (disputed)	25	12	0
TOTAL	**747**	**3**	**7**

The cost was met as follows:

By mortgage	450	0	0
Contribution from Lodge Funds	200	0	0
Donations	97	3	7
TOTAL	**747**	**3**	**7**

The architect's claim was disputed as the trustees were convinced that the architect, a member of the Lodge, had undertaken the work in an honorary capacity, and the dispute was settled arbitrarily in the sum of £15.15s.0d. through the intervention of the Provincial Grand Secretary following threatened litigation in the Court.

The single-storey building provided barely adequate room, and expansion plans for a dining hall and caretaker's cottage were being prepared c.1906. Building and funding advice received led to a limited liability company being formed to take over the lease of the property and responsibilities of the trustees; thus the Okehampton Freemasons' Hall Company Limited was formed in 1909. Of the four building tenders received, the lowest, at £748 from J. Sleeman and Son, was accepted. Freemasons' Hall Co. Ltd repaid the balance of an earlier loan of £450, issued £1 shares, 307 preference and 378 ordinary, and raised another loan of £1,000 on a mortgage of the whole premises. It also offered the Lodge an agreement to take Freemasons' Hall (with cottage) for a term of 14 years at a rent of £52 per annum, which was accepted. The surplus accommodation fronting Station Road was let as offices to Mr G.D. Cann, solicitor, at £30 per annum. (The £1,000 loan was repaid in 1921.) After completion of the work the Freemasons' Hall was reopened on October 31st 1910 and the occasion was marked by the unveiling of a memorial tablet by the Deputy Provincial Grand Master, W. Bro. John Stocker, PAGDC.

One of the three main Principles of Freemasonry is 'Brotherly Love' and every true Freemason will show tolerance and respect for the opinions of others and behave with kindness and understanding to his fellow creatures. This must have been tested during early setbacks and disappointments such as when a founder member was imprisoned for embezzlement but, after 32 years, the Lodge was a healthy body with a membership of 57.

As soon as the building was reopened after building operations, the Masonic Club was formed, and in 1912 a billiards table was installed. In 1917 country membership for members residing outside a radius of 50 miles of Okehampton was accepted unanimously. Freemasons follow 'Relief' as their second Great Principle and are taught to practise charity and to care not only for their own but also for the community as a whole. In addition to the usual charities, both the Lodge and Brethren contributed to the fund for building the Okehampton Cottage Hospital as the Lodge felt it was fitting to identify itself with efforts being made to meet a much-needed want.

By the time of its jubilee in 1928, Lodge membership stood at 103, despite the formation of Lodges at Bude and Holsworthy, but in following advice given to all Lodges not to solicit or press persons to join the craft, the Masons' apparent 'secrecy' continued to be perceived by others.

In 1929 a lych-gate at the entrance of the new burial-ground at Okehampton Parish Church was installed by the Lodge, at an estimated cost of £70 to £80, paid for by subscriptions from the Brethren. On completion, a service of dedication was held at the Parish Church on July 28th 1929, the preacher being Revd the Venerable F.W. Surtees, MA, Archdeacon of Exeter, later to become Provincial Grand Master of the Province of Devonshire.

The third of the Great Principles that Freemasons are expected to live by is truth, since striving for truth requires and builds high moral standards. Building on the foundation of their principles and following in the footsteps of others, the Masons of the Lodge of Obedience in Okehampton have continued to meet regularly in their hall over the past 74 years. They have quietly (often known only to recipients) supported and assisted local groups and charities as well as national and international ones. Yet throughout that time the Freemasonry, rightly or wrongly, has been considered by many to be a secretive, if not secret society. On Tuesday July 2nd 2002 the Mason of Okehampton attempted to sweep away any doubts that members of the public might hold by opening the doors of the Freemasons' Hall and inviting people in; and were soon showing their visitors into their 'Temple', their meeting-place within the Hall. The leader of the Lodge's Masons, the Worshipful Master, was on hand to explain the origins of his own honorary title, which lay with the Master Masons responsible for building cathedrals throughout Britain and the Continent. Anyone entering the Hall with doubts must certainly have left with a clearer understanding and awareness that local charities, including the new hospital, benefit from the unpublicised work of the Masons. Judging by the numbers visiting the Hall on that occasion, perhaps the Lodge might consider inviting senior school groups and community groups to visit them in future to continue to dispel doubts.

One thing that the visitors learned was that a Lodge was formed at Okehampton by French prisoners of war in 1810 – Freemasonry had, in fact, been practised in Okehampton nearly 70 years before the formation of the Lodge of Obedience.

Bro. Henry Luxton welcoming visitors to the Temple, 2002.

Masons

Left: *A volume of Sacred Law open in front of the chair of the Worshipful Master in the Temple.*

Right: *Aprons denoting the ascending ranks through which a member of the Lodge may rise. Left to right, from bottom to top: Entered Apprentice, Fellow Craft, Mason, Worshipful Master, Chapter apron, Provincial apron.*

Below: *Masonic Lodge in the Conservative Club. Included are: George Cornish, Walter William Cornish, Roy Hawkin, Mr Weaver, Andrew Barnados, Fred Mayhurst, Mr Weston, Mr Young, Mr Newton, Mr Scantlebury, Vick Savage, David Vick, Mr Campbell, Micky Dyer, Mr Wyatt and Mr Bates.*

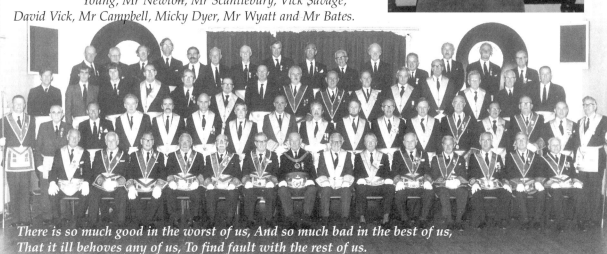

There is so much good in the worst of us, And so much bad in the best of us, That it ill behoves any of us, To find fault with the rest of us.

Rotary Club of Okehampton

Okehampton's Rotary Club was formed and received its charter in 1964 and, as District 1,170, became the local link to Rotary International and in the town began its charitable and social work. Rotarian Les Sweet readily recalled those early days of the club:

The members were carefully chosen by a group comprising Albert Fullwood, a solicitor of long standing, Charles Orsler, Town Clerk, and Mel Bickford, a bank manager. I arrived in Okehampton in 1962 to manage the newly built Post Office and I was approached for membership. I knew few of the founder members, but soon got to know them and what they did. Our first meeting-place was the Okement Café in Fore Street and we dined in an upstairs room which was rather cramped for space. The Thursday lunch was 6s.6d. (32$\frac{1}{2}$p) rising over the years to 10s.6d. (52$\frac{1}{2}$p).

We were a happy, cheerful band of 25 members who quickly formed a good team and soon were joined by Cecil Cole who owned a store in Fore Street; he kindly provided a room on the top floor of his premises which proved a Godsend for our activities, for storing books and providing space for the contents of emergency boxes. Some ten years on Millie and Joe Newcombe, the café

owners, retired and Gerald Rose bought the premises and we sailed on for many years. Later we moved to the Plume of Feathers. Moments to remember include Terry Bennett almost choking on a plum stone from the second course and being helped by our medic Dr Gwyn Jones! A more poignant moment in Bill Cornish's year as President was when one member announced his resignation and that he had only two weeks to live – a long, long silence prevailed. Jon Gilbert died two weeks later.

Within the club the founders soon had a structure of 'special-interest' committees established, through which the expertise and interests of individual members could best be directed. It was a system that became the backbone of the club with committee members assisting people and groups both in the town and in areas overseas.

Officers for 2001–02 are as follows: president Russ Thomas, 1st vice-president Bob Horsley, 2nd vice-president John Stevens, secretary Robin Ward, treasurer Eric Chowing, Imm. Past Pres. Bill Jones. Other members: Ernie Heaysman, Jerome Twomey, Ron Tudge, Denis Mills, John Rattenbury and Chris Powell.

Rotary Council meetings are held on the Second Tuesday in the month at the White Hart, at which

A 'founder member' of Rotary in Okehampton, and its first president, Albert Fullwood, making a point at this meeting.

current activities and future projects are carefully considered.

Committees for 2001/02 were as follows:

Membership Services Committee: Bob Horsley (Chair), John Stevens (2nd Vice) Denis Mills (House and Fellowship), Ron Tudge (Publicity and Youth), Paddy Rowden (Attendance), Peter Sworn (Almoner), John Burgess (Sports), Arthur Ramsey (Classification) and William Jones (Entertainment).
Community Committee: Ernie Heaysman (Chair), Ian Bailey, Mike Luxton, Simon Essex, Micky Dyer, John Whitehouse and John Rattenbury.
International/Foundation Committee: Jerome Twomey, Jack Gregory, Michael Macklin, Les Sweet, Cecil Cole and Chris Powell.
Vocational Committee: Tony Cloke (Chair), Brian Hutchings, Mike Luxton, Bob Ray, John Comyn and Douglas McKenzie.

The range of good work that Rotarians do is illustrated in almost every *Monthly Bulletin* issued to members and the following, from 2001, are a few examples:

Senior Citizen Tea was held at the NAAFI and proved popular... thanks to Okehampton Camp Authorities and NAAFI for use of facilities again.

(Participated in) May Fair held in the park on August 5th. All but 80 ducks were sold outside the supermarkets or by Rotarians before the day, which ensured the event would be financially successful.

Thursday 9th September – President and IPP met the Mayor of Oke. and Cllr Perry Vallance to present the Club's contribution of £250 to provide trees as part of the Town Enhancement scheme.

Letter (received) from Barnstaple RC for help to help a Kenyan Club provide desks for a school which has none – Recommended £50 donated.

£150 donated to town band for its help at May Fair.

No sooner is one project completed than two or more are ready to begin and should they be the organisation of senior citizens' concerts, the arrangements of or funding for children's holidays, or assisting overseas, the Council and committee members of Okehampton's Rotary Club will be quietly and unobtrusively responding to the need.

Okehampton & District LIONS Club

LIONS International was founded in 1917 in Chicago, USA, and with it came the slogan Liberty, Intelligence and Our Nation's Safety. LIONS become the largest voluntary community service organisation in the world by 1986; with a very clear motto, 'We Serve'. The Okehampton & District LIONS Club was formed and chartered in 1974, since when its original aims, to serve the community of Okehampton and district, have been carried out year by year by a steady flow of willing members; and wives and friends and associates whom they call upon to assist them with a multitude of projects.

In 1974 the LIONS were led by president Eddie Langan, Secretary Brian Pinney and treasurer Jim Elson. Members included Lions Brian Barkwell, Basil Bevan, John Beynon, Mike Curtice, Ron Day, Reg Ellis, Archie Fleming, Viv Gammon, Bob Gee, Den Glanville, George Heathman, Lloyd Hines, Jack Kelly, Mike Lavis, Tom Marshall, Mike Phear, Keith Redstone, Gerald Scantlebury MBE, Sam Sheppard and Ray Vallance.

In their first year members raised £1,062.24 and began to use the funds to assist the community, organisations and individuals. They supplied tapes for a 'Pocket Writer' for the local blind, cut grass for the disabled, and obtained a hearing aid as a start to their 'welfare store'. Members came from all walks of life, which helped when the club decided to construct and supply an electric binary calculator for the local primary school. Fund-raising in that first year also helped members to supply two electric razors to Castle Hospital, present two Synchrofax audio playing machines to the primary school, distribute firewood to senior citizens at Christmas and construct two ramps at a local house to enable use of an invalid chair. One particularly successful long-term scheme initiated during that first year was the collection, by members, of waste cardboard from local business people. LIONS were soon collecting a ton per week, which was sold on to raise funds, and in ten years their scheme raised £7,750. In their second year the LIONS constructed a sun lounge at Wardhayes Old People's Home and the spirit of cooperation within the organisation was confirmed when the Chagford LIONS provided furniture for the new lounge. It was at this time that a popular annual collection was initiated; Okehampton and the villages around it, over a quarter of century later, now enjoy the regular return of a sledge drawn by LIONS that brings Father Christmas into their communities as the annual collection continues.

Early in 1977 the LIONS decided to organise a major community project in their area to raise funds for the Children's Hospice (South West), near Barnstaple, North Devon. Their organising sub-committee initially wrote to 200 local organisations, including playgroups, church groups, disabled groups, youth groups, etc., inviting them to organise one function during the year and devote the proceeds, however large or small, to the Children's Hospice, presenting their monies in person at a special gala night in December. Some 65 groups responded positively indicating their support, and the LIONS, for their part, organised a 'Charity Golf Day' at Okehampton Golf Club in September which raised £3,500. The charity gala evening took place on December 5th, at Ashbury Golf Clubhouse, by kind permission of Mr and Mrs S. Essex. Tony Beard, the 'Widecombe Wag' from BBC Radio Devon, compered the evening, and ticket and draw sales of nearly £1,000 helped to swell the final figure to £11,460.19p, which was then handed over to the Children's Hospice.

One of the Okehampton LIONS working closely on this project, among others, was Brian Pinney, a charter (founder) member who was secretary from 1974–89. A former police sergeant, Mr Pinney worked tirelessly to help the LIONS follow and extend their charitable principles. He is remembered as being a 'remarkable man' by some, as a 'determined man' by others, and all agree that recognition was never more deserved than when he was awarded the MBE for charitable services. He devoted many years of his life to helping raise funds and care for those in need until he succumbed to muscular dystrophy.

In their first ten years the LIONS raised £18,630, using the money to assist a great many people. They provided special teaching equipment for educationally retarded children, converted garages into a lecture room for the St Johns Ambulance Brigade, helped provide a portable electro-cardiograph for use by local doctors, a replacement vehicle for local WRVS 'Meals on Wheels' Service, computerised educational equipment at the Royal West of England School for the Deaf and new wheelchairs for the local hospital or old people's home. They have reached out to help set up an eye camp in Northern India, in conjunction with RCSB, provided funds for a 'water-well' project in a village in India, sponsored the 'secondary education' of a bright student in Malawi, among many other international projects. Work that commenced in 1974 is carried forward today by a range of active members, including some of the founders who have served the community for almost 30 years.

Numerous other activities have been undertaken, and, from the funds raised, the LIONS have been able to give financial assistance to local youth clubs, Scout groups, Red Cross, Air Training Corps, Girl Guides and Brownies, Excelsior Silver Band, playgroups, village halls, etc. The list goes on and on. In the field of youth work the LIONS have been involved with the exchange of students from abroad, and the sponsoring of a scholarship to enable selected students to study abroad.

At the dawn of the twenty-first century membership was recorded as follows: president Lion Robert Cunliffe; lst vice-president Bill Addelsee; Lion Roger Alford; Lion Brian Barkwell (P); Lion Gerald Bird; Lion Michael Brint (P); Lion Norman Brock; Lion Ross Campbell; Lion Dave Chapman; Lion Michael Chastey; Lion Norman Cleave; Lion Derek Curtis; Lion Raymond Dean; Lion Viv Gammon (P)(L); Lion Bob Gee (P); Lion David Hollinshead; Lion Martin Jewell; Lion Ron Jewell (P); Lion Basil Jones; Lion Danny Kearon (P); Lion Mike King; Lion Twiggy Lake (P); Lion Chris Langan; Lion Mike Lavis (P); Lion John Mansell; Lion Eric Pengelly; Lion Nick Protheroe; Lion Bernard Sampson (P); Lion Rob Saxby; Lion Nelson Trewin, (P: past president; L: life member).

Projects for the new millennium include: the provision of a new 'delivery-bed' for the local hospital maternity unit, the supply of equipment for integration of handicapped children into the local primary school, and the provision of equipment for a number of primary schools in the district. The *Okehampton Times* of May 9th 2002 reported that the LIONS were already planning a new event to help local young musicians in 2003:

AN EVENT to showcase the best of young musical talent in the Okehampton area and develop skills is being organised by the local Lions' Club. The Okehampton and District Lions Club is proposing to hold the first 'Gift of Music Awards Day' in February or March next year and wants to make it an annual event. It is hoped this event will encourage young people in the area to meet, discuss, learn and help each other realise their full potential in mastering their individual musical skills and provide an opportunity for them to perform to a public audience. Letters are being sent out to schools and organisations in the area inviting them to participate in the project. Funds provided by the audience and other sponsors will be used where appropriate, to support an individual or group developing their skills. The selection process will be made by the Lions Club.

President's projects have included: support for both local hospitals and the new one, televisions for local primary schools, audio equipment for Okehampton Community College, special chairs for Castle Hospital, bath hoist for Wardhayes, fort play-area in Simmons Park and the provision of equipment for St Loye's College, Exeter. Other gifts and support included musical instruments for the town's primary school, Community College and Excelsior Silver Band, computers for children with special needs in Okehampton and North Tawton primary schools, smoke alarms fitted in the homes of senior citizens, Christmas dinners for senior citizens, 'Tacade' packs for schools (teaching aid to help teach skills of life for all ages), sponsorship for youngsters for 'pioneering' trips, etc., holidays for disadvantaged families, medic alert bracelets for people with allergies, diabetics, etc., and the LIONS also have eight wheelchairs which they loan out.

LIONS

Left: *The Wag from Widecombe, Tony Beard* (left) *in celebration mood, with LIONS president Viv Gammon and some of the 'donor groups'. Behind the grand cheque for £11,460.19p, raised from a community project for the Children's Hospice (South West), is Mr David Morris, area representative of the hospice. Ashbury Golf Clubhouse, December 5th 1972.*

Above: *LIONS enlist Jeffe and Peggy Cunliffe's help to get a cheque on its way to the Children's Hospice.*

Below left: *Nigel Knight and Sarah Gailor serve the LIONS and in doing so assist the club.*

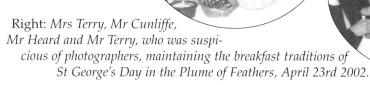

Above: *The LIONS with guest of honour Christine Marsh, town Mayor, celebrating their charter's 26th anniversary, May 5th 2000.*

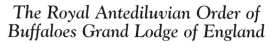

Right: *Mrs Terry, Mr Cunliffe, Mr Heard and Mr Terry, who was suspicious of photographers, maintaining the breakfast traditions of St George's Day in the Plume of Feathers, April 23rd 2002.*

The Royal Antediluvian Order of Buffaloes Grand Lodge of England

Known as the Buffs for short, this international benevolent society has lodges throughout the world. The Buffs came to Okehampton on December 7th 1911, thanks to founder members H.T. Rowe, H. Trenchard and E. Stone who were ready to implement the objects of the order which was then, and remains so today, to render assistance to its members and their families in circumstances of difficulty or need.

For example, the Buffs have two convalescent homes and an education fund, and widows and orphans are cared for. Apart from this its members raise money for many charities and individual cases, including research of medicines and diseases, or many deserving cases that arise in the community; this good work is carried out locally and all over the world.

Among those receiving recent donations from the Buffs are Devon Air Ambulance, Children's Hospice South-West, The Leaze Day Centre, Royal Devon and Exeter Hospital, Okehampton Hospitals, Macmillan Nurses, Okehampton Scout and Okehampton Youth Football Team, to name just a few.

The Association of Inner Wheel Clubs of Great Britain and Ireland

This association aims to promote true friendship, encourage the ideals of personal service and foster international understanding. The Inner Wheel Club of Okehampton held its charter dinner on May 19th 1965. The first president was Mrs Beatrice Fullwood, wife of the local solicitor. Membership was originally intended to be drawn from the wives of Rotarians but in more recent times this has been relaxed to allow sisters and other close relatives to join, although in Okehampton there have only been wives. 'Friendship and Service' is their motto, and in the past this included visiting the local hospitals to take library books, sweets and drinks around and arrange floral displays.

On Inner Wheel Day, January 10th, special events would be arranged such as food parcels for the elderly. A Maypole was presented to Okehampton Primary School and, later, members watched a display of dancing, which they much enjoyed. Coffee mornings and similar events are organised to raise money for charities, and over the years many organisations have benefited, including the Scouts, St Johns Ambulance, cancer and other health charities, the museum, Mencap, and numerous others. The proceeds from two coffee mornings each year are devoted solely to 'local' charities. Inner Wheel members have planted trees, etc. and for many years had a special area of Simmons Park, by the main gate, which they looked after and where they built the huge rockery. Public seats have been donated and sited and besides local charities the branch also supports those overseas and many other worthwhile causes; sometimes by sending garments they have knitted or shoe boxes full of goodies for children, like pencils, writing paper, rubbers and rulers – things which children here take for granted.

The Inner Wheel Organisation has changed over the years, as member Rosina Young explained:

... it's hard to imagine that hats were considered necessary when attending regular meetings held above the Okement Café in Fore Street, where Oxfam is now. The meetings were conducted in a very disciplined way,

On October 5th 1999 the Inner Wheel welcomed the Mayor to their harvest festival in Charter Hall.

to a strict formula, and heaven help any President that didn't keep to the Rules of the Meeting.

Meetings now are held in the evening, to encourage younger members that work to attend, and it is all taken much more lightly with fun being important. Friendship and service are still the aims, but with a lighter touch. Our present membership stands at 24, and although Okehampton is not a big town we have managed to keep going, whilst larger towns like Crediton, Holsworthy and Ilfracombe have had to disband.

Okehampton may be a small town but it has a big heart, and its generosity to various good causes is second to none.

Each year the new branch president has a project to raise money for. Mrs Young's project during her year as president was the summer-house in the grounds of the Castle Hospital for the patients. It is still being used.

St Johns Ambulance Brigade

It is uncertain when a branch of St Johns was formed in Okehampton but certainly it existed by 1921, when it was agreed at a meeting to purchase a motor ambulance from the Red Cross. A committee was formed and Mr Tom Day agreed to garage it for £10p.a. and run it for 9d. a mile. Flag days were to be held to raise the money. By 1937 they reported 126 call-outs in the previous year, and the ambulance had travelled 3,617 miles. Running an organisation whose members are volunteers and meet their own costs was, and remains, a problem for local organisers. Even today, many who ask for St Johns Ambulance to be present at, perhaps, a local show, or any event attended by the public, are often unaware of the voluntary nature of the organisation.

Minutes of the meeting held in the Town Hall in April 1937 stated that the accounts of the branch at that time showed a deficit of £3.0s.4$\frac{1}{2}$d. While new members were being sought, those in the branch the previous year had attended 16 first-aid classes, the lecturers being Dr Price for the men, and Dr Glover Wilson for the women. By the time of the June meeting the deficit had been reduced, but £1.9s.4$\frac{1}{2}$d. remained outstanding for expenses incurred for classes during 1936. His Worship the Mayor, S.J. Rich, contributed £1.1s.0d., Mr Grant 5s.0d., Mr Leigh 2s.6d. and Mr Sprague 1s.0d. to clear the debt and leave a balance of 1$\frac{1}{2}$d. in hand.

In 1938 Mr C. Sprague was elected to the Presidency of the Brigade, Mr H.S. Taylor appointed Secretary, Mr W. Palmer Treasurer and Dr E. Allen-Price elected to be Divisional Surgeon. It was Dr Price, later, who first investigated possible emissions from Dartmoor's granite and came to conclusions which ultimately led to investigations into Radon that continue today.

Membership of the Brigade stood at 23 at this time, and members included Mr R. Balment, Mr E.

Above left: The annual Inspection of Okehampton's St Johns Ambulance group in 1990 coincided with the retirement of Dr Shields. Back row: *Di Slee, Cyril Clark, Andrew Timms, Stanley Stormont, Paul Beer, Tony Brooks;* third row: *Carol Dadds, Di Timms (Nursing Officer), Dr Jean Shields, Dr David Shields, Rose Dadds, Brenda Gerry, Christine McPhee, Laura Beer, Jean Vosper, Anne Meffe;* second row: *Robert Whiteley, Supt. Bob Letchford, T. Chasty, Dr John Riddington Young (County Staff), ?, Ian Gordon, ?;* front: *David Burns, Ian Meffe, ?, Claire Yeo, Wendy Burns, ?.*
Above right: The members of St Johns Ambulance appreciating the support given to them by actor Bernard Cribbens.

Blunt, Mr R. Bragg, Mr Feihn, Mr Heale, Mr R. Horne, Mr S. Hucker, Mr E.C. Lewis, Mr O. Maddaford, Mr R. Maddaford, Mr A.J. Parker, Mr A. Pearce, Mr P.B. Shaddick, Mr R. Sims and Mr K. Smalldon. The first wartime AGM, February 15th 1940, was held in the Town Hall and it was disclosed that the Brigade had gone to war with a financial balance of £5 in its favour. Wartime HQ for the Brigade is recorded as having been in 'East Street' in 1940 with numbers 13 and 15 East Street mentioned as the war progressed. During the early war years, however, membership dropped as many enlisted in the various services. Dances were held to raise funds and uniforms became scarce. Ambulance Officer R. Wilton, of Station House, Barnstaple, was offered £4.5s.0d. for his uniform complete with hat and gloves when he was transferred to Barnstaple Division.

Wartime volunteers, such as Mr Norman J. Bickle, found work imposed on him by the Ministry of Works and came close to resigning. A revision to Compulsory Home Guard Enrolment in 1942 exempted St Johns members from service but some were still drafted into the local force and it was left to the Superintendent of St Johns Ambulance to try to obtain their release. This was perhaps most important at a critical time because conflicting duties could create problems. It was the 'ambulance' part of St Johns that provided ambulance services to the town; a service that continued for a great many years after the war. During 1942 the ambulance dealt with 172 patients and covered 4,742 miles in doing so. Two years later the ambulance was called upon 215 times for civilian use, 15 times for services cases, attended 7 road accidents and covered 5,303 miles. The total strength of the Brigade at that time was 31; out of which 5 were serving in the Armed Forces.

In those pre-NHS days there was no county Ambulance Service. The St Johns Ambulance and Red Cross ran ambulances with volunteers and raised the money locally to pay for the service. At first many of the drivers were not trained in first aid. Nevertheless, they performed a valuable service for very many years, at considerable inconvenience to themselves, as they had to 'down tools' wherever they were in response to a call-out.

During 1942–43, Dr O. Barr was appointed Divisional Surgeon for a short while, before ill health forced him to leave the area and his place was taken by Dr C. Jones. At the 1943 AGM Superintendent Lewis mentioned that it was customary for a member of the Brigade to be on duty at the Carlton Cinema and that the cinema owner, Mr W. Pope, would appreciate it if attendances could be arranged. The following year it was recorded, with appreciation, that 404 attendances had been achieved. While this might conjure visions of St Johns members enjoying the film it should be considered that, from the outset, wartime newsreels were showing the full horrors of war to Okehampton people.

Volunteers continued to come forward to join the Brigade and be trained in first aid. At their new HQ in Market Street in 1944 Supt Lewis proposed and Cpl Blunt seconded a proposal that the Revd Harry Wackett, Charles Bearne Easterling, Arthur Voaden, Albert James Marles and Ernest George Glover be accepted as members of the Brigade. During the war years members of the Brigade Committee, Miss Oag among them, worked selflessly to maintain the group.

St Johns Ambulance drivers had gradually become more professional as the years passed and remained an integral part of the transport of people to hospital long after the NHS was formed in 1948. In

In Service of Communities Near & Far

Dr Andrew Stainer-Smith talking with successor Dr Nicholas Woodall and Mrs Woodall at a gathering to mark Andrew's departure.

Above: *Fund-raising for children in 1999 saw Radio Devon's Douglas Mounce hugging the Mayor, who clung on to Pudsey Bear, and local broadcaster Matt Woodley.*

Right: *On one of his long-distance fund-raising walks, Ian Botham stopped off to sign in to Okehampton for Mayor Joan Pauley and Town Clerk David Voaden, seen here with Mrs White (left) a former Mayor.*

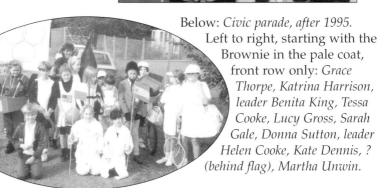

Right: *Carnival in 1982 with leader Shirley Mortimer. In the back row: ?, Samantha Calcutt (pale hairband), ?, Abigail Edwards (helmet); middle: Sophie King, Matthew King, Samantha Durston, Emily Chammings, Marie Ewen, ?, Lucy Hunt; front: James Munkenbeck, Jenny Morris, Hayley Mortimer.*

Below: *Civic parade, after 1995. Left to right, starting with the Brownie in the pale coat, front row only: Grace Thorpe, Katrina Harrison, leader Benita King, Tessa Cooke, Lucy Gross, Sarah Gale, Donna Sutton, leader Helen Cooke, Kate Dennis, ? (behind flag), Martha Unwin.*

Until July 2002, Win Willis fund-raised for Guides and Brownies with her stall in Okehampton Market.

Opposite page: *Okehampton's Red Cross, annual inspection, 1958, Pretoria Rooms. Left to right, back row: ?, Margaret Reddaway, Myra Hodge, Carol Clements, Dawn Preece, Pat Goodanew, Judy Feaver, Diane Pedrick, Frances Wonnacott, Margaret Cook, Eva Down, Beryl Evely, ?, Rosemary Dawkins, Josephine Cox; third row: ?, Gwen Tancock, Joan Pauley, ?, ?, ?, Ivy Aggett, ?, ?, ?, ?; second row: Lil Hosgood, ?, Doris Cause, Ivy Carew, ?, Meneen Kingsford Lethbridge, Sir Treffry Thompson, Matron Hawkins, Polly Finch, Mrs Winterburn, Kath Paveley; front: Rosemary Drew, Enid Bray, Mary Westlake, ?, Diana Winterburn, ?, Doreen Barratt, Miriam Glover, Bronwyn Symmons, Christine Davis, Jane Tolley.*

peacetime, the demands on the St Johns teams continued and at the 1948 AGM Supt Maddaford reported that the ambulances had conveyed 243 patients over 9,578 miles. The Division had been present at two point-to-points, seven gymkhanas and shows, 53 football matches, had performed 379 transport duties and attended the Carlton Cinema 243 times.

On Whit Sunday, May 13th 1951, there was a dedication service, conducted by the Bishop Crediton, in Fore Street in celebration of the new ambulance. The Borough Band under the direction of Bandmaster A.J. Bailey led the singing. It was a much-needed vehicle as the mileage report for the year showed that Brigade ambulances were covering over 1,700 miles annually. Talks were in progress, it was reported at the 1957 AGM, 'with W. Ruby [a local garage owner and businessman] who would perhaps build us a HQ and let it to the Brigade.' It was a matter left to be dealt with by the committee. The president's report for the following year referred to delays in the matter. Major changes were in the air for East Street and they were to the benefit of the Brigade. By April 1959 the president was able to report fully on the changes at Mill Road corner, the relocation of the garage and the building of the new HQ in Mill Road which would also house the ambulances. Only the installation of telephones was needed to allow the HQ to be up and running by June; and it would be one of the best ambulance stations in the county.

August 6th was the important date everyone had waited for. Lord Roborough, president of the Order of St Johns for Devon, with BBC television cameras recording the moment, officially opened the HQ in Mill Lane. The wives of members and mothers of cadets provided excellent light refreshments for over 300 visitors. The new HQ was to witness both rise and fall in membership numbers through the rest of the century, the removal of the ambulances to another station and the introduction of paid staff to operate them.

In 1972 full-time paid staff were beginning to be appointed; even so, in that year 32,943 miles were covered including attendance at 173 emergencies, which necessitated removing 281 patients to hospital. The ambulance service was completely taken over by the NHS in 1975. Names many will remember from those days include Orville Maddaford, Frank Down, Dr Allan-Price, Mrs Marjorie Jones and Dr David Shields among a great many others. Holding first-aid classes for the general public has always been part of the task of St Johns, and initially there was no charge for this. Operating from premises in Mill Road, St Johns continues to play a valuable part in the life of the community, holding classes and supplying first-aid cover at public functions. There is now a Cadet Division, and a Badger Division for younger children, where valuable skills are taught.

On May 12th 1956, the president, Mr Isern-Smith, together with C/Supt Newcombe, Sgt Parker, Privates Pedrick, Glover, Baskerville, and Div./Supt Maddaford were on parade in Hyde Park for the Royal Review by Her Majesty The Queen. One member recalls:

It was a dry day, the sun breaking through the clouds at the time of the Inspection and 22,000 members of the Brigade from home and overseas were present. It was a wonderful sight to see so many men and women wearing the black and white uniform and it made us proud to think that we belong to SJAB though we are only a small band from Okehampton.

That pride continues for members of all ages in the Okehampton St Johns Ambulance Brigade. They continue to be volunteers who pay their own way, they continue to be trained to provide help in emergencies and they continue to serve the community.

Dr David Shields making a retirement presentation to Dr E.P. Jowett. Both doctors served the town for many years and assisted many local organisations including the DRG, St Johns Ambulance and the Red Cross.

The members of Okehampton area Red Cross return from church, August 25th 1958.

13

On The Road to Avalon

While exploring just a fraction of Okehampton's heritage in these pages there remains one link with the past to which we attribute the town's foundation and which should be mentioned. Go to Tongue End and just inside the turning to Belstone look for the old road that led into town. Walk to Okehampton Castle and imagine the stagecoaches that rumbled along that fine high way to the South West and needed extra horses to haul them up the hill. Stand in the castle grounds and look to the tree-covered slopes of the moor and consider those who first came to live here by the rivers that merge. The marks they made were to become pathways for others, tracks for pedlars and traders, routes for carriers and rough roads for coaches. Still the road remains, winding through the town and around it.

For the Romans heading west there were three possible routes down the Dumnonian peninsula to Land's End; via the north coast, south coast or down the central spine. From Gloucester, Bristol and Bath the north coast tracks may, perhaps, have been best. Travellers from the Tiverton or Exeter areas are not at all likely to have reached Okehampton by going via Barnstaple. Reaching it via Plymouth is equally unlikely so a direct route seems likely. It would also make sense if a well-worn track already existed.

Down in the far South West there were, as well as the Celts mentioned, a number of Irish as well. For many centuries BC the Irish incursions on to the peninsula had been regular slave-gathering forays. Since the first invasions by the Gaels, c.800BC, some of these first Celts, to establish themselves down the Dumnonian peninsula, had continued across the Sea of the Severn to settle in a new land – Ireland. Relatives of our own Dumnonii flourished there. The Celts had found yet another home but they, and their descendants as the Irish of Leinster, were to be among the raiding parties that continually returned here to take slaves.

Kings of Leinster like the great Cathair Mår or his successor Fiana Bah Aiccid in the fifth century were still sending out slave seekers. Of course, not all of those who arrived, departed. Many stayed, taking new wives and building new families. The blood of the 'Irish' became an inheritance of the Dumnonii

throughout the peninsula. And it was up and down the peninsula spine that the slave traders travelled, a route which, as well as being within easy reach of either coast, served as a vantage point from which to observe vulnerable communities – without at the same time being easily spotted. Some historians suggest that some of the Roman towns, such as Bath, were destroyed not by the Saxons but by the Irish during their raids. Crimthann, a king who died c.AD483, is reputed to have led repeated invasions that swept up the Dumnonian peninsula to its extreme eastern limits; which, by the best route available to them, means that the Irish invaders then and earlier came through and probably ravaged the area of Okehampton. If the blood of the Celts runs through the veins of the people of Cornwall and Devon today, so must the blood of the Irish.

Throughout much of the Roman occupation the Irish kings of Leinster were making incursions into the Dumnonian peninsula and Wales, taking captives and returning to Ireland to sell them as slaves. One such unfortunate captured during a raid remained in slavery for six years before escaping or being freed. He later returned on a mission and is revered to this day as St Patrick.

A central route up the peninsula served the Irish slave merchants well and the Roman rule of the peninsula was best achieved from a central route down it from which forces could dominate both north and south. We propose, then, that it is not by coincidence that the most important route down the peninsula remains a central one and that such a route has been important for thousands of years. The only thing to defend in the Okehampton area from the earliest times has been that route. The Romans had their fort at Knowle, the Saxons recognised the value of the road, and the Normans put their seal of security beside it.

A Camelot connection with Okehampton arises from the reality that is shrouded within the Arthurian legends. Recent investigation has shown that Tintagel in the fifth century was a major port and royal residence. As such, the knights of old would certainly have gathered there to meet and eat 'around the fire'. Once central fires were superseded, to gather 'around' a table became, and still is, an every-day event. On such simplicities myths can multiply. The roads or tracks then, from the far South West and from Tintagel, converged to the west of Okehampton in the area of Launceston, as they do now, on a high way to Glastonbury and beyond. From Tintagel, Ralfamus or Rietamas, the Supreme High King with his raven insignia rode out with his knights, horse-back warriors, men and foot-soldiers to meet others from down the peninsula and to face the Saxon invaders as they spread westwards.

Along their route they needed rest and food for men and horses and one of the places providing this lay in the valley where two rivers met; on the road to Avalon. It is now believed that at Cadbury the King (who would normally have perhaps 100 defenders at such a fort) was strengthened by a further 400 having come up the peninsula. At his death he is also believed to have been buried on the island that became Glastonbury and a legend was born. As more is revealed by present-day investigation the greater relevance of Glastonbury and Tintagel on a South West way will be confirmed. This also applies to what, until now, has been casually regarded by historians, as a 'skirmish' that took place at Okehampton.

There is still much to learn about Okehampton Castle, the one-time guardian of the high way west.

easily have changed the course of history quite dramatically; even without doing Cromwell learned new tactics of attack and later trained his New Model Army in their devastating use. Recent local discoveries have been made in relation to the battle.

Cornwall at the onset of the Civil War was staunchly Royalist while Devon was divided. Exeter stood mainly for the King while Plymouth stood for Parliament, and a few kept their allegiance to them-selves. For Okehampton, on the main high way into or out of Cornwall, the answer was that it should serve both masters. A Parliamentary force camped at Okehampton in early February 1643 learned of the sacking of Major General James Chudleigh's headquarters at Kings-bridge. Warned that the Cornish Cavaliers responsible were marching on Okehampton, the Round-heads saved the town by saving themselves – slipping away and regrouping at Chagford. It was there on the misty morning of the 8th that the Cavalier horse and dragoons led by Sir John Berkeley fell upon 500 of Sir John Northcote's troops. Lacking infantry support the Cavaliers met more than their match and it was a shaken force that fell back to the safety of Okehampton. During this encounter the Royalists suffered the loss of Sidney Godolphin, one of the school of metaphysical poets, among whose ranks were such men as John Donne and Andrew Marvell. In Okehampton, Berkeley arranged Godolphin's burial in Chagford before regrouping his forces.

Almost as unrecorded by historians as the Chagford encounter was the Battle of Sourton that occurred some six weeks or so later on April 25th. By that time the Cornish Cavaliers consisted of 3,000 men on foot, five 'voluntary' regiments, 300 horse, 300 dragoons and some heavy fire power. Major General James Chudleigh, however, possibly still smarting from his losses at Kingsbridge, felt no fear at the numbers he had to face and his cavalry kept watch over the South West highway to war as he pre-pared for the oncoming army. The battle was graph-ically and quickly reported by the pamphleteers, or 'press men', of the day. By May 3rd 1643, Edward Blackmore, a London pamphleteer, had received and compiled information, had it printed and was selling, to Roundhead readers eager for war news:

'A Western Wonder'
by Sir John Denham

Do you not know a fortnight ago
How they bragged of a Western Wonder?
When a hundred and ten slew four thousand men
With the help of lightning and thunder.

There Hopton was slain again and again
Or else my author did lie;
With a new thanksgiving for the dead who are living
To God and his servant Chudleigh.

And now on which side was the miracle tryd;
I hope at last we are even;
For Sir Ralph and his knaves are risen from their graves
To cudgel the clowns of Devon.

Far from a minor incident, the Battle of Sourton could

A Full Relation of the great defeat give to Cornish Cavaliers By Sergeant Major Generall Chudley. Confirmed by divers letters from these parts to severall merchants in London.

Our Army consisting of 1500. Musquetiers, 200. Pikes, 5 Troops of Horse, under the command of Sergeant Major General Chudleigh, advanced out of Devon. into Cornwall, over Poulson Bridge, neer Lancestone, Sunday morning last, and theere fought with the whole force of Cornwal all that day, till neere midnight, and was in danger to have been cut off, the enemy being so many, and having hemm'd them around to stop their retreat into Devon. which they had done, had not Col: Merricks Regiment of Lond. Gray coats, under command of Lieutenant Col. Calmady, which went of Plimouth the Saterday after noone, and rescued our Army, when the enemy had wel nigh encompassed them round, the gray-coats falling on them bravely, so that our Army themselves killed and hurt them many men, some say 150. so as they made the enemy retreat, and so our men came freely off, making an honourable retreat, not losing any thing, onely having some eight or ten men killed at most.

By Monday morning all our Forces were safely arrived into Devon-shire againe, and whatever the matter was, I cannot learne, some difference there was, so as our Army disperst themselves, the rest being not above 600. Foot and 3. Tropps of Horse, the Tuesday night quartered at Ockhampton, and about nine of the clock at night unthought on, one of the Quartermasters riding out to get quarter to some village neere the towne for their Troopers, met three scouts of the enemies, who fired their Carbines at him, whereon he set spurs to his horse, discovered the enemies Army, which we hear consisted of 4000. Foot and 400. Horse and Dragoons marching towards Ockhampton to cut off our Forces there, who little expected them, the enemie as it seems intending to fall upon them in the dead of night. But now mark and observe the providence of God, most wonderfully and miraculously, in delivering our Forces form these cruel enemies.

The Sergeant major Generall understanding of the enemies neere approach by the Quartermasters relation. Calling a sudden counsell, presently commanded the Horse being but 108. in all (who were going to their quarters before the news came) to divide themselves in sqdrons, having speedily marched first to the brow of the hill where the enemy was to passe, and in that order to remaine till

the enemy came home upon them, and upon paine of death no to shew himselfe, till The eenemy should march full upon them, and when they came, on whose quarter soever they should first light, those squadrons first to charge them through and through, and to shout, crying, Fall on, fall on, They run, they run. This being bravely and speedily designed, was as resolvedly and valiantly put in execution, for it so fell out, that the enemy first approached to Captain Drakes quarter, who having divided those of his Troop, consisting but of 36. into two squadrons of 18. each, commanded them to follow him, and to not give fire until they see him give fire, and so put spurs to his horse, and charged he enemies horse and Dragoons, giving the shout, Fall on, fall on, pistolled the first man he met, knockt out the brains of the next with his pole-axe, and so made way through for the rest of his squadron, who as bravely followed him, and after him his Lieutenant with the other 18. crying Fall on, fall on, They run, they run, and on the other parts, Captain Gold, Captain Pym, Sergeant Major Chudleigh himselfe as bravely fell on the body of the foot, charging them through, making them throw down their Arms, and cry for quarter.

This being done all with 108. Troopers, the Foot remained in the Town being but about 600 in all, who had command to make good the towne for retreat, where also their Ordnance and Ammunition was, after the first rout, againe about midnight our enemy faced about againe, when our Foot also came out upon 400. of them, and together with about 60. or 70. of the Horse so bravely charged them, that they disperst them in a shameful manner, make them turn back, and again to retreat for Cornwall. Our Horse had so far pursued them, that they had almost got their two brasse Ordnance, which they had in possession, but the Foot were not come up to bring them away: So not being of number sufficient, thought it not good to goe too far, but returned back to Ockhampton with honour, being so well employed in the rout, took onely some 20. prisoners, killed some 20. more, and not a man of ours lost. They have taken upon 1000. mens Arms, and 100. in 150. of their horses.

We are now gathering a considerable army together, and intend by Gods help to march into Cornwall. Our men are now all couragious and hearty, seeing the wonderfull mercy of God, who gives the victory to few as well as to many, and fights the battles of his servants, to whom be the glory and honour of his mercy and goodnesse ascribed for ever.

Across Sourton Down – April 25th 2002 and on this day in 1643, with similar bad weather closing in, England's future hung on a battle that history has overlooked.

A NEW-BORN HERITAGE

When I was first contacted by Graham Payne to become Patron of RAPID UK, I was enormously impressed with their aims and objectives. What interested me in particular was the very thorough feasibility study carried out by RAPID UK into starting a much needed Ambulance Service in Albania, a country which holds very fond memories for me. I will always remember the kindness and hospitality shown to me during my recent visit to Albania.

This new and emerging charity has a wealth of wide ranging skills and experience in the field of rescue and preparedness in disaster. I am convinced that they will prove to be a credit to this country and both support and endorse their activities founded upon their motto of Wisdom in Aid. Norman Wisdom, OBE

Since those words were written England's much-loved comedy actor has become a knight and the seed of an idea that was planted by Okehampton people has grown into an organisation that is taking root internationally. Within hours of a natural disaster anywhere in the world, a RAPID UK rescue team of self-sufficient, highly-trained and experienced experts can assemble and be en route to deploy its unique life-saving skills. These often hazardous missions are manned by dedicated volunteers who, through rapid mobilisation and intervention, aim to save lives, and also to teach and train.

In 1995, Christine McPhee was one of a group that decided to form a new rescue-based charity. Not only would it provide rescue teams, but it would pass on knowledge and expertise in rescue techniques to people living in areas of high risk. Local residents, Graham Payne, Barry Sessions, Billy and Christine McPhee, and Brian Blackmar were joined by John Holland, Dave Sleeman, and Paul Blewitt from Gloucestershire, and Chris Port from Hertfordshire. The constitution was soon written up and charity status was gained just 12 months after the first meeting. Thus, in 1996, RAPID UK (Rescue and Preparedness in Disaster) was born, but with no funds, so each member put £10 in the kitty and they were off. Off, that is, to an ex-RAF station at Quedgeley, Gloucester, where they set up their first HQ; purely because their deputy director happened to be a fireman serving there. Each team member was tackling at least two jobs – Christine as fund-raiser soon found out that 'sorry, but no' could be written in three words or three hundred as she received a negative response to her appeals to large firms, trusts, etc. asking for support. The group was growing, nevertheless, and two experienced dog handlers with two trained rescue dogs each also joined.

RAPID UK's help was first accepted after a severe hurricane and floods in Honduras in South America caused disaster. Eight members went as a team and impressed the South Americans with their calm, sensitive approach to the situation. Next came Colombia, also in South America, after an earthquake where, for the first time, trained dogs went as part of the team even though their owners knew that they would have to go into quarantine when they came back. This was followed by a mission to Peru, to two separate earthquakes in Turkey, one in Taiwan and a massive earthquake in India.

During this time more and more members were drawn to the organisation. Volunteers undergo specialist training to prepare for their unique and demanding tasks around the world and people from around the UK with specialised skills were volunteering to commit themselves to the group; some serving in the Armed Forces can be called upon with the cooperation of Commanding Officers.

We had at last been able to acquire some sponsorship and, due to the good reports of our work at disasters, we were getting donations from various sources. The fire station was by this time far too small for our growing membership and equipment needs and we were able to move to another building on the site, affectionately renamed The Kremlin. When the station had been operational it had been the communications centre and was perfect for us as we were able to utilize the various rooms as lecture and meeting rooms, storage for equipment, bunk rooms for men and women and, almost best of all, a kitchen for team mealtimes.

During the Indian earthquake rescue operation in 2001 it was drawn to the team's attention that a woman and her two children had been trapped beneath the wreckage of their home for nearly four days.

The team started to dig and were encouraged to hear faint sounds of life from under the rubble. What they heard was the faint, weak voice of ten-year-old Parth Joshi. He had been trapped with his mother and baby brother who had both been killed. He himself was trapped by his legs, one of which was badly crushed. The team were absolutely determined to get him out so they began the slow, careful job of digging their way down to where Parth was trapped. Any rescue of this kind demands the utmost care as the rubble is usually very unstable and there is always the risk of after-shocks. As the hours passed it became clear that a serious decision was going to have to be made concerning Parth's condition. The first option was to amputate his leg underground to enable him to be rescued more quickly. Team leader John Miller and team medic Nick Spence, who had spent most of the time underground with Parth, consulted with members of the Indian Medical Unit and it was decided that if an amputation was carried out underground it was unlikely that Parth would survive. It had been so difficult to actually reach him and considering the position he was in the rescuers would be unable to give him sufficient medical care to save his life. It was generally decided throughout the team that the best option was to keep digging until they got Parth out. After nine hours of hard, careful digging Parth was eventually extricated and rushed to an Indian Army field hospital where his leg was amputated under hygienic conditions. His father was heartbroken over losing his wife and baby son but was overcome with gratitude in having Parth returned to him. Parth was subsequently moved to a hospital in Bombay for further treatment.

RAPID's experience is now vast: earthquakes in Armenia, Iran, Philippines and Japan; in-training, assessment and logistical work in Liberia, Russia, Rwanda, Peru, Jordan, Tanzania, Austria, Albania and Montserrat; mitigation and preparedness projects in Albania, Peru and Zambia; and members have helped with various incidents in the UK and support the emergency services when requested. They are also prepared to help coordinate multi-national rescues.

The first stage in a rescue operation is for the team to go in prepared to search and locate, search and rescue, or give other appropriate specialised help. Equipment used includes thermal-imaging cameras, sound detectors, fibre-optic probes and thermic lances. Teams also take with them their own tents, food and water-purification equipment, and maintain contact with the UK HQ where volunteers provide 24-hour support. Each team includes a doctor or medic, plus specialists selected for the particular disaster. Team skills include those of mine, cave and mountain rescue, rescue dogs, plus paramedics, police, firefighters and local authority services and the Forces. RAPID volunteers bring to disasters the skills of their own everyday employment, and they come from all walks of life. These include qualified electricians, builders and plumbers, building and civil engineers, ex-Forces with technical knowledge, senior technicians from the Metropolitan Police, specialist drivers, boat handlers, parachutists, nurses, healthcare and social workers specialising in primary healthcare and disaster management in Third-World countries.

RAPID UK is one of the few non-governmentally (NGO) funded response teams in the world to maintain a global response capability to humanitarian disasters. It remains a charity, and a donation-funded organisation, and as a NGO its members volunteer their skills and time to follow its primary objectives; the relief of human suffering and distress in any part of the world resulting from disaster of any kind and the protection and preservation of human life in particular, but not exclusively, by providing suitably trained and experienced response teams free of charge upon receipt of a request for assistance.

There exists also an added dimension that showed itself when the team arrived back from India and said that they wanted to try to help Parth and improve his future prospects. They planned sponsored events to raise money to bring him to this country to have an artificial leg fitted; the media took an interest and the British public reacted in its usual generous way,

Christine recalled with a smile:

Donations started to pour in, from £2 postal orders from pensioners to cheques for £100. Over £12,000 was raised in a very short time and arrangements were made to fly Parth and his father to the UK as soon as he was well enough to travel. An appeal was put out over Gloucester Radio for a family to act as hosts and we were very lucky in the family that came forward as they spoke the same dialect as Parth and Pradip.

While here, between hospital visits for the fitting of the new leg, Parth and Pradip were taken to many places by RAPID members; to Lords for the last day of the England-Pakistan cricket test match, to a speedway meeting in Cornwall where they were guests of honour, and to a children's adventure park in Devon where Parth celebrated his eleventh birthday.

They also spent some time with John Klier and Nick Spence who had fought so long and hard to rescue Parth. When they flew back to India after six weeks, Parth was complete with a new leg and ready for he and his father Pradip to pick up the pieces of their lives. Parth will need to return to the UK every twelve months for the next six or seven years to have his leg replaced as he grows. The money that was donated is held in trust for any expenses to do with his leg and to help with his education in the future.

RAPID now has training and awareness programmes in place in Peru, Colombia, Turkey and Spain and hopes soon to start programmes in India and Bangladesh. Already in place are RAPID Turkey, Peru and Spain, and RAPID France is in the process of being set up and training started. There have also been enquiries from Korea and New Zealand, anxious to be affiliated to and trained by RAPID UK.

Mozambique floods highlighted the need for trained personnel in boat handling as RAPID UK had to co-opt two coxswains from the lifeboat station in Bude in Cornwall. As a result a boat-handling section has been formed and more members will be trained in this skill. The dog section has also grown, with four young Border collies and two Jack Russell tunnel dogs undertaking training. Human membership is more of a lottery. After each disaster and ensuing publicity RAPID UK is inundated with membership applications but, learning that training will require at least one weekend a month for 18 months to two years reduces some people's enthusiasm.

In 1995, people met on the road to Avalon, took a route less travelled on, and by their actions created a new-born heritage, of which they and Okehampton can be extremely proud. Down the centuries there have been many that have given, not taken, helping the town by their actions, yet whose names and stories remain unmentioned in these pages. If nothing ever happens in Okehampton, why is there so much more to tell?

An Okehampton-Born Charity: RAPID UK

Below: *Sir Norman Wisdom approved of RAPID UK's new emergency bed.*

Above: *The western Turkish town of Golcuk as seen by RAPID's team as they arrived on Thursday August 19th 1999.*

Below: *RAPID UK team searching the ruins after the Turkish earthquake.*

Underground it can be hard to get rescue equipment through.

Below: *A Massey Ferguson in a village destroyed by earthquake in India. The only training substitute for a collapsed building is a collapsed building. While the best way to train people to find someone who is buried is to bury someone (all done with the strictest safety measures), requests for access to demolition sites are usually met with, 'You want to do what!'*

Above: *Earthquake survivor, Parth, with Lt/Cdr Alistair Stangroom on the flight deck of HMS Cornwall in Devonport.*

View from Okehampton Castle – the wooded moorland hillside, much as the original dwellers must have known it.

Left: *In 1963 even the river in Simmons Park froze over. Similar conditions were a much more regular occurrence for our ancestors.*

Below: *Approaching Okehampton from the west.*

Subscribers

Helen E. Ashworth, Okehampton, Devon
Mr James (Jim) H. Balkwill, Exeter, Devon
Mrs Phyllis M. Balkwill, Exeter, Devon
Rosemary Banbury, Okehampton, Devon
Brian Barkwell, Okehampton, Devon
William and Elizabeth Batson,
    Okehampton, Devon
Brian Beckett and June Payne,
    Okehampton, Devon
Mr A.J. Berry, Horrabridge, Devon
Pamela N. Binns (née Luxmore), Crawley,
    Sussex
George and Margaret Bird, Sticklepath,
    Okehampton, Devon
Marie C. Bolt, Okehampton, Devon
Christopher J. Bourne, Okehampton,
    Devon
Anthea F. Brock, Okehampton, Devon
The Brooking Society, UK
Margaret Brooks (née Cockwill)
K.J. Burrow, Bucks Cross, Devon
Anita S. Cann, Okehampton, Devon
David Charles Gunn Cann, Crediton,
    Devon
Ernest W. and Helen Cann, Okehampton,
    Devon
Roger Cann, Adel, Leeds, West Yorkshire
Pat and Ron Carter, Northlew, Devon
Duncan Carter, Okehampton Primary
    School, Devon
F. and K. Chammings
Margaret Chastey (née Alford)
Mick and Caroline Childs
A. Chudley, Henlow, Bedfordshire
Lt Col. (Ret'd) A.H. Clark OBE,
    Commandant Dartmoor Training Area
Mr and Mrs G.A.J. Comyn, Okehampton,
    Devon
Kenneth H. Cook, Tavistock, Devon
William J.N. Cornish, Jeweller, Fore Street,

Okehampton, Devon
Olive E. Cosway (née Hain), Exeter, Devon
Mrs S. M. Counter, Okehampton, Devon
George Critchell RAOC (TA), 48 Division,
    Reading, Berkshire
David J. Cushing, Okehampton, Devon
Dartmoor National Park Authority
Murial K. Davies, Bude, Cornwall
Ivy Day, Ashburton, New Zealand
Pamela M. Dean, Okehampton, Devon
The Dog Walker's Appreciation Society,
    Okehampton, Devon
E. Ann Drew, Okehampton, Devon
James Dudley, Germansweek, Devon
Mr R.W. Evans, Boscombe, Dorset
Lilian G. Finch, Okehampton, Devon
Ann C. Finucane, Belstone, Okehampton,
    Devon
Robert A. Gee, Okehampton, Devon
Joan Geering (née Bale), North Tawton,
    Devon
Gilead Foundation, Okehampton, Devon
D.J. and C.M. Gillings, Okehampton,
    Devon
June and Les Gliddon, Okehampton,
    Devon
Captain Robert Glover, Okehampton,
    Devon
Michael Griffin, Okehampton Removals
    and Storage, Okehampton, Devon
Edwin J. Hain, Okehampton, Devon
James F. Hannaford, Mary Tavy, Devon
Philip, Mandi, Darcy, Lloyd and Giles
    Heard, Meldon Farm, Okehampton,
Christine M. Heard, Meldon, Okehampton,
    Devon
Arthur S. Hill, Okhampton, Devon
Alistair D. Hodgson
Carole Holt, Okehampton, Devon
Valerie J. Hood, Okehampton, Devon

John Hubber, Okehampton, Devon
Andrew R. Janes, Taunton, Somerset
W.G. Jeffery DFC and Mrs B.F. Jeffery
Alistair B. Jeffery, Chandlers Ford, Hampshire
John Loveys Jervoise
Mr Roger Jewell, Okehampton, Devon
H.S. Jones, Broadbury
Mr and Mrs D. Joslin, Exeter, Devon
May Joyce, Okehampton, Devon
Mr David John Kelly, Okehampton, Devon
Colin C. Kilvington, Stoke, Plymouth, Devon
Viv and Michael Kirkland, Okehampton,
    Devon
Paul R. Luckett (Curson), Munich
Thornton W.E. Madge, Barking, Essex
Paul R.P. Madge (Madge Family Historian),
    South Petherton, Somerset
John and Kath Mansell, Okehampton, Devon
Christine Marsh, Okehampton, Devon
David and Pauline Marshall, Southway,
    Plymouth, Devon
Janet McCarthy, North Petherton, Somerset
Lita Meardon, Okehampton, Devon
Maurice Meardon, Oxford (from East
    Hook, Okehampton)
David H. Middleton, Okehampton, Devon
T.F. and J.M. Moss, Jacobstowe, Devon
Okehampton Women's Institute
Mr and Mrs D. Paisey
Miss J. Pauley, Okehampton, Devon
Minnow and Geoff Penna, Okehampton,
    Devon
Martin and Jane Perry, Elmfield, Northlew,
    Okehampton, Devon
Mr and Mrs P.M. Perry, Plymouth, Devon
Suzanne Phillips, Victoria, Australia
Jana Phillips (née Stephens), Belstone
Mrs Stephanie Pouya, Honeychurch, Devon
Mr and Mrs D.W. Puttick, Eastbourne,
    East Sussex
Mr and Mrs A. Ralph, Okehampton, Devon
Yvonne Rendle, Okehampton, Devon
Ken Rickard, Lydford, Devon
Mr and Mrs Rolfe, Lower Dimson, Cornwall
Donald and Carol Rooke, Okehampton, Devon
Mr and Mrs L.D. Sampson, Okehampton,
    Devon
The Sampson/Barnes family, Wormit, Fife
Jenny Sanders, Tavistock, Devon
Mrs Jenny Sanders, Tavistock, Devon
Gerald R. Scantlebury MBE, Okehampton,

Devon
Godfrey W. Shellard
Cynthia Sheppard, Okehampton, Devon
Dr Jean N. Shields, North Tawton, Devon
Michael Simmons and Mary Simmons
    (née Felton)
James R. Singer
Brian and Marcia Singleton, Broadbury,
    Okehampton, Devon
Janette Singleton, Okehampton, Devon
Dr Lawrence S. Snell, Peard's Acre,
    South Zeal, Devon
Mr and Mrs J. Squire, Okehampton, Devon
Dr Andrew Stainer-Smith, Sticklepath,
    Okehampton, Devon
Dr J. Stoneman OBE
Norman H. Sutton, Exbourne,
    Okehampton, Devon
Pete and Kit Tarry, Sticklepath, Devon
Mike Thwaites
Kath and Ron Tudge, Okehampton, Devon
Michael P. Tyson, Okehampton, Devon
Ray and Margaret Vallance, Okehampton,
    Devon
Mr David Vick, Okehampton, Devon
Paul and Jill Voaden, St Austell, Cornwall
Mr G. Waldron, Plymouth, Devon
John F.W. Walling, Newton Abbot, Devon
Chris and Marion Walpole
John and Wendy Watts, Bridestowe, Devon
Brian R. Weaver, Okehampton, Devon
Mr C.J. Webb
Mr David Arnold Weekes, Okehampton,
    Devon
John and Mavis Westlake, Okehampton,
    Devon
Hazel and Jim Westlake, Okehampton,
    Devon
Mrs Rose-Marie Williams, Exborne, Devon
Mr John A. Wills, Okehampton, Devon
Revd S.A. Wilson, Bratton Clovelly, Devon
D. Winter and D. Hinds
John Winter, and Jim and Joyce Winter,
    Okehampton, Devon
Margery Wonnacott, Whiddon Down,
    Okehampton, Devon
Hilary and Mike Wreford, Okehampton,
    Devon
Linda Yeo, Okehampton, Devon
Ian and Julia Young, Exbourne,
    Devon

Titles from the Series

The Book of Addiscombe • Various
The Book of Addiscombe, Vol. II • Various
The Book of Bampton • Caroline Seward
The Book of Barnstaple • Avril Stone
Book of Bickington • Stuart Hands
Blandford Forum: A Millennium Portrait • Various
The Book of Bridestowe • R. Cann
The Book of Brixham • Frank Pearce
The Book of Buckland Monachorum & Yelverton • Hemery
The Book of Carshalton • Stella Wilks
The Parish Book of Cerne Abbas • Vale & Vale
The Book of Chagford • Ian Rice
The Book of Chittlehamholt with
Warkleigh & Satterleigh • Richard Lethbridge
The Book of Chittlehampton • Various
The Book of Colney Heath • Bryan Lilley
The Book of Constantine • Moore & Trethowan
The Book of Cornwood & Lutton • Various
The Book of Creech St Michael • June Small
The Book of Cullompton • Various
The Book of Dawlish • Frank Pearce
The Book of Dulverton, Brushford,
Bury & Exebridge • Various
The Book of Dunster • Hilary Binding
The Ellacombe Book • Sydney R. Langmead
The Book of Exmouth • W.H. Pascoe
The Book of Grampound with Creed • Bane & Oliver
The Book of Hayling Island & Langstone • Rogers
The Book of Helston • Jenkin with Carter
The Book of Hemyock • Clist & Dracott
The Book of Hethersett • Various
The Book of High Bickington • Avril Stone
The Book of Ilsington • Dick Wills
The Book of Lamerton • Ann Cole & Friends
Lanner, A Cornish Mining Parish • Scharron Schwartz &
Roger Parker
The Book of Leigh & Bransford • Various
The Book of Litcham with Lexham & Mileham • Various
The Book of Loddiswell • Various
The Book of Lulworth • Rodney Legg
The Book of Lustleigh • Joe Crowdy
The Book of Manaton • Various
The Book of Markyate • Richard Hogg
The Book of Mawnan • Various
The Book of Meavy • Pauline Hemery
The Book of Minehead with Alcombe • Binding & Stevens
The Book of Morchard Bishop • Jeff Kingaby
The Book of Newdigate • John Callcut
The Book of Northlew with Ashbury • Various
The Book of North Newton • Robins & Robins
The Book of North Tawton • Various
The Book of Okehampton • Radford & Radford
The Book of Paignton • Frank Pearce
The Book of Penge, Anerley & Crystal Palace • Various
The Book of Peter Tavy with Cudlipptown • Various
The Book of Pimperne • Jean Coull
The Book of Plymtree • Tony Eames
The Book of Porlock • Denis Corner
Postbridge – The Heart of Dartmoor • Reg Bellamy
The Book of Priddy • Various
The Book of Rattery • Various
The Book of Silverton • Various

The Book of South Molton • Various
The Book of South Stoke • Various
South Tawton & South Zeal with Sticklepath • Radfords
The Book of Sparkwell with Hemerdon & Lee Mill • Pam James
The Book of Staverton • Pete Lavis
The Book of Stithians • Various
The Book of Studland • Rodney Legg
The Book of Swanage • Rodney Legg
The Book of Torbay • Frank Pearce
Uncle Tom Cobley & All: Widecombe-in-the-Moor • Stephen
Woods
The Book of Watchet • Compiled by David Banks
The Book of West Huntspill • Various
Widecombe-in-the-Moor • Stephen Woods
The Book of Williton • Michael Williams
Woodbury: The Twentieth Century Revisited • Roger Stokes
The Book of Woolmer Green • Various

Forthcoming

The Book of Bakewell • Various
The Book of Barnstaple, Vol. II • Avril Stone
The Book of Brampford • Various
The Book of Breage & Gurmoe • Stephen Polglase
The Book of the Bedwyns • Various
The Book of Bideford • Peter Christie
The Book of Bridport • Rodney Legg
The Book of Buckfastleigh • Sandra Coleman
The Book of Carharrack • Various
The Book of Castleton • Geoff Hill
The Book of Edale • Gordon Miller
The Book of Kingskerswell • Various
The Book of Lostwithiel • Barbara Frasier
The Book of Lydford • Barbara Weeks
The Book of Lyme Regis • Rodney Legg
The Book of Nether Stowey • Various
The Book of Nynehead • Various
The Book of Princetown • Dr Gardner-Thorpe
The Book of St Day • Various
The Book of Sampford Courtenay
with Honeychurch • Stephanie Pouya
The Book of Sculthorpe • Garry Windeler
The Book of Sherborne • Rodney Legg
The Book of Southbourne • Rodney Legg
The Book of Tavistock • Gerry Woodcock
The Book of Thorley • Various
The Book of Tiverton • Mike Sampson
The Book of West Lavington • Various
The Book of Witheridge • Various
The Book of Withycombe • Chris Boyles

For details of any of the above titles or if you are
interested in writing your own history, please contact:
Commissioning Editor Community Histories, Halsgrove
House, Lower Moor Way, Tiverton Business Park,
Tiverton, Devon EX16 6SS, England;
email: naomic@halsgrove.com

In order to include as many historic photographs as
possible in this volume, a printed index is not included.
However, the Community History Series is indexed by
Genuki. For further information and indexes to
volumes in the series, please visit:
http://www.cs.ncl.uk/genuki/DEV/indexingproject.html